BECAUSE OF GRACE

Thomas J. Madon

© 2019

All rights reserved

ISBN: 9781798488386

Unless otherwise noted, Scripture throughout the book is taken from the *New American Standard Bible,* © The Lockman Foundation 1960, 1962, 1963, 1968, 1971, 1972, 1973, 1975, 1977, 1995 A Corporation Not for Profit, La Habra, CA, All Rights Reserved

Cover photo by theSOARnet on Pixabay

Painting of our Baxter home on the hill (page 10) by Donna Short

All other photos are from the Tom Madon Collection.

Tom Madon
II Peter 3:18

Table of Contents

ACKNOWLEDGEMENTS

These memoirs would not have become a reality apart from numerous people who heard me preach over the years, suggesting that the life experiences I often included in sermons needed to be preserved that my family and others might benefit.

In addition, what I have included about our three children is done with their permission. Cheryl, Scott, and Christy have encouraged me along the way through their continuing love and support. Though writing is something I had contemplated for the past few years, in the summer of 2018, after gaining a renewed appreciation for life following some life-saving heart stents I was unaware I needed, I sensed the Lord motivating me to begin. As I responded, He enabled me to remain encouraged and to complete the writing in a relatively short period of time. To turn a word document into a published book, however, demands greater skills than I possess, so I am grateful for my proofreaders: my wife Linda, Audrey Bush, our daughters, Cheryl and Christy, along with our granddaughter, Ashlyn, who helped transform my simple document into the appropriate format for printing. My thanks also go to Nancy Bowser who had traveled down the publishing road before us and provided valuable insights. Cheryl also coordinated the cover design and helped bring the final product to fruition, and for this I am deeply grateful.

Finally, this book, and my years of pastoral ministry, would not have taken place without my faithful, praying wife, Linda, who has graciously supported me each step of the journey. The writer of Proverbs captures my sentiments: "House and wealth are an inheritance from fathers, but a prudent wife is from the Lord" (Proverbs 19:14). God's gift of Linda to me is more fully described in a later chapter of Proverbs: "An excellent wife, who can find? For her worth is far above jewels. The heart of her husband trusts in her, and he will have no lack of gain. She does him good and not evil all the days of her life" (Proverbs 31:10-12). While there have certainly been challenges along the way, I am richly blessed by the immense joy Linda and I have shared in our marriage, our family, and our ministry.

DEDICATION

To our beloved grandson, Trent Mabs, enrolled at The Master's University, who is becoming equipped to follow God's call into pastoral ministry

CHAPTER ONE

Where It All Began – Harlan County, Kentucky

"He determined their appointed times, and the boundaries of their habitation." Acts 17:26

Having been blessed to travel to all but one of the lower 48 states in our nation, and to several countries around the world, I have often wondered why I was born in Harlan, Kentucky, in the heart of Appalachia. Why was I blessed to live and grow up when and where I did, as opposed to some other historical period, such as during those more difficult years when my impoverished but courageous forefathers came from England and Scotland to settle in Western Virginia and Southeastern Kentucky?

The Apostle Paul provided the answer in his first century sermon to the citizens of Athens who worshiped an unknown god. Paul proclaimed to them the one true God who created the universe and the world, the God who rules over all things, and who gives life and breath to everyone. He explained that God's sovereignty extends even to the time and place each person would live: "He determined their appointed times and the boundaries of their habitation" (Acts 17:26). In His absolute rule, God had His reasons for me being born just as our country was entering World War II, only weeks after the attack on Pearl Harbor, and growing up in Southeastern Kentucky during the hopeful, healing years as our nation recovered from the war.

My father and mother spent their early years in Lee County, the westernmost county in the Commonwealth of Virginia. My father was born in a small community called Keokee, and my mother near Pennington Gap, in an area named Sugar Run. Their respective families eventually moved across the state line and settled in Harlan County, Kentucky, only a few miles from their place of birth, albeit in a different state.

My parents met when my father was working for Hampton's Dairy, on the Skidmore farm near Harlan, delivering milk to families in our county. One of his regular stops was at my mother's home *in the lane*, as they referred to it. The *lane* was a row of section houses provided for employees of the L & N railroad; and my grandfather, Henry Pendleton, one of the hardest working men I've ever known, considered himself blessed to work for the railroad. The Pendleton home in *the lane* was one of the most anticipated deliveries on my dad's route, and my mother soon fell in love with the milkman! They were married on December 21, 1940. Officiating over the simple ceremony was Reverend Roland Pinky, a loyal friend of my father's from high school.

My birth took place on January 18, 1942, in a small frame house on the Hampton dairy. In those days, doctors made house calls, but I was determined to discover America before Dr. Bailey could arrive. The wife of the dairy owner, Mrs. Hampton, assisted me in making my appearance. My dad loved to tell the story, explaining how Mrs. Hampton had never delivered a baby before, only calves, and he embellished his tale of my birth each time he retold it over the years. Dr. Bailey arrived soon afterwards, and commended Mrs. Hampton for her good work, and my mother for bravely giving birth to her first born, a healthy 8 lb. 7 ounce son.

When I was only a few months old, my father acquired a better paying job at Wardrup's in Harlan, a meat packing company that delivered their product to grocery stores in Southeastern Kentucky. After Dad began working at Wardrup's, we were able to move from our simple home on the dairy to the delightful little community of Baxter, the place I affectionately call home to this day.

My dad holding his firstborn!

6

My parents were able to rent a small white house beside the road and railroad, and near the Cumberland River, which originates in Baxter. The Martin's Fork and Poor Fork rivers merge in our community to form the Cumberland River, recognized as a major waterway of the Southern United States, covering nearly 700 miles.[1] Our new home had *four rooms and a path*, meaning we had no indoor plumbing, only an outhouse.

My earliest recollections are from that simple home, and the photos my mother preserved from those years have helped keep those memories alive. One treasured memory is of our neighbors, Mr. and Mrs. Howard, who were also our landlords. They loved having a little boy next door, and the report is that I loved their attention. Their son, Fred, often asked my parents if I could join them for their special family gatherings, which always included delicious foods I had never seen or tasted, but soon came to enjoy.

Another clear memory from that home is when one of my mother's friends, Dorothy Gregory, came to visit with her daughter, Ava, who was a year older than me. To this day, I have images of us playing in the front yard. Ava and I remain in touch today, and my treasured relationship with her reaches farther back than with any other living person.

It was while we were in that home that I grew to love Mary Howard's grocery, located only a few steps from our home. For only a dime, I could purchase an R.C. Cola and a moon pie, my favorite treat at the time. As the years passed, the front porch of her store became a favorite gathering spot for young people of the community.

One frightening recollection from our first Baxter home was a time when the Cumberland River flooded. Even today, I can visualize how the water came up to our back steps. As a little boy, I was fearful that it would rise higher and wash us all away. Thankfully, the flood waters eventually receded, and we were safe.

Four days after my 5th birthday in 1947, my sister, Linda Gail, joined our family. In the days preceding my sister's birth, I stayed with my Uncle Brit and Aunt Ella Wilder. Aunt Ella was my dad's beloved sister, and their home would become one of my favorite places to visit. Returning home to become acquainted with my little sister, and noticing how excited everyone was, my parents often told how I soon informed them of my desire to return to Uncle Brit and Aunt Ella's. It was clear from my words that in their home I could remain the center of attention! Just how much truth there was in my parent's recollection of that moment will remain a mystery, but in spite of my initial reluctance, I soon came to treasure my little sister.

It was when I began school as a 6 year-old in the fall of 1948 that my horizons began to expand. All the children in Baxter walked to and from the little four room school on the hill, located less than a mile from our home. But I do remember it being *uphill both ways*, as folks older than me like to claim about their trek to school. I also recall walking home in my bare feet once the weather became warm enough in the spring, and often stopping at *Supers*. The owner was a disabled World War II veteran who had a tiny grocery where we could buy tootsie rolls for a penny!

Our red brick Baxter school had four rooms, one for 1st and 2nd grades, taught by highly regarded Miss Middleton, who had also been my mother's teacher when she entered first grade. Another was for the 3rd and 4th grades taught by Mrs. Kelly and a third room for the 5th and 6th where the teacher was Mrs. Howard. All three teachers were passionate about their vocation, and loving but firm toward us as students. The fourth room was used for music, but it was also where we were sent if we were feeling sick or needed to be paddled for misbehaving. While the Baxter school closed some years later, every former student with whom I have spoken has only positive things to say about their years there.

One distressing memory from my earlier elementary years, one which exposed my spiritual deficiency, came when I went to Sunday school with a Baxter friend. The church was located on a hill, as many are, and the classroom was in a dark basement. I have no memories of the class except for how it ended. The teacher announced that no one could leave until he or she had recited a Bible verse. One by one each child approached the teacher and said words that were inaudible to me, yet they were instantly released from the gloomy basement room. Without any concept of what a Bible verse was, my thought was that I would have to remain in that foreboding room forever! The teacher suggested that I just say John 3:16, but I had no idea which John he was talking about or what 3:16 had to do with it. My friend finally ran back down the basement steps and whispered these words, *"Just say 'Jesus wept.'"* As I repeated those two simple words to the agitated teacher, they were like a magic password. The teacher finally smiled and I was immediately released! I later learned that those two words comprise the shortest verse in the Bible. They describe the compassionate response of Jesus to Mary and Martha after their brother, Lazarus, had died. In Jesus' tears He identified with their sorrow, even though He knew He would soon raise Lazarus from the dead, in what is viewed as Jesus' most famous miracle. Little did I know I would soon have an opportunity to learn Bible verses for the first time; help was on the way!

A much anticipated event at our Baxter school was when the missionaries would visit from Camp Nathanael, in Knott County. These two devoted women utilized flannel graphs, a storytelling method that used a board covered with flannel fabric, placed on an easel. As they told their stories, they would aptly place the pertinent Bible characters on the graph, as they skillfully applied the life-changing truths of Scripture to our young lives. The missionaries also introduced us to Scripture memory, and offered incentives to motivate us for the task. Memorizing a relatively small number of verses qualified the student to receive a Gospel of John; an increased number resulted in a New Testament. Memorizing even more resulted in the hard working pupil receiving his or her own personal Bible! The grand prize was a free week at Camp Nathanael in the summer, which only the most serious minded obtained. Though the highest level I attained was receiving a New Testament, in hindsight I see that the seed of God's Word was being sown in my heart. God's unchanging promise is that His Word will produce the harvest He intends in His time. "For as the rain and

9

snow come down from heaven, and do not return there without watering the earth and making it bear and sprout, and furnishing seed to the sower and bread to the eater; so shall My word be which goes forth from My mouth; it shall not return to Me empty, without accomplishing what I desire, and without succeeding in the matter for which I sent it" (Isaiah 55:10-11).

Many years later, I recounted the story of these two missionaries in one of my sermons; my Associate Pastor, Michael Mercer, informed me afterward that these faithful women had been commissioned in the late 1940's by Waukegan Bible Church in Illinois, his prior pastorate. He also stated that one of them, Miss Joy, though quite elderly, was still alive. He was able to contact her and arrange for us to have a delightful phone conversation. In it I was able to express my profound gratitude for the way she and her faithful coworker brought the Gospel to our Baxter school all those years before. She expressed great delight that God had called one of those students to become a pastor.

During the spring of 1949, as I was completing first grade, my parents were able to purchase their first and what would turn out to be their only home. It was one we observed every day if we merely glanced across the road and railroad. Painted an appealing white with green trim, surrounded by kudzu vines, the home had a front porch running the entire length of the house. With memories of the dangerous flood still in my mind, the most positive feature of our new home was its location - high on the hill! Another fascinating luxury was the indoor bathroom, something

Our Baxter home on the hill

entirely new for me and for my parents as well. While the house only had two bedrooms, there was a relatively large living room, dining room, and kitchen. The acre of land on which it was located included a small barn, a chicken house, and a smoke house.

Like most of the houses in Baxter, our home was heated by a coal stove in the living room. This became the gathering place and the center of warmth for our family, especially during the winter months. On extremely cold nights, I can remember wrapping a brick in a towel, placing it on top of the stove, and then taking it into our freezing bedrooms to place under the blankets, keeping our feet cozy for the first part of the night.

There was no TV in those days, but we did have a radio. While I enjoyed some of the classic programs from those years, my fondest memory is of listening to UK basketball games with my dad, but often missing out on some of the action due to annoying reception problems. It was during the radio play-by-play that I developed an intense love for Kentucky basketball that has never faded, and I still *bleed blue* today, as UK fans like to say.

Not long after we were settled on *the hill*, as it is still called today, our family was blessed with a second little girl, Ella Lee, born in March of 1949. As an older brother with two younger sisters, I felt protective toward them. Years later I came to see that I overstepped my bounds at times in giving them advice. While they looked up to me with respect, they also interpreted my protectiveness as an attempt to control their lives. Since I was older, they viewed me as the favorite of our parents, receiving more while they had to do without or settle for less. In hindsight, I believe there was some truth in their assessment.

Our family home was literally on the side of the hill. People from our part of the state have been known to jokingly say that if you get tired, all you have to do is lean against the ground and rest! Having this extra amount of land meant there was space for a garden. As the weather improved in the spring, families would remove the debris from their garden spots. One of my fond memories is of seeing and smelling the fires throughout Baxter as the brush from the previous fall and winter was being carefully burned away. I recall my dad borrowing a friend's mule and plow to prepare our hillside garden for planting. With incomes meager in those days, most families depended heavily on what they were able to grow. My mother, like most women in the community, canned a variety of vegetables, including green beans, cucumbers, corn, and tomatoes. This enabled us to have food long after our garden was no longer producing.

Though we never had cows or horses, we did have pigs, and built a pig pen next to the barn. One of my earliest chores was what

we called *slopping the hogs*. The *slop* was any leftover scraps remaining from our meals, mixed with water. My job was to carry the bucket up the hill and pour the slop into the trough. Our intent was that the pigs gain nourishment and grow into fat hogs, ready to be slaughtered and butchered.

Hog killing time, as we referred to it, was in the fall, when the weather became cold enough so the meat would not spoil during the butchering and salting. In those years there were no

An early school picture

freezers as we have today. A few families were beginning to have refrigerators, but most only had a small icebox. Since Baxter was a somewhat impoverished community, salt was a vital staple, both as a preservative and as a seasoning. Hog killing day was filled with great excitement, at least for me as a young boy. Some relatives and friends came to assist my father with the process. Once the slaughtering was complete, and the meat had been carved, raw mineral salt was rubbed on each cut of meat until the flesh was penetrated and the salt was dissolved. This prevented the meat from decaying, ready to be placed in the smoke house. Through the winter months, assorted cuts of pork were available for us to eat and enjoy: ham, bacon, and shoulder meat. Unidentifiable pieces of the hog were ground into sausage. My favorite part of hog killing day was the fresh tenderloin, deep fried by my mother. All the workers would be treated to as many tenderloin sandwiches as they could eat; a delicious expression of appreciation for their generous labor.

Later in life, as I read Jesus' words, "You are the salt of the earth" (Matthew 5:13), my mind went back to the marvelous way our salted meat was preserved without refrigeration. I learned that Jesus was speaking of the preserving effect His people have in the world when they live in biblical faithfulness and with a passion for His glory.

In time, my parents also put the chicken house to good use. Like most children who grow up on a farm or in a family that raises their own chickens, my sisters and I enjoyed gathering the eggs. While we also loved our mother's delicious fried chicken, seeing her chop off the chicken's head or wring its neck, was far more unnerving than simply gathering the eggs.

Another delightful feature of our home was the long front porch which overlooked the railroad, the road, our previous home, and beyond that, the Cumberland River. In contrast to so many houses with porches today that are only for decoration, ours was always put to good use. We could sit in our porch swing and easily carry on a conversation with friends walking up the road or railroad on their way to the post office, or to some other destination. My mother especially loved the porch swing. During the warmer months, it was rare when we did not spot her watching for us as we walked home from school, or after having been with friends. Even after living away from Baxter for many years, anytime I have returned home, either alone or with my own family, one of my first inclinations has been to sit on the porch and visit, weather permitting. I have also enjoyed quiet times in the swing all by myself. There was something about that peaceful location that enabled me, as in no other place, to reflect on treasured memories from my growing up years, and to give thanks for the countless expressions of grace I have been blessed to receive.

During those early years, my parents did not have an automobile. Dad would generally get a ride to work with a fellow employee who lived nearby, or ride one of the VTC buses that serviced the small towns and communities in our county. Saturday was Mom and Dad's designated day for buying groceries. They would make the two mile walk to Harlan and then have their favorite taxi driver, Charlie Campbell, meet them at A & P or Kroger to transport them and the groceries home.

One of my most infamous acts during those years occurred when I was around 9 or 10 years of age. Like many young children, I became fascinated with matches. One day my friend Jimmy and I were exploring on the hill adjacent to our land, and I decided to show him what matches could do. As soon as I struck the match, the wind took the small pod of sagebrush I set on fire, and it went rushing out of control across the hillside before I could stomp it out. Jimmy and I scrambled down the path to the railroad, and high-tailed it to our homes. I immediately went into my bedroom and pretended innocence to the best of my ability. When my parents asked about the smoke coming over the hill, I innocently asked, *"What smoke?"*

As people began to inquire about the fire, someone reported that they saw Jimmy and me running down the railroad as the fire was starting, and suggested that we were the likely culprits. When my parents asked me about it, my immediate answer was, *"Jimmy did it!"* I did not know the Bible in those days, but I was like the little boy in Sunday school who was asked, *"What is a lie?"* His response was, "A lie is an abomination unto the Lord...and a very present help in time of trouble!" He was combining parts of two verses that did not belong together, always a risky practice. Because of my intense fear of being found out, a lie seemed my only way of escape, *a very present help in time of trouble*. I remained resolute in my contention that Jimmy did it. He, of course, was accurate in his report, declaring that I was the guilty party. With the fire spreading over several acres, fire fighters and all available volunteers were called in to assist. Thankfully, no homes or out buildings were consumed, and no one received any injuries. However, a few days later Jimmy and I, accompanied by our parents, were summoned to appear before the Harlan County Judge. In my guilt and fear, I could never look the judge in the eye, but I can visualize his black robe to this day. Even then, I refused to confess, continuing to place the blame squarely on Jimmy. My fear was that if I told the truth, I would be placed in jail for life! Since Jimmy and I persisted in blaming each other, the judge ordered my father and Jimmy's father to share what I am sure was a stiff fine.

In the days and weeks that followed, my conscience eventually got the best of me, and I confessed my sins to my mother. Being the caring person she was, she graciously forgave me, but then informed me that she had known for some time that I was the guilty one. Mrs. Howard, our former landlord, had been on her porch and saw Jimmy and me on the hillside, and explained to my mother exactly what happened. My mother also knew her son well enough to understand by my pitiful countenance that I was guilty. Years later, I would learn the instructive and encouraging verse: "He who covers his sin will not prosper, but he who confesses and forsakes his sin will find mercy" (Proverbs 28:13).

View from our front porch - Baxter depot and trestle

Without a vehicle of our own, our family was limited to where we could travel, but this did not keep us away from our grandparents, Henry and Flossie Pendleton, my mother's mom and dad. Their home in the lane, where my mother had lived as a child, was not far, but located on the other side of the Cumberland River. Getting there required a walk across the railroad trestle. Many in our community were afraid of it, but for some reason, crossing the trestle never seemed to bother me. Perhaps it was because I was fascinated with bridges and trains, and I loved being able to look down through the cross ties at the Cumberland River as we crossed. A few years later, it was under that bridge where I learned to swim, and often fished with friends.

Going to Grannie and Granddad's home was an event I always anticipated, one reason being the strawberry patch beside their

house. Anytime I have eaten strawberries in the years since, I always compare them with those of my grandmother's. When she gave me a bucket and sent me to pick, she always accused me of eating more than I brought back in the pail, and I am confident she was correct. My grandparents also grew grapes, and they were the only people I knew at that time who were ambitious enough to have grapevines. My grandfather also had bee hives, and it was fascinating to watch him when he was robbing the bees of their honey.

With Mom and Dad at my grandparent's home

Their section house was nicely furnished, although they had no indoor plumbing. Their outhouse was a two-seater and had the previous year's Sears and Roebuck catalogues as a substitute for toilet paper. My grandparents also had an icebox, and Grannie always seemed to have some cool, delicious treat in it when we came to visit. Because my grandfather was a hard

16

working railroad man, they seemed to be somewhat better off financially than other families. Theirs was one of the first households in Baxter to have a television. I would often spend Saturday nights in their home and we would watch Ted Mack's Amateur Hour and General Electric Theater. As a special treat, we sometimes watched one of the Western movies that were so popular in those days. Spending the night there meant sleeping in Grannie's soft featherbed. When we would walk through the house, a fun challenge was maneuvering our way under and around her quilting frames. When her quilts were finished, they were always beautiful. She later quilted one for me when I went away to college, and I proudly put it to good use on the bed in my dorm room. One of my grandfather's hobbies was photography, and he also had a mysterious dark room. My love of photography is likely linked in some way to his passion, even though his photographs were only black and white in those years. Thankfully, I still have some of his old photos in my collection.

Other fond memories from those early years were the regular visits to my Uncle Brit and Aunt Ella's home, across Pine Mountain, near Bledsoe, Kentucky.   Until I was in my teens, my practice was to spend two weeks there each summer. Their home was appealing for numerous reasons. One was going with Uncle Brit each day to milk the cows owned by the Pine Mountain Settlement School where he worked. On one summer visit, Uncle Brit informed me that the school now had *electric milkers*! Though I pondered long and hard to understand, it was impossible for me to wrap my young, uninformed mind around that concept. Even after I saw the *electric milkers* in action, it was difficult to put into words what I had witnessed.

As I grew a bit older, I began to take my bicycle to their home. The school where my father had gone to junior and senior high, and where Uncle Brit and Aunt Ella worked, has one of the most beautiful campuses in Southeastern Kentucky, and it was an ideal location for riding bicycles. By this time I had become friends with other boys and girls near my age who lived nearby, or whose parents worked at the school, so they became riding and exploring companions. The campus had a large swimming pool, but the water was always ice cold since it came directly from a large spring on Pine Mountain. Only in late summer did it begin to feel a little warmer. The central building on the campus was Laurel House, where square dances were held each Saturday night during the summer. My favorite building was the beautiful stone chapel with a pipe organ, viewed as the most hallowed place on campus, and I always felt a sense of reverence each time I entered. A tradition that continues to this day is their annual Christmas pageant. People from Harlan County and beyond come to see the Nativity on one of the evenings when it is presented. What makes it so unique is that the actors are always local people from the community.

Being at Uncle Brit and Aunt Ella's in the summer always included enjoying the red raspberries which grew in abundance by their home, always served on top of vanilla ice cream. Uncle Brit also grew cantaloupe in his garden, and sometimes watermelons. Their most lasting impression on me, however, was spiritual; they were the only people I knew who prayed and gave thanks before every meal,

Pine Mountain Chapel

but it seemed the appropriate thing to do. As I grew older, I came to see their simple gesture as an expression of their quiet faith, and reverential attitude toward the Lord. Some years later, I would learn from the Old Testament book of Proverbs that "the fear of the Lord is the beginning of wisdom, and the knowledge of the Holy One is understanding" (9:10). In hindsight, my aunt and uncle's profound gratitude and humility became additional seeds of truth planted in my young, receptive heart.

When I was twelve, our family again expanded in late September as David Clark was born. We all immediately fell in love with him, and the motherly instincts of my sisters quickly became apparent. Linda and Ella were an enormous help to our mom in caring for David. As he grew older, I also loved taking him with me when I would go to visit my friends in Baxter, and they loved him as well.

By the time David was born, I had been playing Little League baseball for a couple of years. Because my dad loved sports, he saw to it that his first-born son learned to throw and catch a baseball. I could not begin to count the times he retrieved my wild pitches from over the hill. Surprisingly, I eventually became a pitcher known for my control. Dad also taught me how to fish, hunt, and shoot a basketball. Though he had flaws and limitations, as all fathers, he unselfishly invested in me as his son, and I am forever marked by the many hours we spent together. Someone has suggested that children spell love with the four letters T I M E! Because my dad gave his time to me, I benefitted in many immeasurable ways.

During my 6th grade year, while improving in basketball, one of my friends, Alvin, a year older, was on a team coached by Basil Mills, my Little League baseball manager. Alvin suggested to Basil that I had a good outside shot, and would make a nice addition to the team. When I was invited to join, I could not have been more excited. My first game was in a place called Kingdom Come! We rode in the back of Basil's pickup around the curvy, mountain roads to our destination. That was my first time to play basketball indoors. The goals in this primitive gym were attached to the walls with no space to take the ball out of bounds. But even with its limitations, I was thrilled about this new adventure of playing in a gym! Alvin and I would later be teammates on our Harlan High School Green Dragon team that for two years was ranked as one of the top teams in Kentucky. But we often reminisced about him recruiting me and my unforgettable, first indoor game at Kingdom Come!

Our home, like so many others in our county, was near the railroad, less than 50 yards away. Because Southeastern Kentucky was rich in coal, and it was in much demand at that time, the trains ran day and night. The L & N steam engines pulling the heavily laden cars were also fueled by coal. Each time a train passed, we could see the smoke billowing from the engine stack. Our home was also near two railroad crossings, meaning we were constantly hearing the loud blasts on the horn, warning approaching motorists that a train was coming – a sound I loved! Even today, hearing that familiar blast of a train approaching brings back fond memories from my childhood.

With coal being the number one commodity in our region of Kentucky, a number of my friends were coalminers' daughters and sons. I can still visualize the miners from Baxter riding home from work in the back of pickup trucks, with their mining hats still on, carbide lights attached, and their faces pitch black. Working in the mines was extremely difficult, and the risks were enormous. There was always the fear of our miners being trapped underground due to a cave in. Many of the coalminers also developed black lung, and died at a relatively early age, because of having inhaled so much coal dust. The clashes between coal miners and the owners are legendary, and deaths became far too common, one of the factors which resulted in our county being referred to as *Bloody Harlan!*

As a tribute to the vital role of coalminers to our county, a monument was constructed in the center of Baxter, made up of blocks of coal from each of the mines in the county. When it was constructed, there were more than 70 mines in Harlan County. One of my older friends, Charles Johnson, loves to tell of how his father was a member of the group that built it. The coal monument/marker stands as a silent tribute to the miners whose work led to Harlan County being prominently mentioned anytime coalmining in Appalachia is discussed. In those years, the monument stood at the busy intersection of Highways 119 and 421, being passed by traffic going to and from Harlan, the county seat. Now that new roads have bypassed the Baxter we knew in our youth, one could take a nap by the coal monument today and likely not be disturbed. Nevertheless, when former Baxter residents return home, many stop for a photo by the monument because of the prominent place it holds in our memories.

Some from our 2016 Baxter reunion at the Coal Monument

The move from Baxter school to Harlan for junior and senior high was significant, for I was at an age to enjoy more and more freedoms. The truth be told, I never felt a lot of restrictions from my parents. While they wanted to know where I was going, I had freedom to travel everywhere in our little community. During those years, it was common for young people to come in and out of each other's homes. A number of my friends from those years have expressed appreciation for how my parents always made them feel welcome. Though that was something I took for granted at the time, hearing their compliments makes me ever more grateful for the way my mom and dad were always so hospitable to my friends. Thankfully, those of us from Baxter remained amazingly loyal to one another even after our circles of friendship expanded.

As I began attending school in Harlan, and looking at life through slightly more mature eyes, I began to appreciate how uniquely delightful our Baxter community truly was. One business that could not be missed was Modern Bakery, especially when they were baking bread. That unmistakable aroma drifted throughout our entire community. The only other city I have known to rival it is Hershey, PA, where I would later visit; the smell of chocolate was equally enticing. The father of one of my best friends, Ronnie Farley, worked at the bakery; one of our perks was being able to go to the back door and receive a fresh loaf of hot bread, sometimes for free, or only for a few cents. Once our loaf of unsliced bread was in hand, we would often go to Mary Howard's grocery and buy a pound of sliced bologna. This became a frequent practice for my friend, Alvin and me, on our all-day Sunday fishing trips on the Cumberland and Poor Fork Rivers.

Near the coal monument was Coldiron's Service Station. When customers came for gasoline, one of their employees always washed the front windshield, and asked if they could check the oil. It was not uncommon to buy only a dollar's worth. Sometimes it was because we were short on cash, but even that relatively meager amount enabled one to travel several miles, since gas was only 18 to 20 cents a gallon. The face and personality of Coldiron's was Owen. He had served with distinction in World War II as a tail gunner. His job was to use his flexible machine gun to defend the plane against enemy fighter attacks from the rear. All of the boys in the community looked up to him, and we were enthralled by his stories, even though we suspected some were embellished. He and his wife, Effie, were close friends of my mother from childhood, and they later became friends with my dad as well. All these years later, through Facebook, I remain in touch with Owen's son, Mike, and daughter, Sheila.

Baxter was also the home of Chappell's Dairy. Their unforgettable slogan was: *It may be good and not be ours, but it can't be ours and not be good!* In all my years of hearing and seeing commercials, I have yet to encounter one as delightful and appealing; they were not critical of their competitors, but simply affirmed the excellence of their own product. Baxter was blessed to have Chappell's as one of their prominent businesses, and some of the Chappell children became our friends at the Baxter school.

Our community was also blessed with a number of places of worship, but my favorite was the Methodist Church. The pastor in those years, Ralph Leonard, had children in our school. One was a daughter, Laura Jean, who was in my class; and we began to like each other, as much as you can when you are in 4th grade. I have good memories of occasionally giving her a ride home after school on my bicycle. My favorite feature of the Methodist church was the beautiful bell that would resound throughout our community at precise times as church gatherings were approaching. My love for those delightful chimes likely factored into my choice to make this my church home after I became a Christian near the end of my sophomore year of high school.

CHAPTER TWO

When Everything Changed – the Power of the Gospel

"And it shall be that everyone who calls on the name of the Lord will be saved." Acts 2:21

"For the promise is for you and for your children and for all who are far off, even as many as the Lord our God will call to Himself." (Acts 2:39)

There is a famous poem written in the late 1800's by Francis Thompson entitled *The Hound of Heaven.*[1] With great reverence and mastery, he describes the unrelenting pursuit of the loving God for sinners in spite of their best efforts to flee. His insightful sonnet is one of the resources God used to help me later in life to reflect on His tenacious grace which would not give up until I was brought to the end of myself, embracing Jesus Christ as my only hope in life and in death. As is most often the case, this was a humbling and painful process.

As I approached my teen years, I was already becoming aware of my inner spiritual need. In our area of Appalachia, a common thought was that the *age of accountability* was twelve. The belief was that up until that age God would not hold a person accountable for his or her sin; after accountability kicked in, however, each person would have to answer for his sins to a Holy God. As I reflected on that adage, the thought crossed my mind that it would be to my advantage if I could sin as much as possible before I reached that *dreadful age of accountability!*

When I reached my early teens, I suffered a deeply embarrassing incident that exposed how little I knew about the Bible. It occurred in a Sunday school class at the Methodist Church taught by Logan Seales, a highly respected man in our community. Logan often invited me to his class of young people, but I always managed some feeble excuse in refusing his invitation. One day he informed me that the class was going for a picnic afterwards to the fire tower on Pine Mountain. Since this was one of my favorite places, I agreed to come.

As I sat uncomfortably in his class, Logan asked what I viewed as an easy question: *"Should we fear the Lord?"* The regular members all remained surprisingly silent. Since the answer seemed obvious, I naively responded, *"No, we should not fear the Lord!"* Instead of congratulating me as I anticipated, Logan politely explained that my answer was incorrect. He then read this profound verse for his support: "The fear of the Lord is the beginning of wisdom, and the knowledge of the Holy One is understanding" (Proverbs 9:10). Not being arrogant enough to argue with the Bible, I was silenced by the truth of God's Word. I could have been saved from my embarrassment had I followed another verse from Proverbs I would learn years later: "Even a fool, when he keeps silent, is considered wise" (17:28). I also learned the quote commonly attributed to Abraham Lincoln: *"Better to remain silent and be thought a fool than to open your mouth and remove all doubt."*[2] On that unforgettable day in Logan's class, my hasty answer revealed my alarming lack of true, biblical wisdom.

9th grade school picture

During that period, the *Hound of Heaven* seemed to be pursuing me at every turn. It was common to come to a sharp curve in one of our treacherous mountain roads, and be faced with a sign that read, *Get Right with God, Prepare to Meet God,* or *Flee the Wrath to Come!* Each time I saw one of those warnings, I felt God was speaking directly to me, reminding me that I was not right with Him, and certainly not prepared to die.

Though I had older family members and friends who introduced me to certain sins, I quickly discovered that I did not require a lot of instruction. I would eventually learn that sin was at the very core of my nature. In fact, the Bible states that it is an integral part of the makeup of every living person. God's words to the Old Testament prophet, Jeremiah, include this solemn indictment:

"The heart is more deceitful than all else, and is desperately sick (diseased, wicked); who can know it?" (Jeremiah 17:9) Jesus also identified the heart as the root of our problem: "For from within, out of the heart of men, proceed the evil thoughts, fornications, thefts, murders, and adulteries; deeds of coveting and wickedness, as well as deceit, sensuality, envy, slander, pride, and foolishness. All these come from within and defile the man" (Mark 7:21-23). And the Bible repeatedly makes clear that everyone is guilty: "The Lord looked down from heaven upon the sons of men to see if there were any who understand, who seek after God. They have all turned aside, together they have become corrupt; there is no one who does good, not even one" (Psalm 14:2-3). "All have sinned and come short of the glory of God" (Romans 3:23); "There is none righteous, no not one" (Romans 3:10). I later came to see that sin is like a fatal malignancy which plagues the entire human race. In making this point, a friend in Texas loved to say, *"If sin were blue, we'd all be blue."*

In spite of my sin, I now see that my love for sports became one of the restraints that kept me from even greater transgression. My two best sports were baseball and basketball, the ones my father had taught me. Because of this, my favorite teacher in junior high was Joe Gilly who taught 7th grade geography, but was also the coach at

Harlan. His sister, Georgia Howard, had been my 5th and 6th grade teacher at Baxter. Everyone, especially the boys, knew of Joe Gilly, for he was considered one of the top coaches in our state. One of his basketball teams had won the Kentucky state tournament in 1944, when I was only two years old. His best player that year, Wallace (Wah Wah) Jones, went on to star at the University of Kentucky, and was a member of the *Fabulous Five*. This was the nickname given to the 1947-1948 University of Kentucky men's basketball team that won 36 of 39 games, and were national collegiate champions. In the summer of 1948, all five UK starters, along with their coach, Adolph Rupp, were part of the gold medal winning United States team at the Summer

Coach Joe Gilly

Olympics. And Harlan's Coach Gilly was a personal friend of Adolph Rupp! Even today I love geography, and I feel certain that my love for it is rooted in my desire to impress Coach Gilly in 7th grade, and eventually be coached by him as a member of his team.

Once I began junior high at Harlan, I at last had the opportunity to play basketball indoors - in the gym, and become part of the junior high team. The summer between my 7th and 8th grade I grew from 5'3" to 5'10"; all of my pants were suddenly too short. The most pleasing benefit of my new height was how it caught Coach Gilly's attention, along with my developing abilities. Even though he did not coach the junior high team, he kept an eye on the younger players who showed potential, and had a way of giving encouraging words to keep us motivated. After my mother's death in January of 2012, I was going through boxes of keepsakes she had collected over the years, and in one of them I found a post card Joe Gilly had written one summer. In it he was encouraging me to work hard on my game because he envisioned a great future for me on the hardwood. As I look back on those years, he was one of the positive voices God placed in my life and in the lives of my teammates. He regularly admonished his players to not smoke or drink, and to take care of ourselves. While I did not always heed his advice, his words became part of my conscience, and I often seemed to hear them ringing in my ears.

My teachers viewed me as a good student during my elementary years, and I continued to do well through 9th grade. From junior high into high school, most of my teachers considered me shy. I did everything possible to avoid getting in front of the class for any reason. I recall skipping school on occasion to delay giving a book report that was due.

Nevertheless, friends had been important to me during my elementary years in Baxter, and I enjoyed the opportunity to expand my friendships at the larger school in Harlan. Many were established through sports, but there were others, including friendships with a number of girls. My early attempts at *dating* were awkward, but I soon overcame my fears and seemed to always have a girl that I liked.

With increased freedom as I grew older, I began to join my friends in a wide range of sinful activities. Though I had seen the destructive effects of alcohol in others, including my family, I foolishly went down that same path. While taking a drink seems innocent enough in the beginning, the danger is in where it leads. The wisdom of Proverbs contains this sobering warning: "At the last it bites like a serpent and stings like a viper. Your eyes will see strange things, and your mind will utter perverse things" (Proverbs 23:32-33). I once heard a former alcoholic insightfully comment on how commercials for alcohol only focus on the first drink; none reveal, however, the shame and ruin that is so often the consequence of intoxication. Those of us who grew up in the 50's knew nothing about marijuana or other drugs, but we had moonshine – white lightning. It was relatively cheap, and only a small amount was needed for one to become completely drunk! The summer I was 15, I was able, through the influence of my father, to obtain a job at Wardrup's making minimum wage, $1.00 an hour, enough money to spend on beer and moonshine, and I made many foolish and reckless choices. Only the grace of God kept me from permanently destroying my life in that one brief summer. As an aside, three of my friends, two who were on the high school basketball team with me, and the other from elementary school, all died young. Independent reports from family members in all three cases were essentially the same; *"He drank himself to death".* And as the wise adage goes, *"There go I, but for the grace of God,"*[3] or to paraphrase the song loved by all Harlan County folks, written by Darrell Scott, *"I would have never left Harlan alive!"*[4]

During those months, there were five of us from Baxter that ran around together. Kenneth was the one with the car, a black '46 Ford. It was in his vehicle that several of us learned to drive. After we would return from a wild night of drinking and other destructive activities, we would sit in front of Kenneth's house and talk. A bewildering occurrence for which there is no human explanation is that our conversation always seemed to turn to the Lord, to heaven and hell, and how we were not prepared to meet God. The *Hound of*

Heaven was after all of us! As the years passed, most of my friends eventually gave their lives to the Lord.

Another shameful sin was my profanity – foul, vulgar words and dirty jokes. The prophet, Isaiah, when confronted with the holiness of God early in his life, cried out, "Woe is me, for I am ruined! For I am a man of unclean lips, and I dwell among a people of unclean lips; for my eyes have seen the King, the Lord of hosts" (Isaiah 6:5). The cause of the obscene and filthy words, as well as the vulgar jokes commonly told in our group, was an absence of the fear of the Lord. Our culture today is appallingly irreverent with absolutely no shame, and for the same reason. It brings me grief that this was one of the disgraceful ways my sinful nature expressed itself. Again, for reasons I cannot understand apart from God's restraining influence, I never felt free to curse in front of my parents or siblings, or in the presence of girls.

It was during my sophomore year that my life was moving into an almost out of control, downward spiral. While the report cards my mother faithfully kept verify my academic irresponsibility, the grades were only symptomatic of much deeper problems in my life. Though I was unaware of Jesus' words, I was on what He referred to as "the broad road that leads to destruction" (Matthew 7:13). But, thankfully, *the Hound of Heaven* was closing in! The Bible reveals that "It is the kindness of God that leads you to repentance" (Romans 2:4). In His gracious kindness, the Lord brought into my life an attractive young girl who would by her life and words introduce me to the most joyful news ever announced, the Gospel of the Lord Jesus Christ! Though she was a year behind me in school, she was bold in her faith and amazingly articulate. Not surprisingly, it was through my love for basketball that I met her.

One day my friend, Alvin, suggested that we go up to the Shoope home to play basketball instead of playing at our regular spot in front of the Baxter Post Office. The Shoopes had moved to Baxter a year earlier, and had two older sons near our age. Alvin explained how they had put up a nice basketball goal next to their home with a level place to play. This enabled me to become acquainted with Don and Howard, and both soon became close friends. While we were playing, a cute girl was sitting nearby watching us. To say that she caught my attention would be an understatement! I soon learned that her name was Carol Romine. The reason I had not met her earlier was because she went to school in Loyal. The curvy, gravel road that separated the Shoope and Romine homes was the dividing line between the two school districts. From that point onward, the basketball court at Don and Howard's became my favorite place to play, and Carol was often there watching. I learned that she had an older sister, Joyce, and that Alvin already had his eye on her.

One day as Carol and I were talking, I asked her for a date. A date at our age simply meant that I could come to her home for a visit. She agreed, and we set the time for Thursday night. When I knocked on the door that evening, her little brother, Curt, answered, and said, *"You must be Tommy. Carol is getting ready for church!"* While I was certainly not prepared for the news that our *date* would include going to church, I was delighted when Carol entered the room with a friendly smile. As it turned out, her father, a coalminer, was also a lay preacher in their church. While I felt somewhat fearful of him, Carol's mother was warm and gracious, enabling me to feel more at ease. We rode in the back seat of their car to and from church. Afterwards, Carol and I were permitted to sit on the rock wall in front of their home and talk until her parents flashed the porch light on and off, signaling that it was time for Carol to come in and for me to leave.

Though I cannot recall Carol's specific words, I left her home that evening knowing that Jesus Christ was the most important part of her life! Never before had I heard anyone speak of their Christian faith outside of church, in a one on one conversation. While her words of testimony were convincing, it was the attractiveness of her life the Lord used to grab my attention. In His Sermon on the Mount Jesus described how His children are "the salt of the earth" (Matthew 5:13). Salt has many benefits, but if you eat something salty, it also makes you thirsty; it was through Carol that I became thirsty to know more of this attractive life she possessed.

After our first *date,* my pattern for the next ten months became one of attending church with Carol and her family on  Thursday and Sunday evenings. As time passed, her parents permitted us to be together in other settings outside of church, and I especially looked forward to those occasions. Carol became acquainted with my parents, my sisters, and my little brother, David, whom she especially loved. She was also able to come to some of my basketball games in Harlan. Carol was permitted as well to travel with my family to some of the state parks and other popular sites in Southeastern Kentucky. As soon as I reached my 16th birthday, I was able to obtain my driver's license, and there were a few occasions when Carol

With Carol Romine   was permitted to go with me in my dad's black, '51 Ford, on a double date with some of our mutual friends.

In that ten month period leading up to and including my sophomore year, I was essentially two different people. When I was with Carol and around her family, I was on my absolute best behavior; when I was with my other friends, it was the exact opposite. As my friends and I were continuing to pursue a sinful, dangerous lifestyle, I would often ask God to protect me from danger, or to rescue me when I was in a threatening spot, even making promises to turn to Him if He would answer. Sadly, my promises were hollow and of no lasting significance.

My spiritual conversations with Carol were becoming progressively more serious. Though I cannot recall the specifics, I do remember talking often about the cross, and what Jesus did for us. Only recently, while going through a newly discovered box of my

31

mother's keepsakes, I found a note Carol had written while we were dating. It included these words: *"Out of all the good times we've had together, the ones I like best are when we just sit and talk as we've done so often."* I believe she sensed that our conversations were leading to the conclusion she had desired and prayed for all along, my salvation.

After returning from church on a Thursday night, and with a sense of *the Hound of Heaven* nipping at my heels, our conversation was especially solemn. Carol quietly asked me, *"When are you going to give your life to the Lord?"* My response was to ask her to pray that I would do so the following Sunday. Because decisions of a spiritual nature were generally made during altar calls and invitations in our area, I felt it had be this way with me. At that point Carol stopped and prayed for me, a short, simple, sincere prayer, and I was emotionally moved.

Soon the porch light flashed, and it was time for Carol to go inside and for me to head down the hill toward home. It was like a heavy weight was pressing against my heart, and I desperately needed to find relief. Then the thought came to me, *"Why do I have to be in church to give my life to the Lord?"* Being unable to come up with an answer, I suddenly found myself on my knees in the middle of the road! Though I don't remember the exact words I prayed, I do recall telling the Lord that I had a lot of sins, and also questions, but that I was giving my life to Him, as Carol and I had often discussed. While not everyone has tears when they respond to God's call, I certainly did. Because a heavy burden had been removed from my back, and from my heart, I wept tears of joy because I was no longer running from God. *The Hound of Heaven had successfully tracked me down!* The Bible describes it this way: "Therefore, having been justified by faith, we have peace with God through our Lord Jesus Christ" (Romans 5:1). Though I felt an immediate emotional peace as I surrendered my life to the Lord, I later learned that this verse is describing an objective fact, an eternal transaction that forever changed my standing before God. On the basis of faith alone in Christ alone, all of my sins were now placed on Christ, while His perfect righteousness was placed on me! The song writer, Bruce Carroll, refers to this as *The Great Exchange!*[5] The Apostle Paul described it as follows: "He made Him who knew no sin to be sin on our behalf that we might become the righteousness of God in Him" (II Corinthians 5:21).

Though it would take years to begin to grasp all that the Bible says about the miraculous spiritual transformation that occurs at salvation, my new life in Christ had begun.   Years later, I heard someone make this helpful observation: *Becoming a Christian is committing all of yourself that you know to all of Jesus that you understand.*   While there was much more to learn about myself, and infinitely more to discover about Jesus, this was the moment when I was born again - when everything changed!   The date was May 8, 1958, around 10:00 in the evening!

As I am writing about that evening, more than sixty years have passed, but that night is when I first began to experience the miraculous power of the Gospel. Through the diligent study of God's Word I have come to possess a much fuller understanding of the extraordinary ways God works to call sinners to faith in Christ. While the promise of Scripture is that "everyone who calls upon the name of the Lord will be saved" (which I did on May 8th, at the age of 16), the Bible reveals that we are actually responding to God's call. When the Apostle Peter proclaimed the gospel to the large crowd on the Day of Pentecost, including the 3,000 who believed, he highlighted God's call: "This promise is for you and your children and for all who are far off, even as many as the Lord our God will call to Himself" (Acts 2:39). In fact, the Greek word for church (*Ekklesia*) literally means *called out ones*. Through no merit of our own, God graciously calls us out of the sin and darkness of our lives into an eternal relationship with Himself. Every true Christian has a uniquely personal story of how he or she responded to God's gracious, loving call.

With a peace I had never known in my heart, and my sins now forgiven, I joyfully made my way down that gravel road I knew like the back of my hand. From there I walked along the railroad, and then up the hill to my home. My father worked nights, and my mother always waited up until I came home, however late that might be.

In writing about the power of the Gospel, the Apostle Paul states, "With the heart a person believes, resulting in righteousness, and with the mouth confession is made unto salvation" (Romans 10:10). Having believed in my heart and entrusted my life and future to Jesus just a few moments earlier, my mother was the first to hear my initial confession of faith. Again there were tears of joy and relief as I related to her what I had done. She was clearly pleased and went on to relate how she also had desired to be a Christian. Her reason for not surrendering to the Lord was because she did not feel she could live the Christian life in the way she believed it was meant to be lived. At this point my mother said to me, *"Just be sure you are determined to never turn back!"* That is especially wise counsel, particularly when coming from an unbeliever, and the helpful words were also coming from my mother.

In the decades since, I have discovered that there is much more to living the Christian life than my own determination and willpower. The Apostle Paul explained to the church in Philippi the magnificent truth that enables us to continue: "I am confident of this very thing that He who began a good work in you will continue to perfect it until the day of Jesus Christ" (Philippians 1:6). We persevere in our faith because salvation is the faithful, ongoing work of Almighty God in the lives of those He calls to Himself. And the Apostle Paul continues with the same thought in chapter two of his letter to the believers at Philippi: "Work out your own salvation with fear and trembling, for it is God who is at work within you both to will and to work for His good pleasure" (Philippians 2:12-13). Paul does not say that we work *for our salvation*, for "it is the gift of God, not as the result of works, so that no one may boast" (Ephesians 2:9). But we do work it out; that is, we live out our salvation with a reverential fear because Almighty God is working in us, giving us the desire and the power to live in a way that brings glory to Him.

The next person to hear the news of my salvation was my father. He always arrived home from his night shift before I left for school. Dad also was happy for me, but not as expressive as my mother in his affirmation. When I arrived at school, there were certain friends I wanted to tell, but none were as enthusiastic as I expected them to be. Believing in my heart that I still had to go to church on Sunday to make everything official, there was time to reflect and talk more to the Lord about it all. Yes, I had a lot of questions, but I felt confident they would be answered in His time.

One of the first tests to my faith came on a Saturday night, two evenings after I was saved. Following their pattern from previous years, the roller skating business had returned in the spring to set up their tent in Sunshine, a small community similar to Baxter, but on the other side of Harlan. As I had done before, I went skating with my friends. But as closing time approached at the rink, I became deeply troubled as I contemplated what was coming next. This was the time when the drinking would begin, followed by other reckless activities. Feeling a deep repulsion toward what our group always did was a quiet reminder that a change was occurring in me, such as the Bible describes: "When someone becomes a Christian, he becomes a brand new person inside; he is not the same anymore; a new life has begun" (II Corinthians 5:17 TLB).[6] Suddenly, I understood that I had to get out of there, to flee from the evil I knew was just ahead. I quickly put my shoes on, and began to literally run away from the skating rink as fast as I could, leaving my friends bewildered as to what had come over me. They called out as I ran through the streets of Sunshine and then disappeared into the night. I ran past the National Guard Armory, across the bridge, and from there through the streets and back alleys of Harlan. My friends initially pursued me on foot to no avail, and then by car. I was aware that they spotted me a couple of times, but I continued to flee. In my desire to avoid the sin of that evening, I did something none among my Baxter friends would ever do, even in a group. Knowing they would not follow me there, I went through Georgetown, that part of Harlan where only black families lived at the time. This was nearly six years before our schools integrated, and the separation between the races was clearly defined, and the relationships sometimes tense. From there I followed the railroad to Baxter and eventually made it safely into the refuge of my home.

In *The Hound of Heaven,* Frances Thompson writes: *"I fled Him, down through the nights and down the days; I fled Him down through the arches of the years; I fled Him down the tangled ways of my own mind; and in the midst of tears..."* [7] While I experienced some of those identical emotions in fleeing from the Lord, as a two day old Christian I was now fleeing from my unbelieving friends, seeking to avoid the sin to which I could have so easily returned.

Upon arriving home, my parents were not there, and I was thankful I could be alone. Each Saturday night they met with my mother's siblings and their spouses to play cards and to listen to the

Grand Ole Opry. When I was safe in our living room, I immediately fell to my knees and began to cry out to the Lord. While I was praying, I heard someone coming up the front steps, just outside the living room window. Whoever it was would have easily spotted me on my knees. It turned out to be my friend, Alvin, who had been at the skating rink, and had witnessed my bizarre, bewildering behavior. He came by on his way home because he was genuinely concerned. I then informed him about my prayer two nights earlier, and what I intended to do the next morning at church. After he left, I was thankful and encouraged by how sympathetic and supportive my good friend had been toward me.

With my friend, Alvin

The next day was Mother's Day. Because I never went to church with Carol on Sunday mornings, my intent was to go to the Methodist Church. I loved their church bell, and had at one time wondered if perhaps *the Hound of Heaven* was actually calling out to me through the chimes when Alvin and I would have our all day Sunday fishing trips on the river. Carol's church was located beyond Harlan, and for a variety of reasons, I did not feel it was the one for me. The Methodist Church, located just up the lane from my grandparent's home, was where several of my mom and dad's friends were members, and where I believed they would go if and when they became Christians. Much to my surprise, my friend, Kenneth, also was in attendance that day. Though I don't recall anything that was said during the service, as soon as the closing hymn of invitation began, I immediately slipped out of the pew and made my way to the front, kneeling on the floor in front of the altar. When the pastor, Roy Reeves, came to pray with me, I looked up and was surprised to see that Kenneth had also come forward, asking to be saved. While we had been close friends during elementary and junior high, Kenneth chose to transfer to Loyal for his final years of high school, meaning we did not see each other nearly as frequently as before. But seeing him in church on Mother's Day and then having him come forward that same morning brought even more joy to my heart!

When I informed the pastor what I done, he was clearly delighted. His next words were, *"Now next Sunday you will be baptized, and the following Sunday you will join our church."* He did not ask if this was what I would like to do, but simply explained that this was the way it worked. As I left church that morning, I felt a deep peace about everything that had transpired. After joining my family to give honor to our mother on her special day, I followed my normal pattern of going to church with Carol in the evening. She was clearly excited about the events of the past few days as she had witnessed God answering her prayers, and bringing spiritual fruit from our many candid, heart to heart conversations.

While I can't recall a lot from that next week, I do remember reflecting on what an important step baptism would be. While I was somewhat apprehensive, what kept me encouraged was the way my

37

life was truly beginning to change, not only externally but on the inside!

Baptism in our church meant going to the *baptizing hole* on the Poor Fork River. Different churches in Harlan County used that same site because the shore was relatively smooth and sandy, and the depth of the water was just right. Alvin and I often fished through that area of the river, and at times witnessed baptisms, but always from a safe distance. Several people were present that day, including my family, and most from the Baxter church. Carol was also there with her mother. As important as the step of baptism is, it is not the same as salvation. The clear pattern in the New Testament is that belief precedes baptism, and this was certainly true in my case. Just as a wedding ring is a symbol of the commitment we make in marriage to our spouse, so baptism is a symbol of our identification with Christ in His death and resurrection: "Therefore, we have been buried with Him through baptism into death, so that as Christ was raised from the dead through the glory of the Father, so we too might walk in newness of life. For if we have been united with Him in the likeness of His death, certainly we shall also be in the likeness of His resurrection" (Romans 6:4-5).

In those early weeks, the news of my conversion spread through the school, and I was aware that I was being watched. One day a group of us were going off campus for lunch, and I was driving my dad's Ford. As I made my way down Central Avenue, heading away from the school, a car coming off a side street pulled in front of me. While I was able to stop without a collision, a curse word suddenly came out! My first action was to silently ask the Lord for forgiveness, and to ask Him to help me never to do it again. My second thought was to apologize to my friends, affirming what they already knew, namely, that my desire was to live as a Christian. The greatest lesson for me came later as I was reflecting on what had occurred. When I gave my life to the Lord approximately two weeks earlier, I had not promised Him that I would stop cursing, nor had I even determined to put my vulgar way of speaking behind me. It was then that I realized that God was already beginning to change my way of speaking without any conscious effort of my own.

The following Sunday, as the pastor had explained, I became a member of the church. Our Methodist church was of the old fashioned variety that still believed the Bible was the Word of God, and that Scripture alone was our final authority in all matters of faith and conduct, a truth I continue to wholeheartedly affirm today. As I stood before the pastor and congregation, the question from Roy Reeves was this: *"Will you be loyal to our church and uphold it by your prayers, your presence, your gifts, and your service?"* My response was to say that I would.

This chapter about *the Power of the Gospel* would not be complete without commenting on another miracle I observed. On the Christmas prior to my 16th birthday in January, and approximately six months after I began my relationship with Carol and attending church with her family, my parents gave me a Bible for Christmas. I was pleased to receive it, a genuine black, holy Bible! I recall opening it to read at various places, but being completely unable to comprehend anything I was reading. I was pleased to have it, but baffled as to why the Bible made no sense to me. In the days soon after my conversion, however, I opened that same Bible, and it appeared to be an entirely different book! In it I found verse after verse that spoke directly to where I was, verses that brought immediate encouragement for my new life in Christ. The Bible had certainly not changed; rather I was the one who had been spiritually transformed. Later I would discover a passage that perfectly explained what I had experienced: "A natural man does not accept the things of the Spirit of God, for they are foolishness to him; and he cannot understand them, for they are spiritually appraised. But he who is spiritual appraises all things..." (I Corinthians 2:14-15). By the power of the gospel, I was changed from a natural man, completely dead in my trespasses and sins, into a spiritually alive young man whose eyes and heart had been opened by the gracious and sovereign work of God in my life! And my life would never again be the same!

An important piece of information before moving ahead with the story of my journey of grace is that before that summer had ended, Carol and I had gone our separate ways. Thankfully, we did so without any animosity by either of us. One factor in our decision was that we were already going to different schools, but now, following my conversion, we were going to different churches. We both continued to have only positive memories of our relationship that lasted nearly one year, one that I know beyond any shadow of a doubt that God sovereignly arranged.

The Bible says, "But how can they call on Him to save them unless they believe in Him? And how can they believe in Him if they have never heard about Him? And how can they hear about him unless someone tells them? And how will anyone go and tell them without being sent? That is why the Scriptures say, 'How beautiful are the feet of messengers who bring good news!'" (Romans 10:14-15) In His kindness, Carol was the one God chose to communicate the Gospel to me, and she did so in such a winsome way. Though I never carefully studied her feet, in a spiritual sense, I know they had to be extremely beautiful, for hers were the feet brought me the good news of the Gospel of the grace of God!

Carol and I saw and greeted one another a few times during my last two years in high school. After I went away to college, my recollection is of seeing her only one other time. During my college years, however, when I would return home to visit my family, I often saw her mother, and we always shared a warm exchange. Each time I asked her to express my gratitude to Carol for the wonderful role she played in my life.

Carol eventually married a young man from Loyal High School, and they had four children, two biological and two who were adopted. She and her husband were married for 25 years. Though I never knew her as an adult, everything I heard confirmed her love for the Lord, for her family, for others, for needy animals, and her commitment to her church. Sadly, Carol was tragically killed in January of 2000. Upon hearing the news of her death, I wrote a lengthy letter to her family describing Carol's positive influence on my life. This opened the door for me to reestablish contact with Carol's older sister, Joyce, and we

Carol - who pointed me to Jesus!

have enjoyed various opportunities to renew our friendship in the years since. A few months after writing the letter, I was also contacted by Carol's daughter, Alicia, who now lives in her mother's former home in Kingsport, TN. My wife, Linda, and I were able to meet and establish a friendship with Alicia, one we will always treasure. I have a lovely photo from when Alicia and I met face to face. It is permanently and prominently placed in my office to remind me of her mother. As the song says, *I Can Only Imagine,* but I often try to envision what it will be like in heaven to reunite with Carol and express to her my profound gratitude. Whatever it will be like, it is certainly one of the reunions I am greatly anticipating.

CHAPTER THREE

When God's Calling Became Clear – The Vision of My Faithful Pastor

"Faithful is He who calls you, and He will bring it to pass."
I Thessalonians 5:24

The pastor who prayed with me, baptized me, and welcomed me into the Baxter Church, Roy Reeves, was a likeable man, one I was eager to know better. In mid-June, however, when I was only six weeks into my new faith, I heard the sad news that he was moving, and that our church would soon receive a new pastor. The Methodist Church always had their annual conference in June, so this was the time when pastors, for a variety of reasons, were relocated by the conference bishop to a new assignment. The word soon came that Bill Garnett, a younger man, would be our new pastor. His wife was named, Betty, and they had no children. One of the first things to catch my attention was his classy car, a 1957 Chevy, an extremely popular model! My only disappointment was when I learned that his was only a six cylinder, and not the more popular and powerful V-8.

On Bill Garnett's first Sunday, he explained that he would also be the pastor at Yancey, a small coal mining community located a few miles from Harlan. I later discovered that this type of arrangement was not uncommon. Smaller churches unable to afford a full time pastor often share responsibility for the pastor's salary, and both receive proportionally from his ministry. Baxter would be Bill Garnett's primary church, but he would also preach at Yancey in an early Sunday service, then return to Baxter for the traditional 11:00 hour of worship.

When Bill Garnett mentioned that he would be at Yancey for that first Sunday evening, Kenneth and I decided we would go and show our support. As the service came to a close and he announced the closing hymn, our new pastor mentioned how pleased he was to have two young men from the Baxter Church present. And then he said, *"After we sing our final hymn, I would like to ask Tommy Madon*

42

to lead us in our closing prayer!" Suddenly I felt a rush of fear unlike any I had ever known! The thought of *praying out loud and leading in prayer* had never once crossed my mind. After what seemed to be a very short hymn, I mumbled some words to the Lord, though I have no idea what I may have prayed. As I have reflected on why he asked me to pray, knowing I was such a new Christian, I later came to view it as an expression of the potential he saw in me, and of the vision he had for me to grow in my faith.

Bill and Betty Garnet

As a further expression of his interest, that next week my new pastor invited me to accompany him and his wife to Wilmore, Kentucky, the home of Asbury College and Seminary, to attend a few days of the Wilmore Camp Meeting. Bill explained that I could also invite another friend to come along. Since Kenneth was unable to go, I decided to ask Earl, the point guard on our Harlan basketball team, and quarterback on the football team. He was interested, so we set out on what would be a new adventure.

Camp meetings have their roots in the 1800's, and while they were especially prevalent in Methodist churches, some Presbyterian, Baptist, and other denominations utilized them as well.[1] Camp meetings typically meet for ten days each summer, with people often coming from long distances to attend. Originally, those attending camped in tents, as the name suggests, but as time passed, seasonal cottages were built for the adults, and simple dorms were constructed to accommodate the large numbers of young people who would attend. Most campgrounds also have a cafeteria, a snack bar, and typically a book store.

At the Wilmore Camp Meeting, three services were conducted daily, all in the large tabernacle that would seat at least 500. There were also two youth services that met in a structure referred to as the youth tabernacle. One youth gathering was before the morning service, and the other prior to the evening gathering. All meetings included enthusiastic singing, inspiring special music, followed by the sermon. Camp meetings always featured three itinerant evangelists from various parts of the country, and we heard all three every day. There was another gifted speaker for the youth, as well as a music leader. What this meant was that Earl and I heard five sermons a day! Because we were meeting other interesting young people from all around the state, including many cute girls, Earl never once complained. As for my response, I loved everything about the experience, especially the sermons! Because I knew so little about the Bible, I was like a sponge, absorbing as much as I could take in. While the speakers had different styles, each one preached straight from the Bible. All three included fascinating stories to illustrate the biblical truths in their sermons. Bill Garnett explained that the morning and afternoon sermons were typically designed for those who were already Christians, while the evening service was evangelistic, and directed toward those who had not yet been saved. All three services included a closing altar call to invite those who felt prompted by the Holy Spirit to come and pray. I could have gone forward every service, and often did, not only in response to the biblical instruction, but from being so deeply challenged by most every sermon.

As we returned home, my vision of Christianity was significantly enlarged. I had met and interacted with young people from churches across Kentucky, and many, like me, were genuinely excited about their faith. The enthusiasm in our little Baxter church, where the attendance was 70 or 80 on a crowded Sunday morning, was not nearly as impressive as what I had witnessed at camp meeting. But I was growing to love our church because of the spiritual instruction I was receiving, and especially the loving encouragement I was receiving from my first spiritual family. The older ones in the church loved to pray for the youth. One lady, who was simply known as *Aunt Sis,* would often pray, *"Lord, help me not to be a stumbling block, but a stepping stone for our young people!"* As I became more familiar with God's Word, I came to see that she was

44

likely referring to the warning Jesus gave about not causing "the little ones who believed in Him to stumble" (Matthew 18:6). I was also coming to see that when God called me by His grace to be His son, He also called me into a relationship with His people, into His Body, and into His forever family. I was just beginning to get a taste of how wonderful His church could be.

By this time I was also coming to see that being saved and in a relationship with Jesus was the greatest thing that had ever happened to me. It only made sense, then, that the greatest thing I could do for others was to help them know Him as well. While I was deeply concerned for my non-Christian friends, I was especially burdened for my mom and dad, and my entire family. One day as I was reading through the book of Acts, I came across the passage where the Philippian jailer asked the Apostle Paul, "What must I do to be saved?" Paul's answer was simple but profound: "Believe on the Lord Jesus Christ, and you will be saved, and your house" (Acts 16:31). The phrase that seemed to leap off the page for me was *"and your house."* God used the Apostle Paul's words to the jailer to encourage me to believe that my family would one day also be saved.

Youth Tabernacle at Camp Meeting

As we were returning from Wilmore, Bill Garnett informed me of an even larger camp meeting later in the summer called Indian Springs, but this one was in Flovilla, Georgia, south of Atlanta. He invited me, along with a few other young people from Baxter and Yancey to join them as their guests for the entire ten days! Bill's wife, Betty, came from a family who owned a large cottage on the camp ground, with a number of rooms where we would stay. The old, white southern structure had a large back porch with a lengthy table, which I later learned would have on it large bowls of grits all three meals. It was a table with adequate space for us and several others. All I needed to bring was a small suitcase with clothes for that length of time, and also my Bible, which I knew I could not be without!

Everything I had loved about Wilmore Camp Meeting increased exponentially at Indian Springs. By the time I returned home after an exhilarating 10 days, having listened attentively to 50 additional instructive and inspiring sermons, I reflected on how vastly different my life was from what it had been in early May. At that time, I was spiritually dead in my sins, totally lacking in Bible knowledge, and traveling at a dangerous speed on the broad road that led to destruction. And now, only a few months later, I was a new creation in Christ, filled with a living hope, and beginning to sense that God had a larger purpose for my life.

As my pastor was witnessing my hunger for God's Word, along with the excitement I had in sharing my faith, he asked if I would be willing to lead one of the studies for our Wednesday night prayer meeting. Without any hesitation, I agreed. He gave me a study guide, and the lesson included passages that focused on Jesus' sufferings and death on the cross. Though I had frequently given testimonies in church, this would be my first attempt at the more serious responsibility of speaking from behind the pulpit. One of my non-Christian friends, Howard, was there the night I taught. When we sang the closing hymn, I asked if anyone would like to come forward and pray, and Howard immediately responded. My pastor and I prayed with him. Howard became one of my most loyal friends through high school and beyond. Soon afterwards, I took another bold step and invited several friends to our home with my parent's permission, where I led a Bible study on Jesus' parable of the seed, the sower, and the four types of soil. Even today, I can remember most of those who were there, and where they sat.

In the fall, our church formed a youth choir. Since Bill Garnett was a proficient piano player, music was a high priority in our church. As we look back at photos from those days, Howard and I were the tallest members in the choir, even though a couple of girls were near our age. My sisters, Linda and Ella, were also beginning to respond to the Lord, and they also became part of the choir. The director was Dorothy Williams, an excellent vocalist in our church. She loved our youth choir, and we all loved her.

As I entered my junior year, I had a new purpose in life. My desire was to discover how to faithfully represent the Lord wherever I was, in all my relationships, including time spent with Judy who I dated that year, and on the basketball floor. While I was practicing basketball every day after school with a few of my teammates who were not on the football team, I loved being free in the evenings anytime there were church activities.

It was around this time that my pastor began to give me books, ones I later learned were classics: *In His Steps, Fox's Book of Martyrs, The Imitation of Christ, and My Utmost for His Highest.* He also gave me a devotional book by Mrs. Charles Cowman entitled, *Mountain TrailWays for Youth.*[2] One of the daily readings was especially challenging to me: "And David, after he had served the purpose of God in his generation, fell asleep..." (Acts 13:36) Mrs. Cowman's challenge was that we as young people should also seek to *serve the purpose of God in our generation.* Her encouragement was to write in the flyleaf of our Bibles, "*I will seek to serve the purpose of God in my generation!*" And that is what I did, writing those exact words in the front of one of my earliest Bibles. And then she wrote, *"This is life at its highest and best."* I would certainly learn the truth of her statement in the years that followed!

As I have often reflected on our pastor and his wife who related to us in simple ordinary ways, Bill and Betty went on to have an extraordinarily fruitful ministry in our small church, one that spanned more than a decade. They had a genuine love for our church, along with a faithful commitment to the ministry. Their most unique contribution, however, may have been the vision they had for special events, large and small, and how significant they can be in the life of the church. In addition to the summer camp meetings, each Sunday night Bill and Betty invited the young people into the parsonage located next to the church for popcorn. They also purchased a ping pong table for the church basement, providing a fun place where the youth could gather. But other special events for the entire church were on the way. While the Garnetts were there, the church always had an annual revival in the fall with a gifted, guest speaker invited by our pastor.

Our first revival in the early fall of 1958 was led by two passionate students from Asbury College, Bill and Betty's alma mater. Joe Alley was the preacher and Harry Nesmith the song leader. Our church was captivated by Joe's dramatic sermons from the Old Testament book of Exodus, as He drew fascinating parallels between Israel's 400 years of bondage in Egypt, and our slavery to sin. He then compared the children of Israel's miraculous deliverance through the Red Sea to the amazing way Jesus rescued us from sin's bondage. We also loved Harry's special music each night. One of the songs immediately became my new favorite because of the way it captured the essence of the Gospel: *"Jesus my Lord will love me forever; from Him no power of evil can sever. He gave His life to ransom my soul; now I belong to Him! Now I belong to Jesus; Jesus belongs to me; not for the years of time alone, but for eternity."*[3]

The next unique event on our youth group calendar would come in late September. Our plan was to travel to Charlotte, North Carolina, to attend one night of the Billy Graham Crusade. Our youth group leader was Jane Maglia, daughter of the owner of Chappell's Dairy. Because there were eight of us eager to be part of this grand adventure, we were at a loss for a vehicle large enough for the group. One of our youth group members, Edna, had an older brother who was the director of a local funeral home. They had a spacious Ford station wagon which doubled as a hearse. When Edna approached her brother, his response was that if no one died in the days leading up to our trip, the station wagon would be ours to use! We began to pray that God would keep everyone alive, especially those who would require the services of Bianchi Funeral Home. The Lord answered, and that large, luxury vehicle was generously made available to our group.

That trip of nearly 300 miles to Charlotte was in every way an unforgettable journey. We soon discovered that the black Ford wagon had flashing lights on the front grill, as well as an inside switch for a siren. Since I was viewed by this time as *a responsible young man*, and the most experienced driver next to Jane, she asked me to share the driving with her. As the trip unfolded, it became clear that my character was not yet equal to my reputation. Entering one of the tunnels in the Smoky Mountains, someone suggested that we turn the siren on for a few moments, just to hear what it would sound like in the tunnel! Yes, it was an immature and irresponsible choice, but we still did it! Thankfully, the Lord graciously protected us, and also kept the police away during those brief moments of fun and frivolity.

One of the moments forever etched in my mind came as our little group entered the massive Charlotte auditorium. The crusade choir was rehearsing under the direction of Cliff Barrows. Though none of us had ever heard the song, we all loved it immediately: *"To God be the glory, great things He has done; so loved He the world that He gave us His Son; who yielded His life an atonement for sin, and opened the life gate that all may go in! Praise the Lord, praise the Lord; let the earth hear His voice; praise the Lord, praise the Lord; let the people rejoice! O come to the Father through Jesus the Son, and give Him the glory, great things He has done!"* [4] Billy Graham's stirring, evangelistic sermon that evening was from Jesus' Sermon on the Mount: "Enter through the narrow gate; for the gate is wide, and the way is broad that leads to destruction, and there are many who enter through it. For the gate is small and the way is narrow that leads to life, and there are few who find it" (Matthew 7:13-14). One member of our group, Richard, a friend who lived down the hill from our family, made his way forward during the singing of *"Just as I Am"*, and with the assistance of a counselor, placed his faith in Jesus Christ. Our group rejoiced with Richard, and everyone was deeply inspired by that incredible evening. As an aside, after not seeing Richard for many years, we were able to reconnect at a reunion of Baxter friends in 2012, and to reminisce on that memorable, life-changing night for him at the Billy Graham Crusade. While Richard has become a wealthy man, he takes time out of each week to visit a local nursing home in the city where he lives, asking the director to give him the names of the men and women who rarely have visitors. He then goes to the rooms of these lonely, elderly folks where he reads passages from the Psalms, and prays for them. How encouraging it was to see God faithfully continuing His work in Richard!

My junior year of high school basketball was filled with high expectations. Our coach, Joe Gilly, believed we had the potential to win the state. Because his 1944 championship team had worn black tennis shoes, he ordered low-cut, black Converse All Stars for our team, instead of the standard white we had always worn before. As was the case my sophomore year, I was again a member of the starting five. We had a great year with only a few losses, and for several weeks were ranked as one of the top teams in the state. At tournament time, we easily breezed through the district and were crowned champions, and were looking forward to the regional tournament. For basketball purposes, the state of Kentucky has 16 regions, with the regional champs going to the state tournament, held at that time in Louisville's Freedom Hall, which seated 18,000. The regional was held at Clay County, and we won our preliminary games to face them in the final. Though we had beaten Clay County twice during the regular season, we lost when it counted the most, and would not make the trip to Freedom Hall. My only basketball consolation came when awards were announced a couple of weeks later, and I surprisingly received a high honor. The best player on our

Always a Green Dragon

team was Lawyer Partin, but at the end of the year, even though our stats were similar, I was selected for a special honor. One of the most treasured notes in my yearbook that year was from him. It read: *"Tom – I would like to say that I have really enjoyed going to school with a great boy like you, and playing basketball together. I would like to congratulate you on making all – SEK. It sure is nice to have a boy like you on our team. I believe we can make state champs next year if we work hard enough – Lawyer."* Though he won other well-deserved awards, there was no hint of jealousy toward me. Sadly, during our senior year, we again lost to Clay County in the regionals, and our team never fulfilled our dream of playing in Freedom Hall.

Another of my mother's keepsakes from one of those faded cardboard boxes was my first attempt at an autobiography. It was written midway through my junior year to fulfill an assignment from our English teacher, Mr. Terry. While I laughed out loud as I read what I had written about my great-grandfather's moon-shining enterprise, and other unflattering tidbits that should have remained among our *family secrets,* I discovered a few sentences where I had verbalized my new faith: *"At the end of my sophomore year I became a Christian. I feel like this is the greatest step anyone can take in life because you have something to live for, as this is something no one can take away from you. During last summer I attended a lot of church camp meetings, and learned more of who God really is....After I finish high school, I plan to attend college, but I don't know where as of now. I plan to study engineering unless my plans are changed. The only way my plans would change is for me to feel that I ought to be doing more for people. After all, it is a Christian's job to help people."* After the final sentence, Mr. Terry had written: *"How true!"* My grade was B+! In reading my paper again all these years later, and seeing numerous grammatical flaws, there was clearly a lot of grace in the grade I received!

Another unforgettable experience I have enjoyed telling over the years happened in late March. My good friend and teammate, Robert "Buddy" Tweed, secured two tickets to the Final Four to be held in Freedom Hall in Louisville, the same arena where our Harlan team would have played had we been regional champions. Hitchhiking was both common and safe in those days, and that was my primary means of transportation to and from school until I was able to drive my dad's car. But this time Buddy and I were going to hitchhike all the way across the state, 250 miles. His sister lived in Louisville and was the one who helped us obtain the tickets, and we stayed in her home. When we arrived, she made pizza for us; neither of us had heard of pizza, much less tasted it. The teams in the final four were West Virginia, led by Jerry West, my favorite player; Cincinnati, whose star was Oscar Robertson; with California and Louisville rounding out the Final Four. For the semi-finals we sat in our assigned seats, which we referred to as *nose bleed seats* because they were up so high. Neither of us had ever been in a *gym* that large, and it was difficult to see the action. For the championship game on Saturday night, West Virginia was playing California. Buddy and I decided to go down and stand by the floor as the teams were warming up, so we could be close to the players just like we were back home. We were enjoying ourselves so much that we decided to remain where we were until someone asked us to leave. It was not long before we saw a Kentucky State Trooper making his way around the floor. Our immediate thought was that we would be sent back to our undesirable seats in the rafters. Instead, when he came to us he placed his hands on our heads and said with a commanding voice: *"Sit down, boys!"* Because we were respectful, law-abiding young men, we immediately complied! Buddy and I also agreed that if anyone else came to tell us to move, we would simply explain that the state policeman had ordered us to sit there! Because of that unexpected expression of grace from the Kentucky State policeman, we were able to have front row seats for that final game won by California, 71-70, truly a great memory!

Not long after returning from the Final Four, my mother gave me the joyful news that her mother and father, my grandparents, were going to be baptized. They had been attending a Baptist church near their home with their son, my Uncle Eugene, and had been saved. At the baptism, I stood with my dad on the hill overlooking the river. As this wonderful answer to prayer was unfolding, and my grandparents were immersed, Dad began to weep. As I saw his tender response, I was encouraged that God was answering my prayers, and that my family would be saved.

As my eventful junior year came to a close, there had certainly been a marked change in my life. In addition, many of the sins and foolish choices, especially from my sophomore year, had thankfully been done within a small circle of friends. Most of my classmates considered me as *a nice and courteous boy.* In the end of the year awards included in the year book, my loyal friend, Jerry Jayne, and I were voted *"best all-around students"*, and had a memorable photo taken together.

One late afternoon in early June, my dad had been drinking, but was not drunk, and he again began to weep. He surprised me by saying that he wanted to be saved. He asked me to take him to see Roland Pinky, the pastor who had officiated at my parents' wedding. We drove to his home at the foot of Pine Mountain, but he was nowhere to be found. When I suggested that we could go and talk to my pastor, Bill Garnett, Dad agreed. Bill was in the parsonage, and together we went next door to the church. After a discussion about the Gospel, we all knelt at the altar and Dad surrendered his life to the Lord. I will never forget his first words as he stood up after the prayer, *"Now I'm ready to be baptized!"*

As the sermon concluded two Sundays later, my mother went forward during the altar call and was also saved! One week later we all returned to the Poor Fork River and she and my dad were baptized together! God had wonderfully answered my prayers and fulfilled what I had months earlier taken as a promise: "Believe on the Lord Jesus Christ and you will be saved, <u>and your house</u>" (Acts 16:31).

Our family - soon after Mom and Dad were saved

As soon as my junior year ended, I was able to work part time at Wardrup's, where my dad was employed. Most likely because I was his son, I was graciously given time off to attend the same two camp meetings as the previous summer. But this time we had a larger group from the Baxter and Yancey churches. It was during the ten days at Wilmore that my close Baxter friend and teammate, Howard Shoope, was saved. Adding to the joy over his salvation was that the new camp meeting speakers seemed to be even better than the ones I heard a year earlier.

As the time of Indian Springs Camp Meeting drew near, I was sensing in my heart that perhaps God was calling me to preach His

Word. A few of the members of our church family who had witnessed the dramatic changes in my life had already communicated their belief that I would one day be in the ministry. While I did not disagree, I wanted to be sure that this was God's purpose for my life. At Indian Springs, all the teens sang in a youth choir for the evening service. Because of the larger crowds at night, the youth would remain in the spacious choir loft to listen to the sermon. Throughout the service, all I could think about was God's call on my life. So when the invitation was given, I made my way forward to surrender my life to *preach God's Word!* While Bill and Betty rejoiced with me, as did my friends, no one seemed all that surprised. As is often the case, others see what God is doing in us long before we can see it ourselves.

Our Baxter group at Indian Springs when I responded to God's call to preach

As we were making the long return trip to Baxter, my pastor said: *"Now that you're called to preach, it's time to get started!"* Because revivals were so important to him and also common in churches throughout our area, he asked if I would preach a week-long revival at the church in Yancey. It would begin on September 22nd and conclude the following Sunday night, eight sermons in all.

As I was sitting in my first afternoon class before the revival was to begin that night, the girl who made the school announcements entered. As she began to read, I suddenly heard my name; the school was announcing the revival! The choir director at our school, David Davies, would be leading the music for the services, and the student body was invited! Instead of *preaching* to a few folks in this small coal-mining community, it suddenly dawned on me that others were likely going to be present. Things were becoming more serious!

Once my pastor gave me this challenging opportunity, I began to pray, think, and prepare for my first real sermon. I worked on it for a long time, and thought I likely had enough material for two sermons. When that first night came, instead of the 25 to 30 faithful believers from the Yancey community, the little stone church was packed! I learned afterwards that more than 80 people were present. Included were my parents, my sisters and brother, my grandparents, some from my church in Baxter, and several of my loyal and curious high school friends. As I began to progress through what I had prepared, I sensed that what I had said wasn't lasting very long. So I went back over it, attempting to summarize my main points, and had a long prayer at the end – total time elapsed – 8 minutes! Needless to say, I felt deflated, and still had a long week to go! My grandmother, now a new Christian, took me aside and said, *"Tommy, you had a lot of good things to say; you just need to slow down!"* Wise counsel indeed!

After that 8 minute sermon, I was humbled before the Lord, but that is never a bad thing. The Bible says, "God is opposed to the proud, but gives grace to the humble" (I Peter 5:5). Because study hall was my final period of the day, our principal, Mr. Teague, is the one God used to *give grace to the humble*. He gave me permission to leave early during those days of the revival. Upon arriving home, I immediately went in the bedroom and fell on my knees, with my Bible open before me. My pattern was to not leave my bedroom until it was time to go to church. After the service was over and our family returned home, my mother had something simmering on the stove for her famished son to eat!

Having heard so many excellent camp meeting sermons, and through my ongoing study of God's Word, I had ideas of messages I wanted to preach. Thankfully, by God's grace, the second night was better, and I felt increasingly more comfortable as the week progressed. On the concluding Sunday night, I preached for almost 45 minutes! But what was even more encouraging, the attendance had continued to grow, and different ones had responded during the nightly altar calls.

Simultaneous to the revival, another exciting ministry was beginning in our school. The seeds of it had been sown at Indian Springs where I met a girl from Harlan, Ruth Nunnery, whose father was the pastor of the Methodist Church in town. Though she knew who I was, we had not met before, likely because she was two years behind me in school. We shared a common excitement about the Lord, as well as a desire to share the Gospel with our school. As we talked, Ruth and I discussed the idea of establishing an early morning devotional and prayer time before school began each day. As we explored the possibility, we learned that we would need to obtain permission from the superintendent of the Harlan Schools. With some fear and trepidation, but having paved the way through prayer, we made our way into his office. We were discouraged by Mr. Pierce's initial response, but Mrs. Brock, one of the Christian teachers, was standing in the door, listening in on the conversation. Mr. Pierce suddenly turned to her and asked what she thought of the idea. Her response was, *"I think that's the best idea I've ever heard here at the school!"* In His gracious sovereignty, God had one of His servants in the right place at precisely the right time, and our request was granted. We would be allowed to meet in the auditorium each day, thirty minutes before school began. In the weeks after our new ministry was launched, the numbers of those who were coming to hear God's Word and have prayer before school grew to 75.

With the adventure of the revival at Yancey behind us, it was soon time for the fall revival at Baxter. Instead of students from Asbury College as we had a year earlier, Bill Garnett invited a friend of his, Sewell Woodward, a pastor in Campton, Kentucky, to come as the speaker. While I had benefitted greatly from Joe and Harry's leadership a year earlier, as well as other Asbury students Bill Garnett invited to our church periodically, I was looking forward to hearing another pastor preach, and I was not disappointed. Sewell was warm and personable, and a gifted communicator. After one of the first services of the revival, he mentioned that he had a young lady he would like me to meet. She was a member of his church in Campton, had completed one year of school at Morehead State University, but was in nurses' training at the Appalachian School of Nursing located next to the Regional Hospital in Harlan. He also informed me that she would be coming to the service the very next night. In addition to his other qualities, Sewell was also a matchmaker, for I learned that he had also been talking to her about me. When Gloria came the next night, we made a pleasant connection, and she returned to each of the revival services. We soon began to date regularly.

Gloria was approximately 18 months older than me, but two years ahead of me in school. She clearly had a heart for the Lord, and was also attractive, never a bad combination. But what soon caught my attention was that she had a level of maturity beyond that of the girls in my high school. She was simply farther along in her journey toward living as an adult. My parents, my two sisters, and my little brother, soon grew to love her dearly.

By this time I did not need my dad's '51 Ford as before, for I now had my own vehicle, and I still consider it as one of the best cars I ever owned. Without question, it was one of the greatest purchases of my entire life. The car was a four door, 1941 Studebaker, gangster grey in color, and I bought it from a friend for $20.00; yes, twenty dollars! The most obvious problem was that the front grill was missing, due to an earlier accident. But my Uncle Eugene, who was a welder, had an idea. He would create for me a custom grill out of water pipe! After he fashioned and shaped it, and the grill was complete, it needed to be painted. My thought was that it should be grey, to match the rest of the car. But Uncle Eugene, my mother's younger brother, had other ideas; he insisted we paint it a bright yellow. Once that was complete, he remarked that we had no other choice than to paint red flames across the front of the hood, and this is exactly what we did. And, yes, it definitely caught everyone's attention. During those days, the trend was for cars to be lower in the back, but my Studebaker was higher in the rear end. In our attempt to remedy the situation, Uncle Eugene suggested we put large bags of sand in the trunk. In doing that we were able to make the car look close to level, which was more acceptable. One unanticipated benefit of the sand was how it gave me better traction when the winter snows arrived. All through my senior year, I drove that '41 Studebaker with red flames and a bright yellow grill all over the state of Kentucky, and it never once gave me any problems. My friends loved it, and Gloria and I used it on our dates. In fact, for a few weeks the following spring, as part of her training, she was required to serve at the Kentucky State Mental Hospital in Danville. My trusty Studebaker took me there and back on several occasions. One Sunday afternoon Gloria and I drove through the back roads over to Asbury. Surprisingly, we ran into Joe Alley, and had an encouraging conversation. When I sold the Studebaker in the summer of 1960, I doubled my money by selling it for $40.00!

One of our trips in this unique car was to travel to Campton over spring break. Sewell Woodward had asked me to come and preach a short revival in his church. Howard Shoope, my close Baxter friend, was asked by Sewell to lead the youth services each night. Because this was Gloria's home church, she made the trip as well. On our way back to Harlan late Sunday night over those curvy mountain roads, Howard, Gloria and I were singing most of the way home. Even though we were all weary from a busy but rewarding week, I now see that we were experiencing a taste of what Nehemiah described in the Old Testament: "This day is holy to the Lord. Do not grieve, for the joy of the Lord is your strength" (Nehemiah 8:10).

By this time I had made it known that I was going to college to prepare for the ministry. One day my high school English teacher, Miss Garnett, took me aside and said, *"Tommy, I like all these dreams that you have for your future, and I think they are good. But you are going to have to really buckle down in your studies!"* While I had become somewhat more serious in my studies after becoming a Christian, she saw that I was not nearly as diligent as would be required to succeed in college.

Because of Joe Alley and Harry Nesmith, and other students I had met from Asbury College, this was the school I wanted to attend. But because I was a Methodist, and most of the adults in our church presumed I would eventually become a Methodist pastor, there were some who thought I should go to Union College, a Methodist school, located only 50 miles away in Barbourville. One of the wealthy and generous men in the Harlan Methodist Church, Mr. Ed Cawood, was an alumnus of Union, and had taken an interest in me after I had preached in his church. Mr. Cawood invited me to meet him one day for a very serious talk. There had been some discussion that Union would possibly offer me at least a partial basketball scholarship. Mr. Cawood's offer was that whether the basketball piece materialized or not, he would provide the funds for my college tuition and expenses. He added that he would also make sure that I had a reliable car to go back and forth to school. So what would my decision be?

While Mr. Cawood's generous offer was attractive in many ways, and certainly appreciated, the spiritual passion I saw in the Asbury students had captured my attention. One day as Joe Alley and I were talking about college, I explained that my parents were not in a position financially to assist if I pursued my dream to go to Asbury. It was at that moment when he gave me this verse: "Faithful is He who calls you, and He will also bring it to pass!" (I Thessalonians 5:24) He went on to explain that if I would simply trust God, my Father in heaven would provide for my every need. Though I was still a relatively young believer, the promise from God's Word strengthened my faith. Later I would learn that this is how God works; it is through

Scripture that He builds our faith: "Faith comes by hearing, and hearing by the Word of Christ" (Romans 10:17).

By the time my senior year was coming to an end, I was being invited to preach in other settings. One of my most memorable occasions was at a county-wide Easter sunrise service at the Wayne Drive-in Theater. This special event was sponsored by the Harlan County Youth Organization. Our first task was to construct a large stage in front of the giant screen, and have someone knowledgeable in electronics connect the microphone to the speakers that hang on the car windows. But on this Easter Sunday morning, they would be carrying the message of the triumphant resurrection of Christ. That was my first opportunity to preach on Easter but, thankfully, it would not be the last. Many years were ahead of me when as a pastor I would declare the truth that makes Christianity unique from every other religion: *Jesus conquered death, His tomb is empty, and He gave us a living hope; we serve a risen Savior!*

CHAPTER FOUR

When God's Promises Became Real – How He Graciously Met My
Needs

*"And my God shall supply all your needs, according to His riches
in glory in Christ Jesus."* Philippians 4:19

The morning following my high school graduation, I was riding
shotgun in an 18-wheeler bound for Chicago where three Baxter
friends were already employed. My hope was to get a summer job
and save a significant portion of the wages for my college expenses in
the fall. Dad had arranged a ride for me with one of the drivers from
Wardrup's who made a weekly run to the south side of Chicago. It was
an adventure, as this would be my first time north of Cincinnati. As we
traveled through Indianapolis, it was at the exact time of the Indy 500,
so the streets were practically empty.   When we arrived late in the
day at the meat packing plant in South Chicago, my friends were there
to meet me.

Since the next day was Sunday, we decided to attend a
Methodist Church nearby. While it was quite different from our small
church in Baxter, we enjoyed the sermon and were able to meet the
pastor afterwards. He was noticeably surprised to see four young men
from the hills of Kentucky in his suburban church. As we interacted for
a few moments, he asked if he could come by our apartment the next
evening for a visit, and we agreed.

When the pastor arrived, after conversing for a while he spoke
of how encouraging it was to see four Christian young men from
Appalachia in the large city of Chicago. And then he said, *"I assume
you are all Christians, aren't you?"* The three of us who were believers
hesitated for a moment as we considered how we might answer.
Then Don said, *"No, I'm not."* The pastor then asked Don if he would
like to pray and give his life to Jesus, and Don answered *"Yes!"* We
were all delighted, and with the pastor's guidance, Don opened his
heart to the Lord, and we rejoiced to see how God had worked to
answer our prayers.

Early the next week I was able to secure a job in a small factory not far from our apartment. But after only three or four weeks, some physical problems resurfaced. Because of frequent heavy lifting during the summers I worked at Wardrup's, I had developed a hernia. It had given me problems sporadically during basketball season of my senior year, but I could see that this was more serious. After consulting with my parents, we decided that I should return home and have surgery before leaving for college in late August. Thankfully, I was able to heal quickly, grateful to have the issue resolved, and again on the path to enjoying good health.

In the weeks following my hospital stay, Gloria and I had a number of intense, emotional conversations. Though it was impossible to accurately process at the time, I would later come to appreciate that we were at two different points in our life journey. Gloria was older, more mature, soon to become a registered nurse, and anticipating marriage. I was for marriage, and there was nothing negative in her to turn me away. While it was a choice I made against my emotions, the Lord enabled me to recognize that I was not yet ready or mature enough for the level of commitment marriage requires. I could see that I was still interested in other girls, and was eager to discover who I would meet in this new season of life at Asbury. It was a difficult time for us both, and for my family who dearly loved Gloria. In hindsight, I would come to see that God's invisible hand was guiding me because His choice for my life partner was waiting for me at Asbury!

Following my midsummer surgery, I was able to attend the final days of Wilmore Camp Meeting. While there, I met Art, one of the counselors in the guy's dorm, who was a student at Asbury Seminary. When he heard my testimony and how I was relying on the Lord to provide the funds for college, he offered me a job to assist in college registration. This was a responsibility he assumed each quarter, and stated that I could be of help. I simply had to arrive a few days earlier, which was not a problem.

As the time for college drew near, I was concerned but prayerful about my insufficient funds. Approximately three weeks before school was to begin, I stopped by the Baxter post office to pick up the mail. In it was a letter addressed to me, but with no return address. As I opened it and began to read, the writer explained that when I arrived at Asbury, I would find that a certain amount of money had been credited to my account, enough for fall quarter! The person went on to say that additional funds had been set aside for my college education and that each quarter a portion of it would again be given. Still hoping to determine the identity of my benefactor, but seeing that the letter continued on the other side of the page, I attempted to guess who wrote it before I reached the end, but was unsuccessful. It was simply signed, *"A blood-bought friend!"* Two verses were also referenced; as soon as I returned home I looked them up and saw that they were the Apostle Paul's words to Timothy: "Endure hardship with me as a good soldier of Jesus Christ; no soldier in active service entangles himself with the affairs of this life that he may please the One who has chosen him to be a soldier" (II Timothy 2:3-4). There was a P.S. which read: *"In the next few days you will also be receiving a portable typewriter which you will need as you pursue your college degree."* And that is exactly what happened; God had faithfully provided for my first quarter of college far beyond anything I could have imagined, and there was every indication that He would supply everything I would need for the next four years.

As our youth choir was singing one Sunday in late summer, I spotted my mother leaving the service in tears, and could not imagine why she was crying. Though I was oblivious to the significance of that day for her, I learned afterwards that her tears were flowing because this was the final Sunday before her first born son went away to college. Interestingly, I would never live at home again.

When the much anticipated day arrived, my parents drove me the 140 miles from Baxter to the small town of Wilmore in Dad's '51 Ford. It was an exciting day for me, but for them as well, as no one in our family had ever gone to college, much less studied for the ministry.

After unloading my belongings and my parents pulled away, I learned the college knew of my early arrival, and that my room on the fourth floor was waiting for me in East Wing of Johnson Hall, Room 408. The Asbury Guest House was on the first two floors, so East Wing had the reputation of being the quietest dorm. I discovered that my roommate was a sophomore named, Ted, from Ohio, whom I had also met a few weeks earlier at Wilmore Camp Meeting.

The next morning Art and a friend of his, Hugh, an upper classman, asked me to join them for a mid-morning breakfast at the Dixie Diner in Wilmore, a town where everything is in easy walking distance. As we were enjoying our meal, three girls entered the small café and sat at a table by the window. Art and Hugh seemed to know them, so we exchanged greetings. One of the girls caught my attention, but I assumed that she was an upper classman, though each time I saw her after that, my eyes and heart were inexplicably drawn to her.

As I became acquainted with the guys in my dorm, it was surprising that very few were from Kentucky. Instead they were from states such as New Jersey, Florida, Georgia, Illinois, and Ohio. At least two were from other countries. For some mysterious reason, there seemed to always be a group gathered in my room. A few days later I learned the reason; they loved to listen to me talk. Many of us from Harlan County have a distinct way of speaking, and my new friends in the dorm who had never heard anyone with my accent, were certainly fascinated.

The news soon came that in a meeting of the freshman class, officers would be elected. A couple of my new friends suggested that I run for class president, and I agreed. I learned that each of the candidates was to include a testimony in his or her remarks. The other candidates were blessed to have grown up in Christian homes, so their testimonies were similar. Since I had grown up without the benefit of

Christian parents, and was a relatively new Christian, my testimony was quite different. Much to my surprise, I won and became class president. Regrettably, while I was prepared for college life physically, spiritually, socially, athletically, and financially (thanks to my unknown benefactor God had provided), through no fault of my high school teachers, I was unprepared academically; I had simply not applied myself. At the end of the quarter when grades were posted, I had to give up my positon as class president, as did more than half of the other freshmen who had been elected to other positions. To be a class officer, one had to maintain a 2.25 grade point average. My grades at the end of first quarter were one B, two C's, and one D, which translates into a 2.00. Just for the record, though no one has ever once inquired about my grades over these many years, I am pleased to say that they steadily improved each quarter. They were also higher in seminary than in college. Hopefully they have been even better in the challenges of everyday life.

One day in early October, Howard, my Baxter friend who had responded to the Lord after I led a study on the cross in Wednesday night prayer meeting, came to visit. As we were walking across campus, I said to him, *"Do you see that girl walking toward the basement of the library? That's the girl I'm going to marry!"* At this point we had not yet dated, or even had an extended conversation. But I had continued to be drawn to her after our brief exchange in the Dixie Diner on my first full day in Wilmore. By this time I had learned that her name was Linda Gillam, that she had an older sister, Judy, who was in my

The one who captured my heart

psychology class, and that she had grown up in Colombia, South America, where her parents served as missionaries.

Asbury did not play intercollegiate sports during those years, but their intermural basketball program was extremely popular. The teams even had cheerleaders, and the gym was crowded for most of the games. The league was made up of one team from each of the four classes, which alternated playing each other throughout the season. Because my friend from Baxter and high school teammate, Howard Shoope, was also enrolled as a freshman, I felt confident we would have a competitive team.

Once the season began, Linda heard others commenting that Tom Madon was one of the best basketball players on campus, but did not make a connection because she initially thought my name was Jim. My mother's faded clippings confirm that I had a very good year. My friend, Howard, also did well, as did our team. Because Howard and I had a great coach in Joe Gilly, he taught us more than individual skills; he taught us *how to play.* Howard was a strong defender and especially good rebounder. I am thankful that we are still in touch today with him and his delightful wife, Jane. And I am so pleased with how he went on to positively impact the lives of many young people through coaching basketball. I also rejoice that God's faithful work in Howard is also continuing in a beautiful way, and we always enjoy rich fellowship in the Lord each time we are together.

As November arrived, it was time for Asbury's annual missionary conference, and I sensed that the time had come for me to ask Linda for a date. It happened somewhat spontaneously when I spotted her coming out of the library. Meeting her, I asked if she would like to go with me to the Saturday night missionary service, and she agreed. Though neither of us dared to speak about our impressions from that first exchange until some months later, it had been a humorous moment for us both. As the afternoon light was shining on Linda's face, I spotted a faint scar on her forehead that I had not noticed before. And as I turned to walk away, she caught a glimpse of the prominent mole on the back of my neck, a birthmark.

Regardless of what we may think initially, no one is quite as perfect as they appear during that exhilarating season of early infatuation.

Hughes Auditorium

Our first date was in beautiful Hughes auditorium where we also gathered three mornings each week for chapel. The date would include pizza afterwards with some other students in the home of Dr. Westerfield, the Dean of Men. As the challenging sermon concluded, the speaker invited all who were *willing* to be missionaries, if God should call them, to come forward and pray. Independently of one another, Linda and I both responded to make that commitment. The guys in my East Wing dorm knew of my date with Linda, and that she came from a missionary family. They also saw both of us go forward, indicating we were open to Gods' call for missions. When I arrived back at the dorm, several of them were waiting at the top of the stairs singing, *"Where SHE leads me I will follow."* An oft used invitation hymn in our day was, *"Where HE leads me I will follow."*

Sometime later, as Linda and I were sharing a meal in the cafeteria, the conversation turned to our freshman English classes. Though I can't recall the details of how the subject came up, I commented that I was in *"Section L"*, though I did not know what that meant. Someone at the table commented that the section reflected how that person scored on the English portion of their admission test. The sections went from A to L, but there was also an *"Advanced"* section; Linda reluctantly confessed that she had been placed in that elite section! Miss Garnett's words as my English teacher came back about how I would have to buckle down if I was serious about following God's call to become a pastor. Thankfully, my one "B" at the end of fall quarter was in English. And for what it is worth, I still remember my dad asking me over Christmas break, *"Son, where did you get all that fancy talk?"* By being around students who came from different states, though it was unintentional, I was beginning to move away from my careless way of speaking to using better grammar, and also beginning to enunciate my words more clearly. Everyone has to begin somewhere in their pursuit of grammatical competence, and *"Section L"* was mine!

By the time we said goodbye at Christmas break, Linda and I were becoming an item, and we purchased nice Christmas gifts for each other. Linda was clearly the more sacrificial giver for she purchased a beautiful brown, reversible sweater that cost her plenty, and I loved it! Because it was of such high quality, I was able to wear it for a number of years.

For winter and spring quarters, I again received letters from my *blood-bought friend.* While the amount varied, the gift was always significant. The Lord also provided in other ways. There were times during the school year when I was invited to a church in Kentucky, Indiana, or Ohio to preach for the weekend. A song leader and often a girls' trio were also often included in our ministry team. Those weekends were positive times for the churches and for us as students. The church always gave an honorarium for each person, another way the Lord provided. Going to the CPO (College Post Office) also became an exciting adventure as I would often receive letters from friends prompted by the Holy Spirit to send money. The guys in my dorm loved to hear my latest story of God's faithful provision, and I enjoyed telling them of how God was at work. As the first year was drawing to a close, it became clear that God's promise was being fulfilled: "But my God shall supply all your needs according to His riches in glory by Christ Jesus" (Philippians 4:19).

As Linda and I continued our relationship, some of our off campus dates were with her older sister, Judy, and her boyfriend, Dick Amos, who was enrolled at Asbury Seminary. Dick had a VW so we would often drive to Lexington for pizza, and go bowling afterwards. On the way home we would often stop and walk through the large cemetery on Highway 68. Linda especially remembers me praying for us on one of those moonlit evenings, and wondered at that time if I might be the one God had for her.

There were a few occasions during my freshman year when I invited friends to come home with me for the weekend. Though our home was simple, and my parents did not have much financially, they never failed to be hospitable to everyone who came. One thing was certain; my friends always loved my mother's home-cooked meals. On rare weekends when I went home alone, the guys in my dorm knew I always brought food when I returned. They gathered in my room like vultures, ready to devour a piece of my mother's German chocolate cake, or one of her tasty fried pies.

Just before spring quarter ended, it was time to take another giant step and ask Linda to come to my home and meet my family. While Linda's missionary parents were not wealthy, she had informed me that one of their homes in Medellin, Colombia, had a pink bathroom. The missionary organization had purchased a spacious compound from a wealthy engineer, and one of the homes was called simply the Big House. Living there for several years, Linda's family enjoyed that pink bathroom. My question in bringing Linda to Baxter was to see if she could accept my Appalachian home, family, and our way of life. But I was also interested to see if my family would accept her, especially since they had not been pleased when I broke things off a year earlier with Gloria, whom they dearly loved.

Linda's first visit to my home

When Linda and I arrived at my home *on the hill,* one of my dad's first questions to her was, *"Would you like some squirrel?"* A favorite activity with my dad when I was younger was squirrel hunting. It was not uncommon for us to have squirrel on the stove, mixed with gravy, which we ate over biscuits. Linda politely said, *"No, thank you!"* I later learned that a squirrel to her was a rodent, and who would want to eat a rat?

During the weekend, I took Linda to some of my favorite spots in Harlan County, including where I had gone to high school and to Pine Mountain where my father had grown up and graduated, a place I dearly loved. I was also eager to introduce her to my church family who had meant so much to me the first two and a half years of my Christian life. It was a great weekend in every way, and Linda passed my test with flying colors! Every member of my family was gracious in how they accepted Linda, and their love for her would only increase in the years to come.

As we returned to campus, it was time for final exams which would bring my first year of college to an end. Linda's delightful parents were there, and this was the first time I was able to interact with them for any extended period of time. But finishing the year would also mean that Linda and I would say goodbye to one another for three months. She and her sister would make their 50 hour, nonstop trip by car across Route 66 to their home in California. My

71

plan was to return to Harlan and work on a large construction project in the county that planned to hire college students, and I already had my name on the list. Upon arriving home, however, I learned that the project was behind schedule, and there would be no summer work in Harlan for me.

One evening soon after Linda arrived at her home in California, I called to share the bad news that my job plans for the summer had fallen through. She immediately said, *"Why don't you come to California for the summer and get a job out here?"* She went on to explain that a close friend of Dick Amos had just graduated from Asbury Seminary and was moving to Fort Worth, Texas to begin his ministry as a pastor. His name was John Morris, and his wife, Mary Helen, was 6 months pregnant. She would only travel to her home in Mt. Carmel, Illinois, and stay for a period of time until John was settled in their new home. John was looking for someone to help drive their large station wagon, which would be pulling a U-Haul. But the rest of the story is what grabbed my attention. After unloading in Ft. Worth, John would be driving on to Southern California for a church conference. If I helped with the trip, he would deliver me to Linda's front door, and there would be no cost to me, as John would be responsible for my meals and other expenses. I only needed to give him a call quickly if I were interested. But what sealed the deal was when she explained that another Asbury Seminary graduate, Ed Erny, was heading up the paint crew at the mission headquarters where her parents served, and he was looking for someone to assist. Linda even explained that a single man at the mission would make his couch available to me for the summer!

After talking it over with my parents, and calling John Morris to make arrangements, this 19 year-old from Appalachia was on his way to Hollywood! Yes, Linda lived in Hollywood, for that was where the mission headquarters was located. With only a few dollars in my pocket, I set out with my little suitcase and hitchhiked the 140 miles to Wilmore to meet up with John.

In the first leg of our journey, John slept most of the way, being weary from completing seminary and preparing for this major move; so I drove the first part to Mary Helen's home in southern Illinois. She sat in the front with me, and we had an enjoyable time getting acquainted. Before John and I traveled very far, I thought of the section in Reader's Digest where people describe *"My most unforgettable character"*, for this is who John became for me almost immediately, and for a myriad of reasons. I loved his distinct Texas accent, and he was courteous, grateful, a man of high character, and had a delightful sense of humor. He also had a heart for the Lord and for Scripture, believed in discipleship, and was a Texan to the bone! He suggested that we memorize Bible verses as we traveled, and was pleased when he learned that this was a spiritual discipline I was already practicing. I became enthralled and hungry as he described the different places we would stop to eat along the way, especially when he spoke of *Whataburger*! And this Texas-sized hamburger did not disappoint.

John and Mary Helen Morris

Once we arrived and unloaded the heavy U-Haul in Ft. Worth at John and Mary Helen's future home, we agreed that his station wagon drove like a sports car! Our next stop would be Sweetwater, John's hometown, which is famous for its annual "Rattlesnake Roundup". I explained that we had lots of rattlesnakes in Eastern Kentucky but, according to John, Sweetwater had more rattlesnakes than any other place. John nonchalantly commented that his mother would have a steak ready for us when we arrived. At that point I had not eaten many steaks, but when I sat down at Mrs. Morris's table, I was totally unprepared for what I saw, or more accurately, what I did not see. The plate was not even visible because of the enormous size of the steak! Since John's family raised cattle, they could cut their steaks whatever size they wanted, and they preferred them BIG! To this day, that's the largest steak I have ever eaten.

After a good night's rest, we were off toward California, but John's father and brother would join us for this final leg of the journey to attend their church conference. Traveling across Texas had been an adventure, but the brilliant colors of New Mexico and Arizona were unlike anything in Appalachia. By this time, however, my focus was on arriving in California and seeing Linda again. After dropping John's father and brother off in Azusa, the location of the church conference, we were on the famous Los Angeles Freeways. It was not long before we turned off Highway 101 on the Melrose and Normandie exit and traveled only a short distance to Hobart Blvd, past the headquarters of the Oriental Missionary Society to the Gillam home in the next block. At the end of our 2,000 plus long and memorable miles, there she was, waiting for me!

When I said good-bye and expressed my gratitude to *my most unforgettable character*, and new friend, John Morris, I had no way of knowing that in God's astonishing sovereignty, our paths would intersect in a most significant way seven years later. But that story is for later.

Though I had heard Linda talk about her younger siblings, it was great to meet Joan and Rick. I soon met her friend, Vangie, the first person I ever met with that name. It was not long before I also met Ed Erny, who would be my boss for the summer on the OMS paint crew. He and his wife, Rachel, had only been married a year, and their plans were to go to Taiwan as missionaries. Linda also took me over to meet the hospitable single man on whose couch I would sleep while I was in California.

While Linda and I treasured that summer, it was her parents who impacted me the most. The Gillam home was the first Christian family I was able to witness up close and personal. As I observed them and experienced their family dynamics, a desire was forming in me to have that same type of home someday. Prayer was a major part of their family, as was music. Linda's father was an accomplished pianist, singer and song writer, and was fluent in Spanish. The Colombian people once commented that Bill Gillam spoke their language better than the native speakers. Some of his Spanish songs and hymns are in Latin American hymnals even today. A common experience was to

Linda's family in California in 1961

gather in the living room after dinner where their dad would play and sing, at times sharing a new song he had written. Linda and Judy both played the piano, and Joan played the flute, and Rick was learning the guitar, so Linda's father sought to get everyone involved. Though I dearly loved music, I had no special gifts. The best I could offer was to invite them across the street to the outdoor basketball court and have them watch me shoot free throws!

During that summer I was blessed to share numerous meals around the Gillam table. Dick Amos, Judy's boyfriend, was often there as well, as he too was working for OMS, utilizing his capable skills as an upholsterer. Linda's father was generous with their family car, a Pontiac, allowing me to drive us around Hollywood, to Griffith Park, and often to the Santa Monica beach on Saturdays. But Dick still had his VW, which we also used for double dates, as we had done at Asbury. By working at the mission, I became acquainted with many of the dedicated people who served there. OMS began the day with a half hour chapel, and Ed and I attended before we began our work. As an older brother in Christ, Ed became a spiritual mentor to me, along with teaching me the finer points of painting. In the years that followed, I enjoyed referring to him as *the man who taught me how to clean my brush!* The practical skills I learned from Ed that summer proved to be extremely valuable, as painting became my summer job through seminary, and I have painted every house where we have lived.

The time soon arrived for us to make our long cross country trip, driving straight through to Wilmore. Thanks to the gracious generosity of Linda's parents and having a free couch to sleep on, I had been able to save a good portion of my summer wages.

Entering my sophomore year meant that it was time to declare my major, so I chose Philosophy and Religion. Many of the young men preparing for the ministry chose this major as well, primarily because of Dr. Clarence Hunter, the esteemed head of the department. It was in one of Dr. Hunter's classes that I met Harold Shimfessel, who would become one of my closest friends. Harold was also a Kentuckian and had spent his freshman year at the University of Kentucky, but transferred to Asbury to pursue God's call to the ministry.

My second year progressed more smoothly as I was now familiar with college life. The chapel services three mornings each week were highpoints as they had been my freshman year. Hearing 1,000 college students and faculty lift their voices and hearts to the Lord, singing the great hymns of our faith, was unlike anything I had known, with camp meeting singing coming in a close second. Hughes, as we called it, had two large grand pianos on the stage, and Linda was occasionally asked to play one of them for chapel. She always treasured those occasions when her close friend, Jan Fraser, played the other. I always loved the chapels when Linda was asked to play! My friends who were going into pastoral ministry loved to say that the first requirement of a pastor's wife was this: she must be able to play the piano, and I had that box already checked!

Throughout my sophomore year, the Lord again faithfully met my financial needs through my *blood bought friend*, weekend services in various churches, and in other unexpected ways. As we were registering for spring quarter, while in the long line, I realized I was $30.00 short of what I needed. When the break came for lunch, I rushed to the CPO to see if the Lord's provision might be in the letters that had accumulated while I had been away from campus. As I went through the mail, I read the ones I considered the most likely to contain money, but not one of them contained cash. It was then that I spotted a letter from my Aunt Bea, my father's sister, who lived in London, KY. She had never written before, and I wondered about the reason for her letter. As I opened it, three wrinkled ten dollar bills were included, the exact amount I needed to complete registration! In the letter Aunt Bea explained that she and Marshal (her son and my first cousin, also a wounded veteran confined to a wheelchair) had been saving up some of their tithe money, and hoped that their gift, though small, might be of some help! Seeing God faithfully provide the exact amount, and through a totally unexpected source, is always a great faith builder!

Because my previous summer in California had gone so well, Linda and I discussed the possibility of my returning to California to find a job in the area, and that's what I did. While I found employment, along with being able to house sit for one of the missionaries who was away that summer, things did not work out as smoothly as before. My job location was not on the bus route, and it was too far for me to walk. Linda and I were also having some struggles concerning our future, and there were other areas where I felt unsettled. In my discouragement, I made the decision to return to Kentucky. A young man from OMS was driving to Dodge City, Kansas, and said that I could ride with him; from there I could catch a Greyhound Bus the remainder of the way to Kentucky.

The most severe test to my still relatively young faith developed into a full blown crisis on that lonely bus ride. Christians have historically identified their enemies as *the world, the flesh, and the devil;* I seemed to be losing on all three fronts. The world has an entirely different value system than God's Word, and I saw myself being caught up in that worldly way of thinking. The flesh, which stands in direct contrast to the Spirit and the new identity we have in Christ, is always the same, never improving, and I felt I was fighting a losing battle, much as the Apostle Paul confessed from his own experience: "I know that nothing good dwells in me, that is, in my flesh; for the willing is present with me, but the doing of the good is not. For the good that I want, I do not do, but I practice the very evil that I do not want...I find the principle that evil is present with me, the one who wishes to do good" (Romans 7:18, 19, 21). And the devil is relentless, appearing at times as a roaring lion (I Peter 5:8), but on other occasions as an angel of light (II Corinthians 11:14).

By the time I stepped off the Greyhound in Lexington, and was met by my friend, Art, I was at an all-time low. As we were riding along, I said to him, *"I have come to believe this summer that God has not really called me to the ministry, as I had thought, and that it's time for me to return to Baxter and figure out what to do next."* His immediate response was: *"That's a lie from the pit of hell!"* Well, needless to say, his candid and blunt words grabbed my attention, but they also shook me out of my spiritual lethargy and depression, putting me in a position to discuss how I had reached such a low point.

Any time I have been at discouraging points in my life, while God often uses people, as He did that day with Art, it is God's Word and the unchanging truth of Scripture that ultimately has renewed my hope and gotten me back on my feet. The passage God used that summer before my junior year at Asbury was written from the Apostle Paul to young Timothy: "If we are faithless (or unfaithful), He remains faithful, for He cannot deny Himself" (II Timothy 2:13). The unchanging faithfulness of God to His children provides a reliable anchor anytime we are in the midst of storms that threaten our faith.

After surviving that severe test, my passion to pursue God's purpose was restored, and I was excited about the year ahead. I had already been elected junior class president and was excited to fulfil the responsibilities of this role. My basketball season would turn out to be my best one yet, and Linda had been selected as one of the cheerleaders. We were at a point in our relationship, however, where she needed a confirming peace from the Lord that I was the man she was to marry. Vividly implanted in her mind was an admonition her father had given his daughters at the family table when Linda was only eleven years old. He exhorted them saying, *"Girls, when you marry, I want you to remember two things: first, that you marry only a Christian, and second, make sure the person is God's choice for you!"* Linda had easily checked the first box when we began dating, but marking "yes" by the second one did not come so easily. While I had

Enduring wisdom from Linda's father at the family table

been drawn to her from the time I first saw her, and felt in my heart that she was the person God had for me, she was slower in coming to the place of complete peace. Thankfully, after a stressful time of seeking God's will, Linda came to the point where she was at peace that I was the one God had chosen for her, and became genuinely excited about becoming my wife.

Homecoming week is in the fall at Asbury, and I was pleased when I learned that Linda's father would be among the returning alumni, for I had an important question for him. Our team was playing on Tuesday night, and Linda's dad was there. As it turned out, I had one of my better games, scoring 39 points, so I was feeling especially confident and optimistic. After saying goodbye to Linda, her father and I walked back to East Wing where he was staying. As we stood outside on that pleasant fall evening, I asked him for permission to have Linda as my wife, and he graciously granted me that honor. We have a copy of a letter he wrote later that evening to Linda's mother: *"After the basketball game tonight at Asbury, as Tom Madon and I walked back to his dorm, he asked me for Linda's hand in marriage, and I said 'yes', also assuring him that I felt confident that Mary would be in agreement. I also left it to them to work out the timing and other various details."*

As I went to my room afterwards, I was overjoyed! We had already planned for Linda to come home with me to share Thanksgiving with my family. Though our engagement was not one of the perfectly choreographed and recorded ones we often see today, before we went up the hill to my home, we stopped on the same railroad tracks I had joyfully walked along four and a half years earlier on my way to share the news with my mother that I had surrendered my life to the Lord. There I explained to Linda that I had already obtained permission from her father, and I was asking her to be my wife! And she said yes, without reservation! As we shared the news with my family, our Thanksgiving that year was especially joyful as we celebrated God's faithfulness to us, while also discussing the future.

For Christmas that year, I joined one of my closest friends from Asbury, Gary (Gus) Miller, in obtaining a job in New York City with the Salvation Army, to assist in their annual Christmas appeal. Because of the enormity of their task in such a large city, the Salvation Army was hiring college students to assist in their work, and the pay was good. Gus and I, along with several other Asbury students, made our way to the big city. We were housed in the Salvation Army facility in the Bowery, also sharing our morning and evening meals with needy men who came off the cold streets. Each day we rode the subway to and from the heart of the city to work in front of Macy's Department

Dick and Judy's wedding - December 26, 1962

Store. We were provided a microphone to encourage and motivate the people to give, and were also given the freedom to communicate truths about Christ's birth and the wonderful reason He came. During our 20 minute alternating breaks, we went inside Macy's and rode the escalators to get warm. It was a great learning experience for us and certainly an unforgettable memory.

Upon arriving back at Asbury on Christmas Eve afternoon, it was snowing heavily in Central Kentucky. Linda's sister, Judy, was to be married to Dick on December 26; Linda was the maid of honor, and I was to be the best man. Knowing I would love to be home with my family for Christmas, Dick insisted that I take his VW and drive to Baxter, even though the snowy roads were treacherous. He explained that the heater did not work well, and he was certainly correct. Even though I was chilled to the bone, I made the 140 mile trip safely, and my delighted family welcomed me in out of the snow and bitter cold. By the time I returned to Wilmore on Christmas afternoon, it was no longer snowing, and the roads were more manageable. We had an enjoyable rehearsal for Dick and Judy, and they were married the next evening in a lovely wedding.

Since Linda's parents left the timing of our wedding to us, we began to make our plans. While it would have definitely been better financially to wait until we both graduated, we decided that if I could become a student pastor during my senior year, we would take the step of faith and marry in the summer of 1963, enabling us to experience our senior year as a married couple. In the gracious providence of God, the door opened for me to become the pastor of two churches in Southern Indiana. Having married six months earlier, Dick and Judy were a great help to us in many practical ways. Since one of our immediate needs was for a vehicle of our own, we were able to purchase a blue, 1961 VW.

As we discussed the timing and location of where the marriage should take place, my first choice was the Pine Mountain Chapel I had grown to dearly love as a boy, a setting Linda also had come to appreciate. But we soon realized that it would be too far for most of our family and friends we wanted to share in the joy of our wedding. Even though California was Linda's home, it was also impractical, being so far away and too expensive. As we discussed our thoughts and sought counsel from Linda's parents, we learned that they would be in Indiana for a June conference. With that being a guiding factor, it became apparent that we should select a date around that time, and to have the wedding in a location known to all of us. When all the factors were in, the decision was that we would be married in the Free Methodist Church in Wilmore on July 5, 1963!

CHAPTER FIVE

When Two Became One – The Student Pastor Days

"For this reason a man shall leave his father and mother and cleave to his wife, and the two shall become one flesh. So they are no longer two, but one flesh. What therefore God has joined together, let no man separate." Matthew 19:5-6

Church building in Alert

In mid-June of 1963, driving our blue, 1961 VW Beetle, I made the 140 mile trip from Wilmore to Alert, Indiana, to assume my responsibilities as their new student pastor. I would also have pastoral responsibilities at Milford, approximately 15 miles away via the back roads that traverse the Indiana corn and soybean fields. My first act as a 21 year-old pastor was to assist with two weeks of Vacation Bible School. Though I had only limited experience in ministry to children, I loved it, and especially getting to know the dedicated women of Alert who made VBS happen.

The text for my first Sunday sermon was, "Husbands, love your wives, just as Christ also loved the church and gave Himself up for her" (Ephesians 5:25). While it was only two weeks before I would begin learning what it meant to be a husband, my emphasis was not on marriage; it was to highlight John 3:16, the classic verse which tells of God's great love for the world, and compare it with my text from Ephesians on how Christ also loved the church so much that He gave Himself up for her. The Lord had given me a great love for His church through my first spiritual family in Baxter, and my desire was to encourage my first flock to love His church as well. The church structure at Alert was built from Bedford stone, as was the small, attractive parsonage next door where I would live for three weeks before bringing my bride into our first *home.* The loving people at Alert made sure that their short-term bachelor had plenty to eat; they were looking forward to having Linda join me, but not nearly as much as I was!

As the days drew near for our wedding, I returned to Wilmore for the final preparations. Because it was in mid-summer, many of our college friends were away, but our families were present, plus other relatives and friends, more than enough for a memorable wedding. Linda's matron of honor was her sister, Judy. Her bridesmaids were a former roommate, Joan, plus my two sisters, Linda and Ella. Harold Shimfessel was my best man, and my friends, Ted, David, and Gus, were the groomsmen. It seemed only right that Joe and Barbara Alley's daughter would be our flower girl. More than any other, Joe was the person who encouraged me to step out in faith, trusting God to provide the funds for college. Dr. Eugene Erny, President of OMS, a close friend of Linda's family and a man we both respected, would officiate at the wedding.

After completing the rehearsal, Linda spent the night with her sister, and my parents stayed in a small apartment next door, the one where Linda and I would reside when school resumed in the fall. I followed Harold to his family farm near Winchester, about an hour away. While Linda spent the morning of our wedding day making final preparations, Harold and I were in the fields near his home hunting groundhogs. Oh the differences in men and women! On my way back to Wilmore, I stopped in Lexington to reserve our room at the Holiday Inn on New Circle Road.

As the hour of our wedding drew near, Linda later shared that she felt like laughing and crying at the same time, as she contemplated what a momentous occasion this was. As for me, while I felt humbled by the significance of the vows we were about to exchange, as I saw her walking down the aisle with her father, I was overjoyed that this covenant ceremony, one unlike any other, had at last arrived!

One moment in the wedding we were especially anticipating was to hear Linda's father play and sing the song he had composed specifically for us. He had earlier presented his beautiful composition for Judy and Dick's wedding, and this was our moment. His tender and instructive song was entitled *True Love.*[1] *"Sometimes it seems that love is mere affection, and subject to our human imperfection; so seldom do we see the clear reflection of love enduring, strong and true. (Refrain) True love comes down from heaven, true love is selfless giving; true love's a sacred burning, make our love a fire. (Verse two) We cannot love without the love of Jesus; we dare not walk without His presence with us. Tis only in this power divine we stand to face our future days with Him."* (Repeat refrain.) While we were deeply moved during those hallowed moments, it would be years before the total dependence expressed in his inspired words would be worked out in humility and confession before God and one another, a process in which we are still involved.

As our simple but meaningful reception concluded, and we said goodbye to family and friends, we began the 20 mile trip to Lexington and the Holiday Inn where we would spend our first night together in the same room, in the same bed. As I have officiated at weddings over the years for Christian couples who have postponed physical intimacy until marriage (and remarkably many still do), I often say to the couple that this most intimate part of marriage is a wedding gift from God Himself. For those who have not waited, the New Testament includes the good news that Jesus loved and forgave sexual sinners, even as He forgives every other kind of sin. Either way, whatever the starting point, from the moment the wedding vows are exchanged, it is imperative to embrace the truth that God designed marriage to be a relationship of exclusive intimacy between one man and one woman for life! The marriage covenant is such that both husbands and wives are to keep themselves *only* for one another as long as they both shall live. For either to violate that trust places their marriage in serious jeopardy.

Two became one - July 5, 1963

On our second day as husband and wife, we drove north through severe thunderstorms to Columbus, Ohio, where we planned to spend our second night as a married couple. Our final destination would be Beulah Beach on the shores of beautiful Lake Erie. Linda's roommate, before Linda became mine, Jan Fraser, had graciously arranged for us to spend a week in a simple family cottage, at no cost to us, on the grounds of Christian and Missionary Alliance Camp and Retreat Center. An unforgettable memory is of driving into Cleveland one evening, about an hour away, for dinner and to watch the new movie, *How the West was Won*, which we have in our DVD collection even today.

With one week of marriage complete, we drove southwest toward Indiana, with the community of Alert, about an hour south of Indianapolis, as our final destination. I often told people that with Alert being so small, you have to be *alert* or you will miss it! We loved being in our first *home*, already simply furnished, even though we would only spend the summer there, and after that, only the weekends. Beginning my pastoral responsibilities with Linda by my side, those weeks were like an extended honeymoon. I remember how excited I was to be married to her, not even considering the challenges of a more hectic lifestyle that awaited us when we returned to Asbury for our senior year.

An unexpected surprise was that some of the people at Alert were already familiar with Linda's family. One of the men, Paul Jewell, knew that Linda's mother was from Ogilville, about 30 minutes west of Alert, and told of how they met during high school in Columbus. Another family, Norris and Mable Newsom, had heard Linda's father preach and sing at an OMS convention a few years earlier. They recalled her dad telling of playing his accordion and singing in the villages along the Magdalena River in Colombia to gather a crowd to hear the gospel.

Some of the men met for prayer each Saturday night at the church, and I began to join them regularly. The prayers of Mr. Newsom, the oldest, were unforgettable. He seemed to always begin with essentially the same words: *"Father, as we come to you, we feel that we are so far behind in our thanksgiving, so we want to thank you..."* And he would proceed to thank the Lord for one blessing after another; I honestly cannot recall him ever asking God for anything! To this day I consider him one of the most grateful and humble men I have been blessed to know.

Paul Jewell had a nickname for his new student pastor; he always called me *Bishop!* Soon after I arrived, he asked, *"Bishop, do you enjoy visiting people?"* My response was that even though I was new to my calling, I planned to visit people. He then said, *"You'll do well as a pastor. People need to know that you care about them."* Profound words indeed! On another occasion he commented, *"Bishop, if you ever find the perfect church, don't join it, for if you do you'll ruin it!"* While Paul was outgoing and animated, and his wife, Mary, was quiet and soft spoken, both were great encouragers to us while we were there. Once school began and we began driving that grueling 140 mile trip one way between Alert and Asbury, after church most Sunday nights, Paul would say, *"Bishop, before you and Linda*

Paul and Mary Jewell

head back to Wilmore, drop by the house for a minute." We soon learned what that meant. He would have me pull my VW out near the barn, and he would fill up our little VW beetle from his large gas tank. Linda would go with Mary into the house and come out with frozen packages of hamburger, ground steak, and occasionally a roast. Their generous gifts greatly supplemented our annual student pastor salary of $3,000, when we were trying to subsist with a $10 a week food budget.

The entire time we were there, we had a standing Saturday night invitation from Ed and Kathleen Durham to join them for hamburgers. We grew to love our friendship with their family through their gracious hospitality, and are delighted to be in touch today with their daughter, Mary, as we are with the adult children of Paul and Mary Jewell: Sue Ann, John, and Bonnie.

Like all young newlyweds, Linda and I had much to learn in life, and in our marriage. After having been to the Shaw's home one evening for croquet in their spacious back yard, it suddenly dawned on us that we were often making jokes at each other's expense. On the way back to the parsonage, we agreed that this was not a healthy practice, and purposed to change.

By the end of the summer, a young couple closer to our age began attending our church. Dennis and Karen Jones, however, already had young children. Karen was a Christian, but Dennis was not yet a believer. Dennis and I had a lot in common including a love for sports, and even squirrel hunting. When hunting season arrived in early fall, we made a plan to go hunting together. The people in the church heard about it and began to pray that Dennis would be saved during that early morning hunting trip. As we entered the woods, my concern was not as much on hunting as it was on praying for Dennis. As he ventured out to one section of the woods, I sat on a log and prayed. Before too much time had passed, Dennis circled back to where I was. My question to him was this, *"Dennis, when are you going to give your life to the Lord?"* He looked at me with deep emotion in his voice and said, *"Right now!"* He then threw his shotgun to the ground as both of us fell on our knees with the log as our altar! As we prayed through our tears, Dennis responded to God's gracious call, and the prayers of many people were answered. One of my most unforgettable moments came when we returned to his home. His two little boys were outside playing, and he gathered one up in his right arm and the other in his left. I followed him as he hurried into the kitchen and declared to his wife, Karen, *"Honey, I just got saved!"* Many years later we were able to reconnect, and Dennis told of the spiritual multiplication that was set in motion that day, and how their children, grandchildren, and great grandchildren are all following the Lord! He also gave us a copy of a beautiful pencil drawing by one of his grandsons, of Dennis kneeling by the log with the shotgun nearby!

During the fall, the athletic director at Asbury, Cecil Zweifel, approached me about a month long basketball mission trip to Mexico in December. The team would be composed of players from two Christian colleges, Bethel and Greenville, but those who were organizing it wanted Asbury to also be involved. Coach Zweifel had already recommended me to be one of the players, and Howard Biddulph as the other. Howard was also fluent in Spanish, having grown up on the same missionary compound in Medellin, Colombia, as Linda. While I was honored to be asked, two questions came to mind: first, what would Linda think about us being apart for a month, especially on our first Christmas; second, how would the church leaders at Alert and Milford respond?

Because of Linda's heart for missions, she immediately encouraged me to go. Another likely factor in her response was that I had been asked during our junior year to try out for the Venture for Victory basketball team which traveled throughout Asia each summer sharing the gospel. Instead of pursuing what she knew was an appealing opportunity for me, I chose to stay home and get married! When I shared the idea with the churches in Indiana, both thought it was a great opportunity, and graciously gave me their blessing.

When the time came for Howard and me to travel to Mishawaka, Indiana, the home of Bethel College, to meet and practice with our team, our VW was having serious engine problems. Our plan was to leave it in Alert with Richard Shaw, a loyal friend and mechanic in our church. Linda would travel to California for the month long break to spend the Christmas holidays with her family, just as she had before we were married.

This would be my first mission trip, and I was excited about combining basketball with missions. Since none of the other team members were pastors or aspiring preachers, I was called upon when a sermon was needed, with Howard as my capable interpreter. Much of our ministry consisted of team members giving testimonies to those who responded to our halftime invitation to remain after the game to hear more. Our ministry took place in and around Monterey, Saltillo, and Torreon, in Northeast Mexico, but we were involved in much more than basketball. We even had one baseball game in a mountain village, and spent the night among people whose way of life reminded me of the poorest of the poor in Appalachia. The missionary in charge of our schedule also arranged for us to be in a small, remote village on Christmas Day where I would preach. During the invitation, an elderly lady in her 90's responded. According to the missionary who prayed with her, she came forward to be saved! That was a memorable day for other reasons as well. Our team brought Cokes for everyone, and the village people provided an unlimited supply of tamales; that was our Christmas lunch. As we were enjoying the simple but generous hospitality of the village people, my thoughts turned to Linda and I

Group gathered around our "Ambassadors of Friendship" bus in Mexico

wondered how she was spending Christmas Day. She later told me that her father's secretary, Valetta Steele, a young widow in her 30's, had invited her over on Christmas evening to watch the movie, *A Man Called Peter*, the story of Peter Marshal, Chaplain of the U.S. Senate, who, like Valetta's husband, died early in life. While I enjoyed and was deeply challenged by my first mission trip, there were times when I questioned the wisdom of having 30 days away from my bride of only six months, and on our first Christmas! But we survived, and were definitely overjoyed to see one another again!

With only two busy quarters of college remaining, it was also an eventful time at the church. One of the young mothers in her 40's, with older daughters, and also a 5 year-old little girl, was diagnosed with an aggressive form of breast cancer. Her name was Grace Tremain, and her name reflected her character. Each weekend I would join others from the church to visit Grace in the Columbus Hospital. Before we prayed, we would always sing her favorite hymn: *"All the way my Savior leads me; what have I to ask beside? Can I doubt His tender mercy, who through life has been my guide? Heavenly peace, divinest comfort, here by faith in Him to dwell! For I know, whate'er befall me, Jesus doeth all things well."* Her unwavering faith in God's sovereignty was one of my first opportunities to witness the level of trust most believers will be called upon to exercise at some point in their lives.

Soon afterwards, Grace went home to be with her Lord. Her death became the occasion for my first funeral as a pastor. Paul Jewell had arranged for his father, a retired Pilgrim Holiness preacher, to assist; he walked me through the entire process with great wisdom. Before my first year as a student pastor was complete, there would be another funeral at Alert, and one at Milford. Thankfully, all three were believers. The more difficult ones would come later, when I would witness the stark difference between those who die with hope and the ones who do not. "We do not want you to be uninformed, brethren, about those who are asleep, so that you will not grieve as do the rest who have no hope" (I Thessalonians 4:13).

When the time came for graduation, Linda and I were blessed to walk together as a married couple across the platform in Hughes Auditorium to receive our diplomas. We were surprised to be among eight from our class recognized as *Who's Who in American Colleges and Universities,* clearly another expression of God's grace. While my family had to sit in the balcony of

Graduates - May 1964

Hughes Auditorium, along with Bill and Betty Garnett, I knew my parents were proud and grateful. What they were unable to express with words was visible in their faces. Linda's parents were not able to attend, but her eloquent father wrote beautiful letters to us. In one brief paragraph to me, he wrote, *"As I think of your collegiate life, it is always such a rewarding thought to remember the high regard in which your classmates hold you. I know many of the fellows consider you a true example of what the Grace of God can do when He finds a responsive son."* As I read his gracious words, I recognized again that whatever high regard my classmates had for me was only possible because of God's ongoing work of grace in my life. His letter also prompted me to remember again my *blood bought friend* who had given so consistently and generously to make my

Who's Who photo

graduation even possible. Interestingly, to this very day I do not know his or her identity. As I have reflected on the many gifts I received during my college years, the words of Jesus often come to mind: "When you give to the poor, do not sound a trumpet before you, as the hypocrites do in all the synagogues and in the streets, so that they may be honored by men...but when you give to the poor, do not let your right hand know what your left hand is doing, so that your giving will be in secret; and your Father who sees in secret will reward you" (Matthew 6:2-4).

Because our year in Alert had been such a positive experience for us, and for the church, the people wanted us to stay. The Indiana Conference of the Methodist Church, however, had a policy against that happening. While they allowed student pastors from Asbury College, they did not permit students attending Asbury Seminary, where I was already enrolled for the fall. The church board visited the bishop with an appeal, hopeful he would make an exception, but it was denied. While we were disappointed, our one year with the people at Alert remains a wonderful treasure to us, and we are still in touch with some from there even today.

Because we had been so optimistic about remaining at Alert, I had made no plans for a student pastorate in Kentucky. Suddenly we were left without a church, a home, and were uncertain as to what to do for the summer. In contacting the OMS leadership in California, we learned that I could again work on the paint crew for the summer months, and Linda's parents graciously invited us to stay with them. In our highly suspect VW, whose engine had now been out three times, we ventured west. I have always been a *conquer-the-trip* type person, so we drove from Alert to Hollywood, spending $35.00 for gas, and only stopping by the road to sleep a couple of hours. Linda was not yet driving, though that would come soon.

It was an enjoyable summer of work, and everything was going smoothly, except that Linda came down with some mysterious sickness, especially during the mornings! Neither of us will forget that day, not long after our first anniversary, when we learned that she was pregnant! While we were genuinely excited, we also felt a sense of inadequacy as we contemplated the awesome responsibility of parenting. Linda already had a teaching job for the fall at Beaumont Junior High in Lexington, and my plan was to trust the Lord to help me find another student pastor position, even though fall is not the greatest time for such a search.

Because our VW was doing surprisingly well, we decided that our return route would be through the Rocky Mountains. An unforgettable memory from the early part of that trip was driving through Las Vegas at midnight. As we were observing the colorful lights on the strip, we heard the unmistakable voice of Billy Graham on our radio; we were listening to *the Hour of Decision!*

When we had travelled no more than an hour from Las Vegas, I noticed a prominent sign which said *Long's Peak – 700 miles.* What caught my attention, however, was the monotonous frequency of the *Long's Peak* signs: *650 miles...600 miles...500 miles,* and they continued all the way down to *50 miles...10 miles...5 miles...1 mile!* With such attention getting signs, I knew this had to be a spectacular sight.

When we at last reached the peak, I was genuinely disappointed! After all that build up, there were only rocks and trees. Still disheartened, we proceeded east, descending through the countless switchbacks in the Rockies. Suddenly we rounded a turn that left us facing back toward the west, and there it was: *Long's Peak, 14,259 feet, the highest point in Rocky Mountain National Park, and a spectacular sight to behold!*

It was several years before I was able to process a profound spiritual lesson from our experience. Even as we were too close to *Long's Peak* to appreciate its beauty, but were deeply grateful for it from a distance, so it is with many of the events in our lives. Numerous times Linda and I have been temporarily disappointed with things that were happening to us, only to later see that God was working through those same experiences to increase our trust in Him, and to accomplish a higher purpose beyond what we could see with our limited, finite vision.

The very afternoon we arrived in Wilmore and were settling into the basement apartment we had reserved, Harold Shimfessel came with the news that Dr. Patton, one of the most respected district superintendents in the Kentucky Conference, was eager to talk with me. When I reached him later that day, he informed me of a student pastor position waiting for me in Prestonsburg. The pastor who had been sent there in June to serve full time had unexpectedly resigned and moved to Illinois. Another full time pastor was not available, so the church had no other alternative than to return temporarily to a student pastor, and at the exact time I needed a position! I was somewhat familiar with the church in Prestonsburg, for I had spent a weekend there three years earlier with another friend, Charles Lake, when he was their pastor. With our new church being in Eastern

Kentucky, there was also another plus - I already spoke the language! The only drawback was that Prestonsburg, like Alert, was 140 miles away from Wilmore.

As seminary began, Linda was also ready for her first year of teaching junior high history and Spanish in Lexington. Our weekly plan was for me to pick her up after school on Friday afternoon, and then travel on to Prestonsburg, which like Alert, had a furnished parsonage behind the church. A few mice had already moved in when we arrived, but we were thankful for the new opportunity. After the Sunday evening service, we would make the late night return trip to our basement apartment in Wilmore, and Linda would be up early on her way for another week of school, and the process would begin all over again. I had seminary classes, of course, along with the study,

Oscar and Ernestine Collins

and always two weekly sermons to prepare. The people in Prestonsburg loved gospel music, and Linda and I were asked to become part of a quartet with her playing the piano, and me singing soprano (melody), the only part I can sing since I do not read music. In addition to the quartet, another favorite part of church life at Prestonsburg was horseshoe pitching. Having pitched with my dad, granddad, and uncle, I was pretty good. After watching me pitch, Oscar Collins selected me as his partner, and we were usually unbeatable.

Because of her pregnancy, Linda was unable to teach beyond the Christmas break. As the time was rapidly approaching for our child to be born, it became necessary for Linda to remain behind in our

Wilmore apartment for a few weekends. While it was not nearly as enjoyable to drive that long distance alone, we were able to adapt.

As Linda's due date was approaching, we were becoming more and more excited. While the birth of a child is the most common of miracles, like all first time parents, we were apprehensive. One evening as we were at Dick and Judy's apartment enjoying their TV, as we did periodically, it dawned on me that the gas tank of our car, now a Chevy Nova, was on empty, and everything in Wilmore was closed for the night. Dick suggested that I take his car, but I rejected his offer, assuring him that things would be fine. His final words were, *"Now call if you need my car!"* And sure enough, we had to call about 3:00 a.m. for Linda was beginning labor, and the staff at the hospital said she should come in. When I called Dick for his car, it seemed he was on our doorstep by the time I hung up the phone! He and Judy were as excited as we were!

We arrived at Central Baptist Hospital in Lexington a little before 6:00 a.m. In those days, husbands were not allowed in the labor room, and certainly not permitted to be present at the delivery. As I waited with other anxious fathers to be, some were pacing the floor and puffing on their cigarettes, for there were no restrictions against smoking at that time, even in hospitals. Linda's doctor came around 8:45 to inform me that she would likely not deliver until early afternoon, so I tried to prepare myself for the wait. But about 9:45 I heard the doctor again calling my name; as I walked out into the hall, I noticed that he was pushing a little basket, and he said: *"Well, Tom, here's your little girl! What do you think?"* As I looked down on our precious daughter for the first time, all I could see was her black, curly hair. The only words I could muster were, *"What do you think?"* What I attempted to ask was if she was okay; I needed a professional opinion of what the doctor thought before I could even begin to express what I was thinking and feeling! Because it took Linda some time to recover from her anesthesia, she was not alert enough to see our prized newborn until mid-afternoon, and by that time I had called our parents and other family members and friends. When she saw her, Linda's first words were: *"Man alive!"* That was one of Linda's phrases in those days anytime she was astonished, and this was definitely a time of wonder for us both!

Cheryl Lynne Madon was born on March 25, 1965, at 9:36 a.m. at Central Baptist Hospital in Lexington. The first person to come visit us and Cheryl was Alvin, my friend from Baxter who was by this time a member of the Lexington Police Force. Dick and Judy also came soon afterwards, along with Howard and Jan Biddulph. One of my greatest blessings was driving to Louisville to pick up Linda's mother, who boarded the train in Los Angeles as soon as she received the news of the birth of her first grandchild. How wonderful it was to have her share our joy, and how blessed we were to benefit from her servant's heart toward us! A few days later, Linda's father was able to come and join in the celebration as well.

What a delight it was to bring Cheryl home to our small basement apartment! Our friends soon began to visit, and we loved how excited they were about our charming little girl! One of our favorite memories is of taking Cheryl for her first drive on the back roads, weaving through the scenic horse farms of Central Kentucky.

Anticipating the colorful dogwood and redbud trees, so beautiful in the Kentucky spring time, we experienced an unexpected surprise, as mares were also giving birth; on that memorable drive with our newborn, we were blessed to witness one foal after another, some still on wobbly legs, as they struggled to stand near their mothers!

When the time arrived for Linda to again travel to Prestonsburg, and for the church to meet Cheryl, one of my biggest

Cheryl's first trip to our church

adjustments as new father was how much *stuff* was required for a new baby! We had arranged for Linda's parents to join us as well so her father could lead us as we publically dedicated Cheryl to the Lord. Her father had a wonderful gift for making every event extra special, and Cheryl's dedication was no exception. I can still envision him sitting at the piano to sing, and as he sang I saw two little boys on the front row with their hands over their ears. When Bill Gillam sang, he immediately captured everyone's attention!

During our two years in Prestonsburg, I would often visit the hospital in Pikeville, a coal mining town about 30 miles away. It is on the weekends when the poor people of that area, some who live *in those deep, dark hollers where the sun comes up about ten in the morning, and the sun goes down about three in the day,*[2] come to visit their loved ones in the hospital. As you enter through the main entrance, boldly displayed are words impossible to miss: *"I complained because I had no shoes until I met a man who had no feet!"*[3] While I was familiar with that statement, its impact in that setting was extraordinary. Many of the moms and dads who frequent that hospital, like families in Harlan County where I grew up, know what it means to put cardboard in their children's shoes to cover the holes, just to get by until they can afford to purchase new ones.

After two years in Prestonsburg, the church was again able to secure a full time pastor. While our time there was not as positive as it had been in Alert, it was nevertheless a good learning experience. What made leaving there much easier was our next assignment: Mt. Hope and Mt. Gilead. These were two churches where I had preached during my first year of college, and places where we already had friends. An added plus was that our new churches were only one hour from Asbury! One somewhat negative was that there was no parsonage, but as time passed, it became a positive as we always had a place to stay in the homes of our hospitable parishioners.

One confession I must make about our time at Mt. Hope and Mt. Gilead is that this is where I came face to face with gluttony, one of those respectable sins, or so we think, because it is so common. Let me explain. The church members would sign up in advance to host us for the Sunday noon meal. Linda will confirm that I am not exaggerating, but there were always two types of meat, and often three: fried chicken, beef roast, ham, etc. along with several other dishes (salads, vegetables, potatoes, various types of bread) and typically two desserts. We would finish eating around 1:30 or 2:00 and then they would bring the food out again around 5:30 so we would *not be hungry* when we went to the evening service! We often wondered if the families were competing to outdo each other.

My suit pants were getting tighter and increasingly more uncomfortable. After visiting in a home one afternoon, as I slipped back into the car, I heard a rip: the seat of my pants had come apart at the seam! As it turned out, we were to be at Mt. Gilead that evening, and I was not required to return and eat again before church. Linda and Cheryl were spending the afternoon with the family where we had lunch, and would ride to the service with them. But what could I do about my pants? My first thought was that there surely must be a needle and thread among the VBS crafts in the church basement. Sadly, there was none to be found. The only thing I could find was a stapler, but I thought that would work. So I took off my pants, put them on one of the Sunday school tables, and stapled the seam together again. It worked, though I did feel the need to stand with my back to everyone all evening!

Our two years at Mt. Hope and Mt. Gilead were almost equal in joy to what we had experienced at Alert. We grew close to the people, and they expressed their love to us in numerous ways. One of our dearest friendships was with Kurt and Lillie Fryman, and their two daughters, Becky and Marsha. Staying in their home on Saturday nights became our most frequent destination, and they absolutely loved Cheryl, who by this time was able to sit quietly in church. One of our favorite photos of Cheryl at that age was taken on their piano bench. Becky, the oldest, was skilled on the organ at Mt. Hope, and she loved to play with Linda at the piano.

One weeknight while we were in our seminary duplex in Wilmore, we received the troubling news that Kurt and his youngest daughter, Marsha, had been hit head on by a drunk driver. Kurt was a muscular 6'6" farmer, and was taking Marsha to band practice when the accident occurred. Kurt was uninjured, but Marsha hit her head on the dashboard. Their first thought was that the blow was not too severe. But when she did not respond, they took her to St. Joseph's Hospital in Lexington. When we arrived from Wilmore, Kurt and Lillie were emerging into the lobby with the news that Marsha had just died. We were all in shock and deeply distraught over this sudden loss. By this time, Becky was a student at Eastern Kentucky University in Richmond, southeast of Lexington and Kurt and Lillie asked us to accompany them as they broke the news to her of Marsha's death. It was a most difficult evening, and a season of life we will never forget.

Marsha Fryman

When the facts were revealed, Kurt was familiar with the drunk driver, a young man in Harrison County who was known for his lifestyle of drinking. After the accident, he was locked in the country jail. Kurt, a deeply bereaved father, asked me to accompany him to the jail. Kurt's purpose in going was to let the man know that he forgave him, that he loved him, and also admonish him to turn his life around. Kurt asked me to go so I could pray for the man who killed his precious daughter. As we arrived, the jailer would not permit us to be very close to the prisoner, fearful of what Kurt might do. But he did allow us to stand perhaps 15 to 20 yards away, looking across a dimly lit hallway to the cell where the prisoner stood. As I listened and observed Kurt's words of forgiveness and love, I felt I was standing on holy ground, in the presence of astonishing grace! When he said, *"And now, I want my pastor to pray for you"*, I was so overcome by emotion that it took me awhile to find my voice. As I gave the message later that week at Marsha's funeral, approximately 800 students were present. Marsha was not only an attractive and sweet 15 year old; she was also verbal about her faith, and this gave me greater freedom as I spoke. I felt that in a very real sense, my sermon was her voice sharing her faith with her classmates. Her genuine faith also gave comfort to her family and to those of us who were friends, for we knew we would one day see her again. That season surrounding Marsha's death was one of those challenging, bewildering experiences God used to teach and prepare me for other difficult ministry valleys in the years ahead.

During that period when Linda was teaching and I was in seminary, Cheryl was cared for by a loving lady in Wilmore we called *Mama Jane*. Linda would drive to school, and I would carry Cheryl, her diaper bag, and my books from our duplex, along a little path through the Wilmore cemetery, and on to Mama Jane's, before heading to class or to the library. Cheryl was dearly loved by Mama Jane and her family, and was later asked to be a flower girl in her daughter's wedding. And our little daughter, not quite 3 years old, did it perfectly without any miscues. She went on to have quite the career as a flower girl in her early years.

Having the added responsibilities of a student pastor meant that it would take me four years instead of three to complete my degree. One of my favorite professors was Dr. Robert Coleman, author of *The Master Plan of Evangelism*, and I came to know him as a friend as well. I also had great respect for Dr. Dennis Kinlaw, my Old Testament professor. My classes on missions under Dr. J.T. Seamands were also challenging and instructive. Dr. Seamands had become one of Linda's father's closest friends during a year long trip around the world, singing in the same quartet, supporting the ministry of evangelist, Dr. John Thomas.

The seminary professor, however, who most impacted my personal life and future ministry, was Dr. Robert Traina, [4] who joined the faculty as I was beginning my third year. Dr. Traina introduced us to inductive Bible study, the idea being that you simply approach the Biblical text and allow it to speak for itself. The three main steps are *observation, interpretation, and application.* Careful observation includes learning the historical and cultural context, the grammatical structure of the passage, as well as the precise meaning of the words in the text, Greek words from the New Testament, and Hebrew words from the Old Testament. Once careful observation has been made, you move on to interpretation and ultimately to application. What I came to see about inductive Bible study was that it was necessary for me to lay aside whatever previous ideas or assumptions I had about the passage. It was simple but profound, yet so refreshing; in the months and years to come, it would be life changing.

As I began to practice this stimulating method of study, I saw that there were two factors which made it difficult for me to look at God's Word objectively - one cultural and the other theological. The cultural issue came from my Eastern Kentucky roots where so many have great difficulty accepting the absolutely free gift of God's grace. During my growing up years, I had often heard my father say, *"Son, we don't accept charity!"* People in our culture will barter or trade to get something, but there is a prideful resistance against accepting a gift without giving something in return. After I later came to understand the grace of God in truth, as Paul expressed it in Colossians, (1:6), I had a serious discussion with my dad about this issue, and said to him, *"Dad, before God we have to accept charity! There is nothing we can give to Him in return for our salvation!"* I quoted to him that wonderful phrase from the old song, *Rock of Ages*, which he knew: *"Nothing in my hand I bring, simply to the cross I cling."* In my mind I knew that *grace is the unmerited favor of God,* and I also knew that my life was being transformed by grace, but it was not until I was out of seminary that the magnificent truth of the *Gospel of the Grace of God* forever captured my heart!

As for the theological issue that made it difficult for me to study God's Word inductively, Asbury College and Seminary were in the Wesleyan Armenian theological tradition, as were the vast majority of camp meeting preachers who had been so influential in the first two years of my Christian life. If I were to follow Dr. Traina's inductive Bible study method as he taught it, I needed to lay aside, at least temporarily, my Wesleyan Armenian glasses, so to speak, and this is what I did. Dr. Traina's approach enabled me to begin to study the Scripture with greater objectivity and freshness. Prior to Dr. Traina's class, there were certain verses I tended to avoid, feeling those passages belonged to our theological adversary. For example, I had never heard any of my Wesleyan friends recite John 10:27-29 as their favorite memory verses: "My sheep hear my voice, and I know them, and they follow Me; and I give eternal life to them, and they will never perish; and no one will snatch them out of My Father's hand. My Father, who has given them to Me, is greater than all; and no one can snatch them out of My Father's hand." The reason I viewed Jesus' great promises about the security of the believer as belonging to our theological rival was because the position of Wesleyan theology is that it is possible to lose one's salvation. While I admit that my thinking may seem somewhat extreme, that was how I felt; but Dr. Traina's teaching on inductive Bible study freed me from my somewhat restricted way of approaching Scripture.

This new approach to Scripture became the tool God used to motivate me to dig into God's Word with greater passion and confidence than ever before. Early in my Christian life I had memorized Romans 12:2: "And do not be conformed to this world, but be transformed by the renewing of your mind, so that you may prove what the will of God is, that which is good and acceptable and perfect." As unbelievers, our minds are filled with many incorrect thoughts about God, and flawed ideas about other areas of life. But when we come to Christ, His plan is to *transform and renew our* minds, to correct our defective way of thinking, and He does this through His Word, which is the final authority for all matters of faith and conduct. As I write these words, I am grateful to say that so many of my false ideas about God, along with my incorrect views about other crucial areas of life, have now been consumed in the flames of biblical truth, and the process is continuing!

While Linda and I were enjoying the ministry and the people we were seeking to serve, along with our friends at Asbury, and certainly Cheryl, who was our common delight, as a couple we had been gradually drifting apart. While we had numerous joys, we were not truly sharing life together. As Linda and I have often reflected on those years, we now see that we were in an extremely vulnerable season of life, both of us having numerous responsibilities and extremely busy lifestyles, making it difficult to experience the marriage God intended, and that we both desired. In addition to her teaching, class preparations, and grading, Linda had numerous home responsibilities, being a wife, and a new mother. I had my seminary courses, of course, along with the study and various assignments, two sermons to prepare each week, other relational responsibilities of pastoral life on the weekends and, oh yes, learning what it meant to be a husband and a father. The fly in the ointment, so to speak, was my love (obsession) for sports. Asbury College had just opened a golf

Like all young couples, we had a lot to learn.

course where students at the college or seminary could play 9 holes for 50 cents, and 18 holes for $1.00; I was learning to play, and enjoying it. While it was a poor joke, I used to say that it was cheaper to be on the golf course than to stay at home. Sadly, while I could not see it at the time, there was a high price to pay. One of the questions in the heart of my young, loyal, hard-working conscientious wife, and mother to Cheryl, was this: *just where did she fit in the day to day priorities of her husband? How valuable was she in my heart?* As the years have passed, I have discovered that this is the foremost question in the heart of every wife; *she wants to know she is cherished by her husband!* I have yet to meet a wife who felt otherwise.

Adding to my misplaced sports priorities, during my final two years of seminary, I was on the student counsel with the important role of being the intramural sports director. This included organizing a flag football league in the fall, a basketball league in the winter and, of course, a fall and spring golf tournament, which I won both years. Something, or more accurately, someone needed to change. And I, of course, saw areas in Linda's life where I felt she needed to be transformed as well. Because of God's love for us, and His commitment to our marriage, in His perfect timing He would put us in exactly the right place and at the right time, to bring about the changes we both needed to begin to build a healthy, growing marriage that would endure.

During Asbury's annual Minister's Conference of my final year of seminary, John Morris, *my most unforgettable character* from seven years earlier, reappeared in our lives. While visiting Wilmore, he came to our duplex, inviting us to join him in ministry in Tyler, Texas, where he was the founding pastor of a new church. Because the congregation was still in its infancy, he could not offer me a staff position, but he did promise to find me a job and a place for our small family to live. By this time, though my five years as a student pastor had been positive, I had come to see that being a Methodist pastor was not God's plan for me. In praying about John's offer, for a variety of reasons, we sensed this would be a helpful next step before moving on into our future ministry, which we sensed at the time, would be missions.

In May of 1968, after 20 consecutive years of schooling, I was at last a seminary graduate, and it was a wonderful time of celebration for me and my classmates, many of whom had become dear friends. My pastor and his wife, Bill and Betty Garnett, who had been my loyal supporters for ten years, and were still serving in Baxter, came to rejoice with us. My parents and siblings were also there, along with Linda's parents, and it was a marvelous time of jubilation and giving thanks, all because of *God's amazing grace!*

CHAPTER SIX

When Our Marriage and Ministry Were Saved – God's Faithful Servants

"Reprove a wise man, and he will love you. Give instruction to a wise man and he will be still wiser; teach a righteous man and he will increase in learning." Proverbs 9:8-9

While *commencement* marked the completion of my seminary degree, it more importantly announced the beginning of what I had been preparing for since my senior year of high school, namely, pursuing God's purpose for my life. Before we left Wilmore, however, and departed for Tyler, Texas, the Lord had a message of supreme importance He had sovereignly arranged for me to hear. Dr. Dennis Kinlaw, my respected Old Testament professor, was speaking at a retreat of OMS missionaries on the campus of Asbury College. Since Linda and I were anticipating serving with OMS, we were invited to attend. Dr. Kinlaw's text was this: "'Not by might, nor by power, but by My Spirit,' says the Lord" (Zachariah 4:6). The Lord spoke these words to Zerubbabel, the governor of Judah, to encourage and assure him of divine enablement in the rebuilding of the temple. Dr. Kinlaw explained that the Hebrew words for might and power were used to refer to various types of force: *military might, financial wealth, a charismatic personality, physical strength, or the power of sheer numbers.* He explained that God's words to Zerubbabel, while spoken in a specific historical context, were applicable in all ages; though God uses people, it is His power working in and through them that ultimately accomplishes His work – *"by My Spirit!"*

There are times in our lives when the Holy Spirit speaks through His Word with such power that our hearts are profoundly pierced, and this was one of those occasions, an unforgettable moment that became a treasured spiritual marker in my life. In response to Dr. Kinlaw's faithful exposition of God's Word, I was prompted to prayerfully express to the Lord that any eternal value that would come from my future ministry would not be the result of my own gifts or abilities; it would come about only *by His Spirit!* I have often returned to this truth, and used it as my own text on many occasions over these decades of ministry.

After eight years in the village of Wilmore, the day finally arrived when Linda and I, along with our rapidly growing and vivacious three year old, Cheryl, left our familiar surroundings in the bluegrass of Central Kentucky for the piney woods and lakes of East Texas. My only memories of the Lone Star state were of my trip with John Morris across the dry, desert-like terrain of West Texas. Though I had heard positive reports, it was difficult to imagine how East Texas could be any different, but we were in for a pleasant surprise.

True to his word, John Morris found employment for me and a house for our family. My job was to work as a carpenter's helper on one of the crews of James Landrum, a respected builder in Tyler, and a member of the church. Our home was on Birdwell Avenue near Green Acres Shopping Center, and had been referred to by the neighbors as *the haunted house.* Approximately five years earlier, the man of the house died, and his wife left with his body the next day for West Virginia, and never returned. Apart from a few minor break-ins, the house simply sat vacant all that time. One of the men in the church, Ray Vanderpool, who was a neighbor across the back fence, contacted the woman and worked out an arrangement for us to move into this long vacant house. It was actually a nice home, pleasantly furnished, but somewhat run down because of the neglect. John had arranged for some of the church members to do an initial cleaning before we arrived to take occupancy.

After purchasing a hammer, I began work immediately, and remember losing 8 pounds that first day working outside in the East Texas heat and humidity. Meanwhile, Linda and Cheryl were seeking to make *the haunted house* into our *hallowed home.* In addition to John, Mary Helen, and their two children, we also met John and Kay Prestridge that first week, who in the years to come would invest in our lives in countless ways, becoming some of our closest and most loyal life-long friends.

In contrast to the multi-cultural dynamics of our college and seminary years where students came from all parts of our nation, including several from other countries, Tyler had its own distinct culture. While there were differences, the East Texas culture, including the accent, reminded me of my roots in Southeastern Kentucky. Another refreshing characteristic of Tyler was the enthusiastic patriotism we witnessed, more than we had observed in any other location, and our hearts responded to it.

As I began my job in construction, my primary task was to assist the foreman - a gifted master carpenter. Ours was a relatively small crew of no more than five or six, but we were involved in all phases of construction, enabling me to be exposed to the entire process. There were times when I thought of my hard-working grandfather in Kentucky who built a three story home, with only used lumber he had accumulated from tearing down old, unwanted buildings, and how he did it all without the luxury of power tools! Working with these men was considerably easier than what he experienced. These were positive months for me, being outdoors and doing manual labor, while also having the opportunity to share my faith with unbelievers.

During this time John Morris also asked me to lead one of the mid-week Bible studies that rotated between various locations. One evening we met in a home where the father had a trophy white-tailed buck over his fireplace. After the study, as we were having refreshments, Cheryl shouted from across the room, "*Dad, why does Mr. White have that donkey over his fireplace?*" That became a hilarious story that would be retold many times in the years to come. John also asked me to begin reaching out to the young people in the church, and gave me a list of names. Since I was only 26 at the time and Linda 25, we were not far removed in age from those in their teens. What a wonderful time we had building what would become lifelong friendships, while also helping teens discover the joy of a personal relationship with Jesus, and of being involved in the life of the church.

We had not been in Tyler very long until Linda began experiencing that identical mysterious sickness as a few years earlier, except this time we were able to diagnose it more quickly. Near the time of Cheryl's birthday in March, we would become parents again, and Cheryl would have a little brother or sister. We were all overjoyed!

One of our new friends in the church, Charlie Featherston, worked for the Billy Graham organization. Soon after we arrived, he organized an evangelistic outreach targeting several towns in East Texas. The plan was to show the Billy Graham film, *The Restless Ones,* in theaters in the various locations for an entire week. At the end of the movie, we would give an invitation for people to come forward and give their lives to Christ. Charlie recruited men from our church to teach counselor training in each town as we prepared for the event. My assigned town was Jacksonville, located to the south of Tyler. It was astounding to see what the Lord did during those days through that simple yet compelling movie to bring people to Himself.

As Thanksgiving was approaching, John informed me that my days on the small carpenter crew would soon come to an end. Years later I would learn that working in a secular job was part of the discipleship vision John had for me. While it gave me an opportunity to labor alongside unbelievers in the workplace, I also learned skills that would benefit me for the rest of my life. But now I would be in full time ministry. The plan was for me to split my time between what I was already doing in Tyler, with a church in Jacksonville where the pastor was Charles Fries, a friend from seminary who had been in my graduating class. Even more surprising was the news that a new church was beginning in Greenville, Texas, 80 miles to the northwest, and they had asked for our assistance. My role was to drive to Greenville each Sunday morning to preach and help the church to become established. John Prestridge would fill the pulpit on Sunday evenings while I returned to our youth group in Tyler. It all worked very well, as we were able to establish strong friendships in all three churches.

After returning from a gathering in Jacksonville on Christmas Eve, John Morris called to say that he had some news, and that we might want to sit down. John knew our circumstances and was aware that I had a seminary debt of $1,800 dollars, which in today's economy does not seem like a large amount, but it was significant at the time. One of the reasons we accepted John's earlier offer to come to Tyler was to give us time to pay off that one debt before completing the final application with OMS, with whom we hoped to serve as missionaries. John's news was that an anonymous person had graciously given the money to pay the entire amount, and had also given extra funds so I could attend a conference on evangelism at Arrowhead Springs in California. He also mentioned that a young man from the Jacksonville church, Danny Robertson, a new Christian, was going as well. In contrast to my *blood bought friend*, where I never learned his or her identity, Linda and I heard some years later that this generous Christmas gift was given by the mother of a young man in our youth group. Her financial investment was her way of thanking us and the Lord for how the life of her son had been transformed in such a positive way.

While we were overjoyed with this completely unexpected gift, there was uneasiness in my spirit, and I understood why. In anticipation of this moment, I had been looking over the final application we needed to complete with OMS. One part was a simple signature indicating that we were in agreement with the doctrinal statement, the one area where I had reservations.

While there are honest disagreements between Bible believing Christians, differences I respected then and now, those of us who are committed to Scripture as the final authority must come to our own conclusions through prayerful and diligent study of Scripture. The biggest issue with me at that time was the security of the believer. While I was excited about the Lord and the work I saw Him doing in my life, at times I felt an inner anxiety, fearing I could lose my salvation. One of the passages God used to bring me great encouragement was in Hebrews 12 where the writer describes God's discipline. One of my questions all along was how bad a sin had to be for God to kick me out of His family. And if He did, would I have to repent and then be born again and perhaps even again? Would I be required to receive *eternal life* all over again if and when I repented? In this passage I came to see that getting rid of me when I did wrong was not in God's heart at all, for I was His child and loved by Him unconditionally. "My son; do not regard lightly the discipline of the Lord, nor faint when you are reproved by Him; for those whom the Lord loves He disciplines, and scourges every son whom He receives" (Hebrews 12:5-6). In these verses which are actually quotes from the Book of Proverbs, two warnings are given: the first is to never take God's discipline lightly, for it is not a trivial matter to be disciplined by our loving Lord. But second, we are not to faint or become discouraged by God's discipline, even when it may be severe, as it will be at times. The overarching truth is that, because of His parental love, God will discipline (correct, train) us, but never disown us! "It is for discipline that you endure; God deals with you as with sons; for what son is there whom his father does not discipline? But if you are without discipline, of which all have become partakers, then you are illegitimate children and not sons." (Hebrews 12:7-8) This expanded passage on the subject of discipline, along with numerous other passages such as Romans 8:31-39, gave me a sense of security I had not yet come to know in my heart. The question then became, if we were not going as missionaries with OMS, what was God's plan for us?

As Danny Robertson and I traveled to our evangelism conference in California, it exceeded my expectations, giving me a new tool in sharing the gospel, along with greater confidence in my faith. While our conference was directed toward lay people involved in the ministry of the local church, Danny and I also learned about the ministry of Campus Crusade on college campuses. One afternoon while Danny was attending another of the elective seminars, I chose to watch a film by Bill Bright, Founder and President of Campus Crusade for Christ, called, *Come Help Change the World.* During those moments, an unexpected spiritual encounter occurred. As much as at

Linda's parents – Bill and Mary Gillam

any other time in my life, I sensed that God was calling us to join this ministry and serve on a college campus!

When I returned home and informed Linda, who by this time was eight months pregnant, she was remarkably supportive, even though this meant going in a very different direction than with the mission of her parents. While I had been somewhat apprehensive about sharing the news with Linda's mother and father, when I related to them our change of plans, any disappointment they may have felt was not expressed, only love and support as we moved toward Campus Crusade - truly a display of grace!

John Morris was also supportive, as was the church in Jacksonville. The church in Greenville, while understanding, was not as enthusiastic. Their hope was that I would become their full time pastor. Nevertheless, we began the application process with Campus Crusade for Christ and were soon accepted with plans to attend new staff training that summer of 1969, with the goal of being on campus by September. In the interim, there was still work to be done in Texas before stepping out in faith into our new ministry adventure.

Meanwhile, in the midst of these major changes, there was also a child to be born. Even though four years had passed since Cheryl's birth, fathers were still banished from labor and delivery rooms. When the days for her were accomplished, Linda gave birth to our first born son, Thomas Scott Madon, 6 lbs., 7 ounces, on March 14 of 1969, in Mother Frances Hospital in Tyler. The waiting room had a simple display on the wall with the words: Girl and Boy. Once the sex of the child was determined, the delivery room nurse would flip a switch, and the appropriate light would come on. After hours of waiting, I rejoiced when I saw the light for *BOY* indicating that Linda and I had been blessed with a son! Cheryl was overjoyed as well as we brought her little brother into our home.

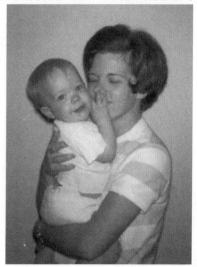

When the time came for our three weeks of staff training at San Bernardino in July, the most difficult part was leaving Cheryl, four years old, and Scott, only four months old, behind with loyal, loving friends. Linda and I were two out of several hundred who were joining the staff that summer, and apart from missing our children, it was a very positive

A mother's love

experience. At the end of two weeks, we would learn our assignment. As Linda and I discussed the locations where we could be sent, we imagined every state - except California. When we opened the envelope with the hundreds of others who were shouting and crying upon learning their assignments, we were shocked: *Northern California/Berkeley District, with a specific assignment in Sacramento.* Our District Director at Berkeley would be Warren Willis, and our Campus Director, with whom we would work most closely, was Bill Hansell, whose wife's name was Margaret. A significant portion of that third and final week was spent in meeting and becoming acquainted with our staff team. Warren's assignment was for all members of the team to memorize the first chapter of James from the J.B. Phillips paraphrase of the New Testament, which turned out to be an enriching experience. He also voiced his expectations that all staff would have their support raised and be on campus by the first of September.

When we returned to Tyler to reunite with our children, the most heart-wrenching moment came when Scott did not remember us, even his mother! Thankfully, as our family was reunited, that changed very quickly, but our hope was that we would never again have to be apart for that length of time. With the blessing and counsel of John Morris, as well as the church, we began the humbling, yet faith-building process of trusting the Lord for the support we needed, $1,200 per month, although we would only receive $900 for living expenses. The additional amount was designated for insurance and other administrative costs. Even as He had faithfully done in the past, God provided what we needed, and in record time, making it possible for us to arrive on the first of September. The majority of our support came from the three churches we were serving: Tyler, Jacksonville, and Greenville, plus other individuals. We also made a trip to Kentucky and Indiana to visit family, where others became part of our support team, including the Jewell family from our first church in Alert.

Bill and Margaret Hansell

With this new venture before us, we traded in what had been our most reliable car to that point, a 1966 Chevy Biscayne, a stick shift, for a new 1969 Chevy Impala – our first car with air conditioning! As we left Tyler, we were pulling a U-Haul with all our belongings, but by the time we reached Lubbock in West Texas, the shocks on our new Impala had worn out, and we had to purchase oversized ones to handle the load.

Upon arriving in Sacramento, Bill and Margaret had arranged for us to stay with friends from their church until we could find housing. The best we could do on our limited budget was to rent an unfurnished duplex close to Sacramento State, and trust the Lord for furniture later. Soon some friends in our new church who owned a cabin near Lake Tahoe gave us a limited amount of furniture, and it was adequate until we could add more.

Bill and Margaret already had a strong ministry underway at Sac State, as we called it. They also were reaching out to Sacramento City College as well as American River Junior College. While Linda's primary responsibility was with Cheryl and Scott, I went to campus each day with Bill, and began to experience ministry on a secular campus. Up to this point I had gone to a Christian college and seminary. Other than working as a carpenter's helper alongside a few unbelievers, this was a new but very encouraging experience. I soon learned that special events were a major part of what we did with Campus Crusade. In addition to a weekly evangelistic meeting called *College Life*, we had fall and spring retreats, a Christmas and Easter conference, as well as summer outreach projects. The retreats were always planned in conjunction with our ministry at Berkeley. We also met weekly with individual students, and in smaller gatherings called *Action Groups.* Throughout the week, we were also sharing the Gospel with unbelievers, seeing a number of them come to faith in Christ.

As our very positive first year with Crusade was coming to a close, Warren Willis from Berkeley came to visit. His purpose was to ask me to become the Campus Director at San Jose State University. Since Linda and I had only been on staff for one year, I felt somewhat hesitant. But after he said a number of very positive things about me in the course of the conversation, I began to feel more encouraged about the challenge. But then Warren paused, and his next word was *however;* I wondered what could be coming next. He went on to explain that he was confident I would respond positively to what he was about to say and he quoted these verses: "Reprove a wise man, and he will love you. Give understanding to a wise man and he will be still wiser; teach a righteous man and he will increase in learning" (Proverbs 9:8-9). With such a complimentary *set up*, how could I not respond? These were his words: "*Tom, as I have watched you this year, my impression is that you appear to be putting the ministry ahead of your marriage; if you are, the time will come when you will not have a ministry, and the time will come when you will not have a marriage."* He proceeded to give two examples of why he said what he did. The initial, inner response of my flesh was to justify myself, to rationalize, and convince him that he was wrong; but I kept quiet, especially since he had prefaced his *difficult but loving words* by calling me a wise man!

As I was seeking to prayerfully process what Warren had said, first about my attitude toward our marriage and second, about the new responsibility I would assume in San Jose, the weight of leaving Bill and Margaret left us with a bit of sadness. We had learned much from them and had become good friends. Thankfully, as it turned out, we were able to stay in touch as fellow campus directors. Bill and I were also able to go to two Rose Bowl games together in the years that followed, and we remain in contact today. But now it was time to turn our attention to summer staff training, where we would discover who our team members would be, and begin strategizing about our fall ministry in San Jose.

Dr. Howard Hendricks

What we did not know was that our loving Heavenly Father, who was committed to our marriage and family, had a life-changing experience for us just ahead. When we arrived at Arrowhead Springs, we learned that one of our classes would be on Christian marriage and family, a two week course taught by Dr. Howard Hendricks of Dallas Seminary. While there were other classes, this one was held in an outside amphitheater in the evening so all staff could attend. While Linda had grown up in a Christian family, and had a better grasp of God's design for marriage and family life, most of what I was hearing was entirely new. Dr. Hendricks was a gifted communicator of God's Word, and delightfully humorous. From his

119

vast experience he also included many unforgettable stories of how these profound biblical truths were to be worked out in the demanding realities of marriage and parenting. Each class was filled with both laughter and tears, and God was clearly at work.

After returning to the small apartment in San Bernardino we had rented for the three weeks of staff training, we put Cheryl and Scott down on their little mats on the floor, and they were soon asleep. Because of the Holy Spirit's work through the Biblical messages from Dr. Hendricks, I knew in my heart it was time for a change. As Linda and I sat around the small old fashioned dinette set, my words to her were essentially these: *"During this class I have come to see how far short I have come from what God intends for me, both as a husband and a father. So I want to ask if you would forgive me for not being the man God intends. By God's grace I want to change, but based on all we are learning, I know it cannot happen overnight, so I also ask if you will be patient with me as I change."* Linda graciously forgave me, but also asked me to forgive her for the areas where she had failed as a wife. We then prayed and wept together, sensing God was giving us a new beginning.

As I have spoken on repentance over the years, I have often compared it to a U-Turn. Repentance literally means a change of mind, the idea being that you recognize you have been on the wrong road, going in the wrong direction, and need to make a change, a U-Turn. As Linda and I look back on that unforgettable evening seven years into our marriage, we are so thankful that God "granted us repentance, leading to a knowledge of the truth" (II Timothy 2:24). The word *granted* is essentially another word for grace, and we know it was God who graced us with repentance that evening in San Bernardino. The result was an inner desire to embrace the Biblical truths about marriage and family as the blueprint we would seek to follow.

Linda still felt a measure of hurt for a time, but it was soon gone as she looked to the Lord for grace to change, even as I was doing. As I began to conscientiously seek to fulfill my high calling as a husband, described so clearly in Scripture, amazingly, Linda began to come around! But it was not just because of me; the greater reason was her new and sincere response to the Lord.

Linda and I are forever indebted to God's faithful servants. The first was Warren Willis, who courageously came with great wisdom to confront me about my marriage and ministry. *"Better is open rebuke than love that is concealed. Faithful are the wounds of a friend, but deceitful are the kisses of an enemy"* (Proverbs 29:5-6). The second was Dr. Howard Hendricks, who faithfully taught us God's Word. Because of the significant way God used him in our lives, Dr. Hendricks became a highly respected mentor.

Our plan immediately following staff training was to leave for Texas, driving through Friday night and all day Saturday to arrive in Tyler where I had four speaking engagements on Sunday: two in Tyler, one in Jacksonville, and one in Greenville. After a few additional days

My friends had all loved David.

of reconnecting with friends, our next stop was Kentucky to visit my family in Baxter. While Bill and Betty Garnett had recently moved to a different church, the new pastor was a respected man from Harlan County, Alvin Boggs, and he invited me to preach in my home church. As I was speaking, my eyes were drawn to my brother, David, who was listening attentively. Later that afternoon he needed a ride to visit his girlfriend who lived in Cumberland, 20 miles away. On the way, I said, *"David, I could not help but notice how attentive you were when I was preaching today, so I have a question. With our being 12 years apart, we have not been able to see one another nearly as much as I wish we could, but what I would like to know is, do you consider yourself to be a Christian?"* David's immediate response was, *"No, I'm not, but I would like to be!"* As we drove along, I shared the good news of the Gospel, beginning with God's love before explaining our common problem of sin. From there I described how Jesus died on the cross to pay the full penalty for our sin, and how our response to such great love was to simply open our hearts to Him in faith. We pulled off the road and prayed together as David opened his heart and responded to God's call. The Bible says: "Behold, now is the acceptable time, now is the day of salvation" (II Corinthians 6:2). That Sunday afternoon in late August of 1970 became David's *day of salvation,* and it was a special moment for us both. Included in my mother's memorabilia was a letter I had written to David after our return to California, assuring him of my prayers, and sharing various Bible verses to encourage him in his new faith.

When we visited Linda's parents in Greenwood, Indiana, where their mission headquarters was now located, her father was not well, and we were deeply concerned. The previous spring he had been flown back to the US from Haiti, where he and Linda's mother had been serving with OMS. He was soon diagnosed with cerebral malaria. In the fall of that same year, her father began experiencing double vision; after further testing a brain tumor was also discovered. This proved to be a very difficult time for the family, but a season in which each one took significant steps of faith. In January they were able to remove a portion of the tumor at St Francis Hospital in Indianapolis.

When we returned to San Jose after our eventful summer, it was time to begin my new responsibilities. We moved into a small apartment about 3 miles from the campus, and it was from here that Cheryl began kindergarten, a tiny girl riding a huge yellow bus with a driver named Myrtle. Being the campus director meant having our own staff team, a group we came to dearly love. Among them was a newly married couple, Greg and Denyse Gripentrog, and two single girls, Kirsten and Deanna; they all loved our children. The Lord blessed our ministry in wonderful ways, with numerous students responding to the gospel. Our staff began to meet with those who were eager for discipleship, helping them also become involved in action groups, and encouraging them to attend one of our special events. Greg and I concluded the week each Friday afternoon on a secluded part of the campus lawn, studying a harmony of the gospels called *the Life of Christ in Stereo*. Our goal was to discover all we could about how Jesus conducted His ministry, and what the applications were to our lives. Many of the truths we discussed are ones I have shared in sermons and with individuals over these many years. Though I had no way of knowing at the time, Greg and Denyse would leave for Dallas Seminary two years later, would eventually serve as missionaries in Indonesia, and be supported by a church where I was the pastor. Greg would go on to serve eight years as President of OC International, before he and Denyse returned as missionaries to Indonesia. Nor could we have known that Kirsten Beeler, who grew up in the San Francisco Bay area and introduced our staff to some of the wonderful restaurants in the area, would still be serving with the same ministry, now called CRU, with Athletes in Action, all these years later!

March 24, 1971, is a day I will never forget! Just before 6:00 a.m. I received an unexpected call from Pastor Alvin Boggs in Baxter with the alarming news that my brother, David, only seven months into his Christian faith, had been injured the day before in spring football practice. He had been taken to the UK Medical Center in Lexington where he was undergoing surgery, but the physicians were not hopeful. After receiving encouragement from God's Word during my quiet time, but with a deeply troubled heart, especially for my family, I went to campus to keep my scheduled appointments. About noon I received the heartrending news that David had died.

As we looked in our checking account, there was enough for me to purchase a one way ticket to Kentucky, but not enough for a round trip. Because of a spring conference I was to lead at Arrowhead Springs in April, I had an early afternoon appointment with a friend from our church, Conn Bauer, who was also on lay staff with Campus Crusade. Conn was a giant of a man with an intimidating appearance. He had been a former wrestler, and always wore a black patch over one eye.   When I entered his office, he greeted me and asked how things were going.   When I informed him of my 16 year-old brother's sudden death in Kentucky, Conn asked if I had purchased my ticket; I responded that I had not.   Even before I could give the details, he picked up his phone and asked his secretary to purchase a round trip ticket for me to the nearest airport to Harlan, Kentucky!   Just for the record, this was the only time I ever met with Conn in his office.   But my loving Father arranged for that one meeting to be less than two hours after receiving the news that David had died.   It was because God would prompt one of His generous servants, a wealthy one, to pay for my round trip ticket!   "Remember the former things long past, for I am God, and there is no other; I am God, and there is no one like Me,

David, not long before his death

declaring   the   end   from   the beginning, and from ancient times things which have not been done, saying 'My purpose will be established, and I will accomplish all My good pleasure'" (Isaiah 46:9-10).   Through Conn Bauer's Spirit-prompted generosity, I was again the recipient of *God's grace and generosity, as I have been throughout my entire life!*

That overnight flight to Kentucky was the most beautiful I have ever experienced.   Flying at 33,000 feet, I was able to witness the continuous   lightning   strikes   that   were   fueling   the   Midwest thunderstorms below.   When I arrived in Harlan to share in the deep grief of my family, and then spoke at David's funeral, I shared with his classmates the same message I had communicated with him only seven months earlier, the *good news of the Gospel of the grace of God!*   The crowd of nearly 800 was reminiscent of the memorial service I conducted only three years earlier for 15 year-old Marsha from Mt. Hope when I was a student pastor. As I was interacting with various ones afterwards, I spotted Marsha's parents and older sister, Becky, who had come to share my family's loss. Among the many cards of condolences my parents received were tender notes from two of my former girlfriends, Carol and Gloria, who dearly loved David when he was only a little boy, and they loved my family as well.

Immediately after my return from Kentucky, we received the alarming news that Linda's father was being flown to the City of Hope hospital in Duarte, CA. in greater Los Angeles in hope of curtailing his aggressive brain tumor. Because it was near the time when we would be traveling from San Jose to Arrowhead Springs where I would lead our spring conference, we were uncertain about what to do until we discovered affordable one way fares, even for our budget, where Linda, Cheryl, and Scott could fly to LAX and be met by Linda's sister. This enabled Linda to be present for her father's second operation. Because of some delays at the hospital, when I arrived by car, he was still in surgery. Her family insisted that I be in the first group to greet him in recovery. Amazingly, his initial words to me were not about himself; he expressed how sorrowful he felt when he learned about the death of my brother, another expression of grace to add to my long list of unforgettable memories of my beloved father-in-law!

Like the Apostle Paul, Bill Gillam "fought a good fight, finished his course, and kept the faith" (II Timothy 4:7). When his work was done, the Lord called him home on June 29, 1971, at the young age of 57. Linda flew to Indiana for his memorial service. Because his death

occurred at the time of the OMS annual convention, the service became a treasured celebration of his life and ministry. Cheryl, Scott and I remained behind in San Jose. My only memory of those long days with Linda away was our trip to the drive-in movie one evening to see *The Lady and the Tramp!*

Meanwhile, our marriage continued to grow in many encouraging ways. One of

Growing together!

Dr. Howard Hendricks's suggestions to husbands was to save money so you could take your wife away for a weekend, and I began that practice soon afterwards; it is one we have continued throughout our marriage. Linda especially remembers a time when Scott had been sick for several weeks, and she had been unable to even leave the house. At that time, without her knowledge, I had arranged for one of our trusted college young ladies to come and stay with our children while I took Linda away for a weekend on the Monterey Peninsula. She has never forgotten that trip!

While our first year in San Jose was spent in a small apartment, thanks to the Lord's provision, during our last two years there we were able to rent a house with 3 bedrooms and 2 baths. This gave us greater freedom to have students into our home. This included a weekly meeting with our Master Action Group, made up of our key leaders, with a meal prepared by Linda. One of the unique features of our ministry in San Jose was the large numbers of married students who became involved in our ministry, some from San Jose State, and others from San Jose City College. We also were able to purchase all of the life-changing messages by Dr. Hendricks, and listen to them in our home with these couples on our reel to reel recorder. After hearing those sermons over and over again, I came to know them about as well as Howard Hendricks. Even now they are permanently etched in mind and heart, and have influenced all of the teaching I have done over these many years about marriage and family life. Interestingly, one of the couples in that group was Ron and Joan McLain who live just north of us in Fresno. Ron is the founder and director of Healthy Marriage Coalition, and the author of *The Resurrection Marriage,* an Amazon

With Ron McLain in 1972

best seller, and a book I highly recommend. It has been a joy to reconnect with Ron and Joan after all these years, and to rejoice in God's faithfulness to us as couples.

During our three years in San Jose, we became members of Los Gatos Christian Church, which became one of our supporting churches during our final two years with Campus Crusade. Marvin Rickard, the pastor, became a friend and I went to visit with him on more than one occasion, seeking counsel and prayer, two things we all need at some point from our pastor.

Special events were always a part of our ministry, but none was larger than Explo '72. This evangelistic conference was sponsored and planned by Campus Crusade. It has sometimes been referred to as the most visible event of the 1970's Jesus movement. Explo was held in various locations in and around Dallas, TX, from June 12 -17, 1972, with nightly gatherings in the Cotton Bowl with crowds close to 100,000. Our entire California staff was assigned to what was referred to as *Tent City*, near Arlington. This is where those who had campers or tents could stay, and daily activities were held on site. Because our supporting church in Tyler was only 100 miles away, one of the members, Burtis Lloyd, allowed us to use his camper for that week. Because *Tent City* was such a unique part of Explo, Billy Graham came to speak one afternoon, and each member of our staff was able to meet him, and shake his hand.

As we returned to San Jose following Explo, some of the young men in our ministry invited me to join them for a backpacking trip in

The backpacker

the High Sierras. Even though I had no equipment, they provided everything I needed with the exception of a good pair of boots, which I was able to purchase on sale. The first part of the trip was near Tuolumne Meadows in Yosemite National Park, but we were not prepared for the rain that came the first night. After taking an entire day to dry out, we drove to another location farther north, and had an unforgettable experience. I will never forget hiking with Peter Wood from our base camp to a location high above the tree line where we were overwhelmed by the unspoiled magnificence of God's creation. It was an extraordinary, life-changing experience. While I had hiked and camped in the hills of Kentucky, with the demands of my college and seminary years, I had been unable to pursue my love for the outdoors. During that trip I purposed to involve Linda and our children in exploring the marvelous world God created. In May of the following year, Linda, Cheryl, Scott and I spent three memorable days and two wonderful nights in Yosemite, experiencing as much of the stunningly beautiful valley as was possible with an 8 and 4 year-old. From that time on, camping became a summer activity for us, and all of our children have a deep love for the outdoors still today.

In addition to life-transforming teaching on marriage we received through Campus Crusade, Linda and I also benefitted from the practical, Biblical instruction on the Spirit filled life and learning what it means to walk in the Spirit. While we had often heard messages about the Holy Spirit and sanctification in our past, the most frequent emphasis seemed to be on a crisis, rather than the life-long process of sanctification. There was also a strong emphasis on living by faith which we appreciated, because this was such a central part of our lives. Learning to confidently share the gospel, and having to deal with some of the difficult questions of skeptical college students helped to strengthen my faith even more. One of Dr. Bill Bright's wise statements that will always be part of my thinking was this: *Success in witnessing is simply sharing Christ in the power of the Holy Spirit and leaving the results to God!* While I confess that I have attempted to convert a few people over the years, not once have I ever been successful. For a new spiritual birth to occur there must be a work of God in each heart, enabling a person to respond. While I dearly love sharing the good news of the Gospel of the grace of God each time I have an opportunity, it has helped me to simply pray and leave the results to my Heavenly Father, trusting Him to work in His time.

As our third year in San Jose was progressing, Linda and I sensed that another change could be on the way. Dan and Mike, the two young men who were on our staff, were capable and ready to be directors, so I knew the ministry in San Jose would be in good hands. At that time, Campus Crusade was seeking to build a ministry team to go to Ireland, and we expressed an interest in possibly being included. At this time, I had been meeting with leaders from other Christian groups on campus, including the Navigators, Inter Varsity, and the leader of the Baptist student ministry. Our discussions were centered on spiritual gifts and other truths related to discovering the unique ministry God had for each of us. As all this was happening, I received an unexpected call from Darrell Brown, on behalf of the church leadership in Tyler, our primary supporting church where John Morris was the pastor, and where Linda and I had been involved for 16 months before joining the staff of Campus Crusade. Darrell said this: *"Tom, we would like to invite you and Linda to come back to Tyler and be part of the church. We all see pastoral gifts in you. You will have an opportunity to preach and teach, for John Morris is planning to transition into a counseling ministry."* We talked more about the logistics and timing of the move if we were to come, and then the conversation was over. As I hung up the phone, I immediately put my head in my hands and wept, for in my heart I had long embraced the significance of the local church in God's plan. In discussions with my ministry colleagues, I had also voiced how I identified with the words *pastor and teacher. Pastor* refers to the relational side of the ministry which I saw to be vitally important; *teacher* refers to one who is called to faithfully communicate God's Word which He has entrusted to us. By this time I had come to understand that both were desires God had placed in my heart, even during my years as a student pastor. Linda and I were soon at peace that the Lord was calling us back to Tyler.

Simultaneous to this new development, my old friend, Warren Willis, again came for a visit. Three years earlier his purpose was to confront me about putting the ministry ahead of my marriage; this time he came to ask if I would be part of the Summer Institute of Biblical Studies faculty in Cuernavaca, Mexico, where he would be the dean, and I would teach a two week class on Christian marriage! Warren and I had remained in contact, especially through the periodic meetings for campus directors, but he had also been observing me from a distance, witnessing the changes God was faithfully bringing about in my life. I agreed to his offer, though teaching that two week class on Christian marriage would be our last official responsibility with Campus Crusade. Once the class began, filled with responsive college students from across the U.S., some wives of the Latin American staff asked if Linda would translate my material into Spanish and teach it to them. While it was challenging for her, it was also deeply rewarding. Even though my class was only for two weeks, the IBS was for three weeks, so we were able to stay on for the additional week to enjoy the unique culture of this beautiful part of Mexico.

After returning to California, it was time to gather our belongings and return to our beloved friends at the church in Tyler, ready to begin another new chapter for our lives. Our four years with Campus Crusade had been amazingly fruitful while also providing additional training that would serve us well for the rest of our lives. The most significant benefit by far was the miraculous change in our marriage and family, a major turning point, for which we are eternally grateful!

CHAPTER SEVEN

When EMC Became a Grace Community – Our First Home

"And when they had appointed elders for them in every church, having prayed with fasting, they commended them to the Lord in whom they believed." Acts 14:23

"Prepare your work outside and make it ready for yourself in the field; afterwards, build your house." Proverbs 24:27

After a challenging but memorable move from San Jose to Tyler, we were blessed with a wonderful place to live. Herbert and Janet Rainey, members of the church, graciously rented us a beautiful three bedroom brick home, for a generous price, on Waunell Ave. It had a lovely yard and was in a good location. Soon after moving in, while having my quiet time one morning, Jesus' words captured my attention: "And if you have not been faithful in that which is another's, who will give you that which is your own?" (Luke 16:12) Hopefully we would have been good stewards of the Rainey's home even without Jesus' probing question, but it certainly gave me renewed motivation to *be faithful in that which was another's.* I can recall at least two occasions in the years we lived there when neighbors commented positively, in Herbert's presence, how well I was taking care of the house, and I was thankful.

The first Sunday evening we were in church, for the closing song, Martha Graham, whom we had not yet met, sat down at the piano and beautifully sang these words written by Andrae Crouch: *"How can I say thanks for the things You have done for me, things so undeserved that you gave to prove Your love for me; the voices of a million angels could not express my gratitude; all that I am or ever hope to be, I give it all to Thee! To God be the glory, to God be the glory, to God be the glory, for the things He has done; with His blood He has saved me; with His power He has raised me; to God be the glory, for the things He has done! Just let me live my life, let it be pleasing, Lord, to Thee, and should I gain any praise, let it go to Calvary!"*[1] That song was exactly what I needed on our first Sunday back in Tyler! Though I had heard Andrae Crouch sing his song while we lived in California, I thought Martha sang it better! I later learned that she and her husband, Van, had also recently moved to Tyler. In time they would become dear friends, ministry partners, and even neighbors.

Van and Martha Graham

When the church heard that I had taught a class on marriage with Campus Crusade, the ladies' ministry asked if Linda and I would teach some of that material in their fall study, and we welcomed the opportunity. I was in the back of the class one morning as Linda related to these young women the three greatest needs she felt as a wife. *First, she needed someone who loved her perfectly; second, someone who would be available to her on a 24 hour basis; and third, someone who would make the right decision every time.* The ladies all laughed and agreed that having a husband like that would be wonderful. But she went on to say, and this was my favorite part, regardless of how hard Tom tried, Tom would never be able to meet those needs. She went on to explain how she discovered that those needs could only be met by the Lord. Not only had her discovery taken the pressure off of me; her words communicated a profound truth that every wife (and husband) needs to understand. Marriage was never designed to cure all of our loneliness, or to heal all our brokenness. Nor was it designed to meet the deepest inner needs of our hearts. Only God can do that! Husbands and wives, if they work hard at their calling, and depend on the Lord, can become good marriage partners, but no spouse can ever be God!

Our church in Tyler was an Evangelical Methodist Church, called EMC by the members. John Morris was a pastor in this relatively new denomination that began in 1946 after breaking away from the Methodist Church. EMC, however, was never an accurate description of the Tyler congregation. The church began when a small group of families from diverse backgrounds met with John Morris to share their vision of beginning a new church. In time they sensed that their dream was compatible with John's philosophy of ministry, so they asked him to become their founding pastor. Becoming part of the EMC denomination was simply a part of the package they accepted.

Soon after we returned from California, it became clear that a change was in the works for the church. The EMC had a congregational form of government, meaning that the members vote on the pastor and other matters of major importance. But John and other church leaders came to see that the pattern in the New Testament was for a church to have elders who would give oversight, and provide shepherding care for the people. "And when they had appointed elders for them in every church, having prayed with fasting, they commended them to the Lord in whom they believed" (Acts 14:23). As the members studied the expansion of the first century church in the book of Acts, along with the teaching in the Epistles, their desire was to follow God's Word as they understood it. It is one thing for us as individuals to humbly submit ourselves to the teaching of God's Word and *be transformed by the renewing of our minds*; it is quite another when an entire church makes such a choice. The day came, however, when the members *voted to give away their authority,* in favor of an elder form of government. The beautiful part of this extraordinary transition was how no one was angry toward the denomination. In fact, some of the EMC leaders were present when the change occurred, and it was a smooth transition.

Once EMC was no longer a denominational church, there were two important questions: first, how would the first elders be selected; and second, what would our church have as its new name? It was determined that John Morris, as the founding pastor, should prayerfully select the initial elders. As I recall, there were seven John selected, and Van Graham and I were the two youngest. The entire group was deeply challenged as we studied and discussed the high qualifications we saw in the New Testament, and not one of us felt we fully measured up. As for the new name, it was decided that anyone with suggestions could submit them to the new elders.

During this time Linda and I, along with Cheryl and Scott, visited my family in Southeastern Kentucky. As I was sitting in my favorite front porch swing one morning, having my quiet time, these words from Acts captured my attention: "And the congregation of those who believed were of one heart and soul; and not one of them claimed that anything belonging to him was his own, for all things were common property to them. And with great power the apostles were giving testimony to the Lord Jesus, and abundant grace was upon them all" (Acts 4:32-33). I was impressed that the generous actions described in the passage were in no way coerced; they were prompted by the *abundant grace that was upon them all!* I wrote in the margin of my Bible: *"This was a Grace Community!"* Though it was not my

intent to name our church, the moment eventually came when it was appropriate to tell the other men about my quiet time, and what I observed. Amazingly, there was an immediate sense of unity! Our name would be *Grace Community!* I would later learn that there were other churches in our country by that name, but as my understanding of grace has increased, it is now my conviction that every church, regardless of the name or denomination, is meant to be a community where grace is always prominent and on display! Because of his heart for the larger body of Christ in our city, John Morris suggested a subtitle: *A Part of His Church in Tyler!* For many years that phrase was included in the name. The two other churches where I have served since leaving Tyler have also been community churches with an elder form of government. Like Grace Community, they too sought to relate to the larger Body of Christ in their respective cities. While I believe having multiple elders is biblically correct, I would hasten to add that it takes much more than having the

134

correct form of government for the church to be strong. Whether yours is a denominational church or an autonomous community church, for it to be healthy, there must be a genuine commitment on the part of the leaders to seek to "walk in a manner worthy of the calling with which you have been called, with all humility and gentleness, with patience, showing forbearance for one another in love, being diligent to preserve the unity of the Spirit in the bonds of peace" (Ephesians 4:1-3). We had some challenging lessons to learn about this in those early years in Tyler, and this has been the case in the other two churches where I have served. My experience is that this is true in varying degrees in every body of believers.

Very soon after we arrived, Grace Community School began with Van Graham as the capable Headmaster. Our vision was broader than the children, in that it included Biblical teaching and practical support for parents as they sought to embrace the high calling described in God's Word. I have fond memories of the excellent fathers' workshops developed by Mike Henderson, a good friend from Asbury, who served in Tyler for a period of time. While the founders and initial leaders of the school had lofty dreams, no one could foresee that in the years to come Grace Community would become one of the most respected Christian schools in East Texas.

Another vision of John Morris which we were able to implement in those years was a missionary internship, a place where candidates for the mission field could come, be part of a healthy church body, grow in character, and enhance their ministry skills before going to their field of service. Doug and Jane Haltom, along with Bob and Sydney Biddulph, were two couples out of several who came, and went on to fruitful years of missionary service.

During 1974, as we were making our summer trip to Kentucky, Linda and I had some exciting news for Cheryl and Scott; we decided to make the announcement in a game of 20 questions. While we enjoyed watching their suspense and hearing their probing questions, we were excited to let them know that they would be having a little sister or brother! While we thought she might be a Christmas baby,

Rachel Christy Madon was born on December 26, 1974, and she brought a new level of joy to our family!

Christy

With Christy and Cheryl being nearly ten years apart, and Scott six years older than Christy, Linda and I were praying that the Lord would give Christy a playmate, and before too many months, we were again expecting. Everything was progressing normally, and Linda was in her fifth month. As her husband, I felt that Linda always seemed to have a special glow in her countenance when she was pregnant. As I walked into the kitchen one morning, I immediately knew something was wrong. As I went over and gave Linda a hug, she began to weep. Even though we had already felt the baby move, something had changed. Because Linda was so far along, it was necessary for her to go to the hospital and be induced. Even though it was a time of intense sorrow, Linda has positive memories of us walking through that valley together, and of how she felt supported. Another miscarriage would occur a year later, and there had been one when we lived in California. We are not fully sure just what this will mean in heaven. While we are blessed to have three children on earth to enjoy and share their lives, we ponder at times about the three in heaven, and the joy of future reunions.

When it became apparent that Christy would not have a playmate as we had hoped, the Lord did an amazing work in Linda's heart, so much so that I continue to see the results today. The thought God seemed to place in her heart was that the time she would have given to a new baby should now be invested in our other three, especially to Christy as the youngest. And that's what she did, not only being Christy's mother, but her playmate. Christy is marked today because of Linda's selfless investment during the early years of her life. From that point on, Linda has continued to display an extraordinary heart for little children, giving to them above and beyond anything I have ever witnessed. I often tell her that I'm never going to compete with her for the affection of our grandchildren; for I know she will win hands down without it even being a contest.

As the church was growing, one of the positive qualities of John Morris was his willingness to share the pulpit. Part of this was his transition into counseling, but it was also an integral part of his vision for discipleship. In the first few years after our return from California, four of us were part of the rotation. In addition to John, there was Danny Robertson, also on our staff, and John Prestridge, one of our elders and a gifted preacher. I was thankful to be in the rotation as well. While we all had different styles, the people responded, and the Lord blessed our church with continued growth.

One of our greatest memories from those early years in Tyler is the Scripture *songs.* Having now been in ministry for six decades, Linda and I have witnessed the ever-changing styles in church music; thankfully, we have appreciated most of the changes. But singing Scripture was a wonderful season, and also an excellent way to memorize God's Word. While some of the songs came from outside sources, the majority came from Martha Graham, who seemed to have an unending supply. They became part of our worship in church, but our boys and girls in the school were also singing them. A couple of years earlier, while still in California, a friend once encouraged me to compose a song to the Lord using Scripture, but I was reluctant to attempt it, though I never forgot his challenge. One evening, while on my way to pick up one of the high school girls, Cindy Porter, to watch our children, I began to sing a favorite portion I had memorized from Lamentations 3:21-25, and it actually sounded like a song! When I finished with two verses and a chorus, I was not sure I could repeat it, but amazingly, I did! The next step was to visit with Martha Graham so I could sing it for her, knowing she would write it down in E flat (Martha's key), and it would be official. While Martha has gone home to be with the Lord, and is now harmonizing with the saints in heaven, we are blessed to have CD's containing many of her delightful Scripture songs from those years.

Our staff singing around the piano with Martha Graham playing

As a pastor, my strongest motivation is to preach and teach, and be involved in the relational side of the ministry. But the Lord has also placed in my heart deep convictions about the place of music in the church, and how it should be done. Because I was the most musical of the pastors, it was my responsibility to plan the order of worship, including which songs we would sing, and then lead our Sunday worship. *Lead* is too strong a word, for the direction came from the piano, always our lead instrument in those years. Sometimes it was Martha Graham, but often Mary Helen Morris, an outstanding pianist. Anytime our staff met in homes or in small groups during those days, music was included. Some of my fondest memories from our Tyler years are of singing with Martha Graham and Jerry Burgess. They were able to harmonize and let me sing the only part I knew, but

I loved it! When Tom and Shirley Porter came to the church, they also made a wonderful contribution to our ministry, with Shirley organizing and directing various musicals featuring our young men and women. In 1976, in conjunction with the bicentennial of our nation, we presented a musical drama called *If My People,* written by Jimmy and Carol Owens. Afterwards we received numerous invitations to travel and present it in other churches. Those who were part of that experience will never forget it.

As Associate Pastor, I was given a great amount of freedom to carve out my own ministry. One of the first areas where I saw a need was in missions. While the church was generously supporting several missionaries, most in the church did not know them, and my goal was to see that change. Because John Morris and Dick Amos had grown up as friends together in Sweetwater, Texas, Grace Community supported Dick and Judy's ministry in Japan. This connection opened the door

for one of the most positive and memorable mission experiences our church ever experienced. A highly respected leader of the church in Japan came for an extended, six month visit to observe and learn from our ministry. We called him Brother Matsumura, while in Japan he was called Matsumura Sensei, a title of utmost respect. Our family hosted him for one month, before he rotated for other month-long stints with five other church families. On his first Sunday, through his broken English, Brother Matsumura said to the

Matsumura Sensei

congregation: *"Since I have been in America, I have seen many things with the words, 'Made in Japan'. I was also made in Japan – made by God in Japan!"* The church instantly fell in love with him, and we made a wonderful connection that continued for several years.

Grace Community also soon became involved with our friends and co-workers from Campus Crusade, Greg and Denyse Gripentrog. Greg had completed his seminary training in Dallas, and he and Denyse had been appointed to Indonesia as missionaries. They spent a few months in Tyler, and worked with Harris and Gail Nobles to establish a children's church ministry. Grace Community, along with other believers in Tyler, became part of their support team, and that partnership continued for many years.

As I began to concentrate on missions, different ones stepped forward to serve, including Carl Weber and Tom Hanson. Both had worked at Xerox and to say that they had not been friends would be an understatement. But after they came to know Jesus, their hearts changed and they developed a loyal friendship, serving together in our missions' ministry. One of the early years we invited Dr. Sam Kamalasen, from India, to come as the speaker for our annual missionary conference. He had been a seminary classmate with John Morris, and was serving with World Vision. In our first session on a Thursday night, Dr. Kamalasen spoke for about 45 minutes and then prayed; we were all ready to go home after a wonderful sermon. There was only one problem - that was only his introduction! The real sermon came later, about 75 minutes in length, and we discovered that other nations and cultures have a vastly different concept of time than most of us here in the USA.

By this time we were beginning to camp as a family, following through on the conviction that was planted in my heart during my backpacking trip in the High Sierras with some of the Campus Crusade young men in San Jose. Our first venture was with Jerry and Virginia Burgess and their family, tent camping at Camp Albert Pike in Arkansas. The next year John and Kay Prestridge invited us to join them in Colorado, near Pagosa Springs, along the middle fork of the Piedra River. Again we camped in a tent, and woke up the next morning with ice in our water bucket. Eventually, John and Kay allowed us to use their pop-up camper. They would often pull it to Colorado and stay for two weeks, and we would join them on their final day, stay two weeks ourselves, and then pull the pop-up back to Tyler. Later, the Prestridges, along with Dr. Dick Knarr, generously made their campers available to us anytime they were not using them, so we took advantage of their offer on numerous occasions. Even today, our grown children have fond memories of those trips, reading around the campfire at night, sometimes from *Treasures in the Snow,* and later, *The Chronicles of Narnia.*

John and Kay Prestridge

One day John Prestridge approached me about the possibility of us owning our own home, explaining that he, John Morris, and others had discussed it, and believed it would be a wise and helpful move for our family. The thought of home ownership had never once crossed my mind. I assumed we would trust the Lord to provide housing as we had always done. Sometime before that, I remember Cheryl asking one evening, *"Dad, are we poor?"* While I did not give her a definitive answer, I recall telling her that even if we were poor, "God has chosen the poor of this world to be rich in faith, for the kingdom of heaven is theirs" (James 2:5). But with this possibility of owning a house before us, and with John's assurance that others wanted to assist, our vision was expanded, and we were encouraged.

After investigating various options, it became clear that the most economical approach would be for me to build the house myself, with help from our generous and gifted friends. John Prestridge accompanied me as we went to see James Landrum at the savings and loan institution to discuss interim financing, which we would then convert into a long term loan. James had previously been my

141

employer for six months in 1968 when I worked on one of his crews as a carpenter's helper. While it was obvious to James and to me that I did not possess the skills to be a master carpenter, with John Prestridge, a respected man of integrity by my side, our loan was approved. We were able to purchase almost two acres of land near

Scott and Christy enjoying the bulldozer

Gresham, a small community about seven miles south of the church. While clearing enough trees to get a road and house site prepared, Jerry Burgess, a friend who was elementary principal at Grace Community School, but a draftsman by trade, was drawing the house plans with input from us. It would be a simple, 2,000 square foot house, with four bedrooms and two baths. The living room, dining room, and kitchen would all be open, making it conducive for hosting groups. There were far too many who assisted to name them all, but Danny Robertson, my friend and fellow associate pastor, would do the plumbing, a business he had learned from his parents. David Florey, an electrician in the church, generously volunteered to do all of the electrical work. I assisted both, of course, but they provided the knowledge and skill. Orin Davidson brought the various nail guns I needed for each phase of the project. During this time, one of the men in the church commented that what he saw happening reminded him of this proverb: "Prepare your work outside and make it ready for yourself in the field; afterwards, then build your house" (Proverbs 24:27). His point was that the Lord had blessed me with a ministry; now it was time to build our house! And we liked that!

The building phase I had most enjoyed when working as a carpenter's helper was framing, so I was comfortable when that stage began. Once the framing was completed, the pre-engineered trusses soon arrived. One of my most memorable days was the Saturday when a large group of friends from the church came and worked to lift and nail them into place. By the end of the day, our house was *in the dry!*

Since I was still Associate Pastor, the elders encouraged me to not take on additional responsibilities until the house was complete, and if it was possible to take off after lunch to work on the house, that was what I should do. What a blessing it was! For maximum savings, I did all the labor that I could, hanging the dry wall (with help from various friends), shingling the roof, and even building the kitchen cabinets. I was able to do this because we used rough sawn cedar, which is easy to work with, and this matched how we had finished out the interior of the windows and doors. This gave the house a nice rustic look, which had been our intent. We also built a spacious deck around two large trees in front, and added a back porch. We hired a professional brick layer, and I enjoyed interacting with him and his helper about the Lord throughout the project. When they completed the final work, his helper asked me to come up to see what they had written in the cement on top of the chimney. These were his words: *"God bless this home!"* God had already blessed us through the people who helped make it a reality, and our new home opened the door for additional years of memorable ministry within those walls, all richly blessed by God!

When the Lord led us away from Tyler some seven and a half years later, we were able to sell our home for more than twice the amount we had invested in it, and this enabled us to become involved in the home owning process. While I could never list all those who assisted, and am not even aware of everyone who helped with the land purchase in the beginning, none of it would have been possible without the Lord putting it in the hearts of John and Kay Prestridge to support us so generously!

143

Friday Fellowship on a Colorado ski trip

In addition to missions, another deeply rewarding ministry the Lord opened to us is what came to be called *Friday Fellowship,* a ministry comprised of young singles. A small college/career group had been meeting sporadically but with little success. Linda and I invited them and other singles we knew into our home for six Friday nights, as a short term experiment to see what might happen. The evening would include singing, a devotional I would share from God's Word, along with prayer requests and praises, and a time of prayer. Afterwards we would have refreshments, and everyone could stay and visit for as long as they wanted. Those six weeks went so well we continued on for several years, most of the ministry occurring in our new home. While we called it Friday Fellowship, it was significantly broader than Friday evening. We became involved in a myriad of activities: camping trips, canoe trips down the Guadalupe River in the Texas hill country, and numerous snow skiing trips in Colorado. Some of the singles even joined us for our summer family camping trips to Colorado.

One of the greatest blessings was having our children involved, as many of these young single adults became mentors to them, remaining friends today. The Friday Fellowship resulted in numerous engagements, and I was blessed to officiate at more weddings than I can remember, most after pre-marital counseling. Thankfully, through Facebook, Linda and I remain in touch with many of these couples today as they celebrate wedding anniversaries, all over 30 years, and some even 40!

While we were in Tyler, Linda and I often received affirmation about our ministry to singles. My response was to point out that at the heart of it all was the often *lost art of hospitality*. In her intensely practical but highly instructive book, *Open Heart, Open Home,* [2] Karen Mains shares a profound insight on the difference between *entertaining* and *hospitality*. She writes: *"Entertaining says, 'I want to impress people with my beautiful home, my clever decorating, and my gourmet cooking'. Hospitality, however, seeks to minister. It says, 'This home is not mine. It is truly a gift from my Master. I am His servant, and want to use it as He desires'. Hospitality does not try to impress, but to serve."* Our home was definitely a gift from God, and our desire was to utilize it in a way that honored Him.

What we discovered was that these single young people loved being welcomed into our home and family, into an atmosphere where they felt valued and accepted. It became an environment where they thrived spiritually. In reflection, Linda and I agree that our passion for hospitality was rooted in our respective families. For Linda's parents, having people into their home was a way of life, so I am blessed with a wife who does not know what it is like to say *no* to people. And my parents, before and after they became believers, were never reticent when I invited friends into our simple Appalachian home. And we are richly blessed as we have watched our oldest daughter, Cheryl, and her husband James open their home each Friday night for nine years to essentially the same age group we hosted those long years ago!

In 1977, I received a troubling call from Kentucky that my father was in the hospital, in a coma, and not expected to live. Immediately I made plans to fly to Knoxville, Tennessee, the closest airport, where my brother-in-law would meet me, and drive me the remaining 100 miles through the curvy mountain roads to the Harlan Appalachian Regional Hospital. That trip became an occasion to reflect deeply on the difficult but resilient life of my father.

Dad was born a twin on March 30, 1917, but his brother died at birth. As a result of complications, his mother also died a few days later. His father soon remarried a younger woman with no experience in caring for a little boy. When he was still very young, Dad contracted polio, and the entire right side of his body was affected, being smaller in size and weaker. This meant that he always walked with a limp and had limited use of his right hand, being unable to grip things well, or even to shake hands in a normal way. When he was only five years old, his father also died, leaving him extremely vulnerable. While there was talk of putting him *in a home* (orphanage), his older brother, John, newly married, took his needy little brother in to live with him. From stories Dad would tell later, that was not a good arrangement, and he was soon being passed back and forth between his four older sisters, never finding a place to truly call home. When Dad was in sixth grade, he enrolled In Pine Mountain Settlement School where his sister, Ella, worked with her husband, Brit. It was in that school where he found the home and family he lacked and Dad began to thrive. Like most students at the school, he received room and board, and he loved and was loved by the teachers and his classmates. Because the school was founded on Christian principles, Dad was exposed to God's Word, even memorizing passages he would later quote to us as his family. He also learned numerous songs and grew to love music, including many classical pieces, especially the *Blue Danube Waltz.* His love for Pine Mountain School was passed on to his family, and to this day it remains one of my most loved places in Harlan County. At Pine Mountain Dad grew to love sports, and became a remarkably good athlete, even with his physical limitations. He became a very good fast-pitch softball pitcher, and had a great shot in basketball.

146

On my trip to visit Dad in his coma, I reflected again on how he had given his time to me so unselfishly, teaching me a variety of sports, often taking me with him and his friends to Norris Lake in Tennessee, and teaching me to fish and hunt. And I could never forget his tall tales that seemed to become more extravagant with each telling, along with his unique sense of humor. I also remembered his wonderful conversion, and how well he did in his faith for approximately seven years, during which time he showed extraordinary kindness to everyone I brought into our home. I reminisced on how beautiful it was to witness him enjoying life with my mother, with both of them believers! I also remembered him being wounded by the unkind words of someone in the church, and how he failed to deal with it very well, soon dropping out of church and eventually going back to his drinking. I also remembered my critical attitude during those times when he drank too much, but was thankful that by this time my criticism had turned to compassion. A major factor in my change of heart took place when I was able to understand and acknowledge that there was very little difference in his struggle with alcohol and my struggle with food. The Apostle Peter gives the underlying truth about addiction: "For by what a man is overcome, by this he is enslaved" (II Peter 2:19), and the enslaving masters are too numerous to count. But I also remembered Dad's love for his family and how, when he was sober, he was one of the nicest and most likable men in Harlan County. How deeply thankful I was to God for giving him to me as my father.

When my brother-in-law, Ralph, and I arrived at the Harlan hospital, it was well past midnight. My mother and two sisters had the waiting room on the 4th floor all to themselves. Their update indicated that Dad was not expected to awaken from the coma. Around 2:30 a.m. I went into his room alone by myself, and began to pray. I remember telling my Heavenly Father how wonderful it would be if I could talk with my earthly father again, and especially to pray with him and confirm that he was at peace spiritually. After I had prayed for a while, my Heavenly Father who delights in giving good things to His children, answered my prayer in such a gracious way! Though I had made this emergency trip to Harlan questioning if I would ever see my father alive again, I suddenly heard the soft but familiar voice of my dad, *"Why hello, son, how are you doing?"* As I looked into his eyes, I immediately assured him that I was okay, but went on to express how sorry I was when I learned of his condition. In what was a relatively short conversation, I went on to say to him, *"Dad, my prayer is that you will pull out of this; but if you do not, and the time comes for you to stand before God, and He were to say to you, 'Tom, why should I let you into heaven? What do you think your answer would be?"* Dad became deeply emotional, and almost in a whisper he said to me, *"The cross; the cross!"* I assured him that the cross would also be my answer, for we have no other hope apart from Jesus, but Jesus is

enough! I prayed for him and thanked God for being so gracious to give us those treasured moments, and Dad went back to sleep. When the nurses came in the next morning, Dad was awake, asking for food, and continued to improve and regain his strength, eventually being able to return home. The Lord gave him 18

Dad and Mom a few months before his death

additional months of life without any need for alcohol, and with a renewed assurance of his salvation. All this was a wonderful gift to my mother, as he often let her know how sorry he was for the times he had failed to treat her well. They both enjoyed those final months, as did our entire family.

When we received the news of Dad's death a year and a half later, Linda was in the hospital recovering from surgery. When her physician learned that I would be going to Kentucky for the funeral, he said, *"I think we'll just keep you here in the hospital, so we can care for you until Tom gets back!"* Yes, those were the years when doctors made that decision, not the insurance companies. With Christy being only 5 at the time, she and Cheryl stayed with friends in the church, while Scott, 10 years old, made the trip with me to Kentucky. Amazingly, the Lord had just provided a beautiful Chevy station wagon our growing family needed, and this would be our first trip in it of any length.

My focus throughout the time of the funeral and burial was on being a support to my mother, and there was little emotion on my part. As Scott and I were returning to Tyler, we stopped at a newly opened Wendy's to get a Frosty. As we were driving along with darkness approaching, I began to explain to Scott what God had promised if something would ever happen to me, and he was left without a dad. "A father to the fatherless and a judge for the widows is God in His holy habitation" (Psalm 68:5). The combination of the Frosty and a conversation that was probably a little too deep for his age, Scott soon fell asleep. As I drove west across Interstate 40, I began to reflect on my words to Scott, and as I did, it was if the Lord was saying to me, *"This promise now applies to you!"* Yes, while God is the Father of all true believers, His special promise to the fatherless now applied to me as a 37-year-old son, and I wept! My tears came because I had said a temporary good bye to the man God had sovereignly chosen as my earthly father, but they also came because my Heavenly Father was refreshing my heart through one of the remarkable promises of His Word! He had done this countless times in the past; He continues to do it to this very day, and He will do it until the day He calls me home. "For as many as are the promises of God, in Him they are yes; therefore also through Him is our Amen to the glory of God" (II Corinthians 1:20).

CHAPTER EIGHT

When God's Call Came into Sharper Focus – Pastor Teacher

"And He gave some as...pastors and teachers for the equipping of the saints for the work of the ministry, to the building up of the body of Christ." Ephesians 4:11-12

Luis Palau, the Argentine evangelist, while speaking at our church in California, made a simple but profound statement I have never forgotten: *"Big doors often turn on small hinges!"* His point was that there are times when God works through an unexpected comment or a casual conversation to set in motion something of monumental, even eternal significance. It was through one such occasion that we met Andrew and Ann Sims.

Jack Prater, who had been a part of Grace Community, but was at the time assisting a small Baptist church in the area, informed me of a young couple he had just met, and his belief was that our church would want to meet them as well. They were in Tyler making a presentation on behalf of Wycliffe Bible Translators. Jack arranged a breakfast appointment for John Prestridge and me to meet with them, and we immediately fell in love with the Sims and their vision for Bible translation. Andrew and Ann had graduated from Oklahoma University, and during their years there had been involved in a denominational church they loved. But when the Sims informed the pastor that God was calling them into Bible translation with Wycliffe, he indicated that they would not be able to raise support in their church, for they only gave to those in their denomination. As a result, Andrew and Ann were praying that one or more churches would *adopt* them and become their ministry partners in Bible translation.

After discussion and prayer, we began to set things in motion for Grace Community to become one of their supporting churches. In the months that followed, Andrew and Ann spent several weeks in our home, and our children loved them. During that time we arranged various home meetings, church gatherings, and even a retreat, where they explained how they, as trained linguists, would go about learning a spoken, but not yet written tribal language. They creatively illustrated how they would form an alphabet, reduce the language to writing, and develop a literacy program, all with the ultimate goal of translating the New Testament into the heart language of the people. In the case of Andrew and Ann, their people group would be in Indonesia. While it was an enormous and highly specialized task that would require many years, their conviction was that God would honor His Word and establish a church within that language group.

When it came time for the Sims to leave, our church was excited about the deep commitment Andrew and Ann displayed toward their future ministry, and we were committed to being their ministry partners. What would take place in the years that followed would be extraordinary, beyond anything we could have ever imagined, and their ministry continues to flourish even now. More of this incredible story will come later!

One of the blessings of having a wife who is fluent in Spanish is getting to know the unique people the Lord brings into her life. Even when we lived in San Jose and Linda had to go to the laundromat, she always seemed to come home with stories of meaningful spiritual conversations with young mothers from Mexico. In our first Tyler home on Waunell, the Lord sent to our door an Avon lady from Colombia, where Linda had lived as a child. Our most unforgettable cross cultural experience, however, came through Isidro and Maria from Mexico, a young couple living in East Texas, and both came to trust Jesus as their Savior. Soon after we met them, Maria became pregnant. We learned that she was in touch with a Jewish midwife who would assist her through the pregnancy and deliver the baby. Because Maria spoke no English, Linda often met with her and the midwife about how Maria was progressing, and the upcoming birth.

Immediately upon arriving home from church one Sunday, we received a call that Maria was at the rural home of the Jewish midwife, west of Tyler. The news was that she had delivered not one but two daughters, identical twins, *one alive and the other dead*. That call set in motion one of our most unforgettable Sunday afternoons ever.

When we arrived at the simple home in the woods, my task was to assist the grieving father, Isidro, and the husband of the Jewish midwife, in digging the grave. Meanwhile, Linda was inside preparing one infant daughter for burial, while also interpreting for Maria and her midwife as they sought to assist the living baby in need of care. If there was ever an occasion to "rejoice with those who rejoice, and weep with those who weep" (Romans 12:15), this was it, and at the same time! After the grave was prepared, the plan was to have a short funeral service and bury the little girl. I obviously had no time to prepare for what was undoubtedly the most unique funeral message I would ever give in my entire life. No thought was given to what I wore or how I looked for I, along with the two other men, was wringing wet with perspiration after digging the grave in the East Texas sweltering humidity. As a young pastor in my late 30s, my task was to comfort the young couple, Isidro and Maria, also new believers, while also rejoicing with them over the living daughter in her mother's arm. I was keenly aware that this was a *Divine Appointment* arranged by God so I could also share Jesus and the Gospel of the grace of God with the Jewish midwife and her husband, in whose lives Linda had already been planting seeds of truth. My sermon came from the words grieving King David had spoken following the death of his son who was born from the adulterous affair he had with Bathsheba: "He cannot return to me, but I shall go to him!" (II Samuel 12:23) And I was seeking to be the Lord's spokesman while Linda was interpreting for me! One of the advantages of speaking through an interpreter, as I have now done on countless occasions, is that after a sentence or two, you have a brief moment to prayerfully reflect on what to say next. On that day I welcomed that short reprieve, for my desire was for the truth to be clearly understood. By God's grace we made it through that extraordinary afternoon. Upon returning home, we had time for a quick shower before the evening service. When we arrived, a friend asked, *"Well, Tom, did you and Linda have a relaxing Sunday afternoon?"*

A few months after my dad died, the Lord brought a father figure into my life by the name of Ken Stine, who at age 65 had

152

become a new Christian; his conversion was the answer to the faithful prayers of his wife, Blanche. At the time of his retirement, Ken heard and responded to the Gospel, was born again, and entered into an entirely new life in Christ. In his enthusiasm, Ken wondered why every sermon was not about *being born again.* He would come to my office each Thursday in his large Buick to pick me up for lunch at our favorite Mexican restaurant. Even though Ken and Blanche were too old to camp, they drove to Colorado one year, stayed in a motel near our camping site, and drove out during the day to be with us and others from the church that were part of the trip. Like many at Grace, Ken came to love the music of Bill Gaither. Groups from our church would often travel to Shreveport, Dallas, or Ft. Worth to attend the popular Gaither music gatherings. We enjoyed them as well, and Ken and Blanche rode in our van on a couple of occasions. On our last trip, Ken had difficulty getting in and out of the van. Medical tests soon revealed that he had aggressive, extremely painful bone cancer, and it was so difficult to witness his pain; Ken died several weeks later. At his funeral, I used a quote I remembered from years before: *"Once born men die twice; twice born men die only once!"* I explained that Ken, while his body had died, because he had been born twice, he would not face spiritual death for eternity; instead he was rejoicing in the eternal life given to him when he was born again. Some weeks passed, and Blanche asked me one day in church, *"Have you been out to see Ken's tombstone?"* I said that I had not, but promised to go soon. When Linda and I drove to the cemetery, Ken's epitaph appropriately read, *"Twice born!"* In the great doxology of praise that begins his first epistle, the Apostle Peter writes: "Blessed be the God and Father of our Lord Jesus Christ, who according to His great mercy has caused us to be born again to a living hope through the resurrection of Jesus Christ from the dead" (I Peter 1:3).

For the first seven years after we returned from California, Linda and I felt settled, and absolutely loved our Tyler church family. Many had children similar in ages to ours, and we were thankful for the supportive friendships we enjoyed. We loved our Friday Fellowship group, our growing involvement in missions, and I was grateful for regular opportunities to preach. One day, however, I received a call from a relatively new church in Arlington, TX, looking for a pastor. They invited Linda and me to come and meet with them, and we made a very positive connection with their leadership team. At the end of the meeting, they invited me to come and preach, *with a view toward a call*. In other words, if they liked what they heard, and we were agreeable, I would become their pastor. While we loved Grace Community dearly, the thought of having the opportunity to preach weekly and be a senior pastor, was appealing. The elders at Grace were fully aware of all that was transpiring. Following an elders' meeting when I was not present, three of the men approached me with the news that they did not believe I should go and preach in Arlington. The consensus of the group was that I should become the Senior Pastor at our church, Grace Community. By this time, John Morris was deeply involved in counseling, and much of the ministry I was already doing was consistent with the responsibilities of a senior pastor. My initial question was to ask if John was in complete agreement with this decision, and they assured me that he was. Even so, I knew I had to meet with John, look into his eyes and know for sure that my older brother in the faith was truly in agreement. During our meeting, he assured me that he was!

Before accepting the position of Senior Pastor, I needed to know I had Linda's full support, which she immediately gave. I also wanted to have peace that this was God's next step for me. Soon afterwards, I was driving on the Loop that surrounds Tyler, and listening to the music of Don Francisco, one of my favorite artists. His song was one I already loved entitled, *"I'll never let go of your hand."*[1] The closing lyrics are: *"The life that I have given you, no one can take away; I've sealed it with My Spirit, blood and word. The everlasting Father has made His covenant with you, and He's stronger than the world you've seen and heard. So don't you fear to show them all the love I have for you; I'll be with you everywhere in everything you do; and even if you do it wrong and miss the joy I've planned, I'll never, never let go of your hand."*

Though I already knew the lyrics by heart, the phrase that struck a chord was this: *"And even if you do it wrong, and miss the joy I planned; I'll never, never let go of your hand."* At this season of my life, I was not at all discouraged, but I did feel the need for a reassuring affirmation from the Lord, and He sent it through Don Francisco! Whatever our calling, not one of us does it right all the time; what keeps us going is knowing that our Faithful God will never let go of our hand! (John 10:27-29)

Jack and Marcy Dean

Upon becoming Senior Pastor, Linda and I sensed that it was time to give up the Friday Fellowship ministry. We were at peace about entrusting the ministry to our dear friends, Jack and Marcy Dean. After joining the group as singles, they eventually were married, yet chose to remain, assisting us in leading the group. It was a smooth transition, and the ministry continued to thrive.

Soon after beginning my new responsibilities, I thought it would be good to write my job description, listing my responsibilities as I understood them from Scripture. It was enjoyable in the beginning, but as the list grew increasingly longer, my enthusiasm began to wane. By the time I finished, I wondered if accepting the call to be Senior Pastor had been the correct decision. But as I continued to reflect on my intimidating list, it suddenly dawned on me; what I had written was the job description of the church, not of the pastor! While I had a challenging responsibility, I was simply one part of the Body of Christ. At the time I was in a

155

sermon series from I Corinthians, and approaching chapter 12, the most detailed description in the New Testament of how the Body of Christ is meant to function. When I taught through that chapter, I shared about the impossible job description I had written. Affirming those helpful Biblical truths brought needed relief to me, and instructive encouragement to the church.

The numerical growth at Grace Community was never spectacular, but always steady. Soon after our return in the summer of 1973, we built a new worship center that would comfortably seat 300, but had to go to two services the very first week. By the time I moved into my new role early in 1980, both services were full, and a larger multipurpose building was under construction across the parking lot that would also be used by our school. Because we were proceeding only as funds became available, there were a few delays along the way, and we had to go to three services during the final two years before taking up occupancy in the new building.

With John Morris engaged in his counseling, and Danny Robertson having moved on to begin a new outreach ministry, the elders sensed that we needed at least three additional pastors: Christian Education, Youth, and Music. It became my responsibility to search for the men the Lord had for us, and in a relatively short period of time, Scott Pierce, Larry Kent, and Bob Arthur became part of our pastoral team.

It was while I was speaking at a ski retreat in New Mexico that I met Scott and Dee Pierce, and we made an encouraging connection. Scott was a teacher at a Christian school in Greenville, but as we interacted during the retreat, I sensed that he had the personality, gifts, and character to be our Youth Pastor. When I broached the subject, he expressed a sincere interest. We soon arranged for him and Dee to come to Tyler to meet with our elders, and we were in unity about inviting him to join our pastoral team. When he accepted, I was pleased and looked forward to our working together. If I remember correctly, the job description I wrote for him had ten points, with the final one reading, *"and other duties as assigned by the*

156

Senior Pastor!" Scott loved to tell people that 90% of what he did was in the *"other duties"* category! Scott had a fruitful ministry, and he

Scott and Dee Pierce

and Dee impacted many lives, not only during his years on staff, but in the years that followed. Their ministry continues today, and for many years he has served as one of the elders at Grace Community. Scott was a man of wisdom, and I quote him from time to time even today. He once said to me, *"Tom, do you know how to tell if Sunday morning was any good? If everybody hangs around afterwards until you have to basically run them off, you know it was a great morning. But if the church empties quickly, you know that the morning was a dud!"* My observation after all these years is that there was a lot of wisdom in his assessment.

It was through Charlie Featherston, one of our elders, that I first heard about Larry Kent as a possible Pastor of Worship and Music. Larry and his wife, Mary, lived in Paris, Texas, and had a music studio in their home. After contacting them, Linda and I drove to Paris to become acquainted. It was a pleasant meeting, and I was encouraged by Larry's wide range of musical gifts, but also with his heart for ministry. Like Scott Pierce before him, our next step was to invite him to meet with our elders, but also to lead worship, and present a Sunday evening concert. Everything went extremely well, and Larry soon became the next member of our pastoral team. While he possessed many obvious gifts, what we could not see in the beginning was Larry's ability to involve the musically gifted people at Grace in the ministry. He was soon able to establish an excellent choir, and to

Larry and Mary Kent

this day I remember their first selection: *Jesus is the Cornerstone!* Larry and I had a good working relationship, and it was such a blessing to have someone who could, even on short notice, put together any song I wanted to include that went along with the sermon.

Bob Arthur was already a member of our church, a graduate of Dallas Seminary, and with pastoral experience. He also had the training and heart for our Christian Education ministry, and we were thankful to have him on our team. Bob and his family later returned to his home church in Manhattan, Kansas, where he served for several years as the Pastor of Christian Education. More than 25 years later, as a surprise to Bob, the senior pastor of his church invited Linda and me to fly to Kansas where I would preach on a special pastor appreciation Sunday where they planned to honor Bob for his many years of faithful service. It was truly a delightful weekend!

A couple of years later, we also added Rick Tillman to our pastoral staff. Rick and I were close friends, and he had been a faithful member of Grace Community and one of the respected leaders in our Friday Fellowship. During his time at Grace, he sensed God's call to Dallas Seminary to prepare for ministry. When he completed his work, we invited him to return to Grace as our Pastor to Single Adults.

Anytime I comment on the many years of ministry God has so graciously given to me, I always speak of serving with Scott, Larry, Bob, and Rick during those final years in Tyler as one of my most delightful seasons. Even though more than 30 years have passed, we remain in touch today and often reminisce about that period.

In the early 80's my mother took a bold step and came to visit us in Tyler, by plane! To that point she had not ventured far from home, and had often said that she would never fly. But as she began to regain confidence following my dad's death, she agreed to make the trip. She loved seeing our new home, visiting our church, and meeting many of our friends. Our black lab had nine puppies at the time, and our children have great memories of how the puppies followed my mother anytime she went outside, especially when she walked to the mailbox.

One of the major sports in Tyler was soccer, and all three of our children eventually became involved. Cheryl was on a talented coed team, while Scott was a member of an excellent traveling team that won a number of highly competitive tournaments. He later was a member of the Lee High School team, and became a gifted offensive player. Christy's first position was goalie, and was selected for that role because she could kick the ball farther than any of her teammates. Linda and I loved being soccer parents, and appreciated the opportunity to build positive friendships with the other moms and dads. This became a major part of the sphere of influence the Lord provided where we could share our faith.

After rarely playing golf for approximately ten years, I began to pick it up again. In contrast to my earlier years, this time it was under control. Jack Dean and I had identical days off and shared many memorable rounds together. From the time Scott was around 10 years old, he began to join us. As an expression of their friendship, Jack asked Scott to be in his wedding a few years later. As it turned out, golf is the sport Scott and I have enjoyed most over these many years, and we try to make time to play anytime we are together. It has been great for our relationship, and we have many unforgettable memories from out time together on the links.

After serving as the Senior Pastor at Grace Community for a couple of years, a friend whom I had long held in high regard was in church one Sunday after having been away for an extended period. When we spoke following the service, he said to me with deep sincerity, *"Well, the Lord has given His church a pastor teacher!"* His words were a great encouragement, not only because he was someone I respected, but because of the high value I place on the ministry of a pastor/teacher.

One of the most memorable adventures of my life took place in the spring of 1984. With the blessing of our families, the elders, and our church family, I, along with Clyde Powell, who was an elder and close friend, were commissioned for a month long trip to visit three of our missionaries: Greg and Denyse Gripentrog, Andrew and Ann Sims, and Dick and Judy Amos. The outward bound route would take us from Dallas to Seattle and from there to Bangkok, the Philippines, and on to Jakarta, Indonesia.

While our first visit was to be with the Gripentrogs in Jogjakarta, we had to enter Indonesia through Jakarta, where we were met by Wycliffe friends of the Sims. While Andrew and Ann had been in their village for four years, were making great progress in the language, and having also constructed their home, their friends gave us the unsettling news that the Sims had been flown out to the coast

Greg and Denyse Gripentrog and their children

because of villages being burned in the area. Though it would be ten days before we were scheduled to meet them, we began to wonder if they were okay, and if we would be able to see their work in the village first hand.

But the first step was to fly to Jogjakarta for our days with Greg and Denyse, who now had children, and were well established in their ministry. Greg had arranged for me to preach in the seminary chapel where he served, and there were other opportunities to speak in the villages he had arranged for us to visit. One memorable evening was riding several miles on the back of a small motorcycle with an Indonesian worker to preach in an oft persecuted church in a remote village. Clyde and I were encouraged as we witnessed the ministry the Lord had given to the Gripentrogs. My mind could not help but go back to when they were newlyweds on our Campus Crusade staff team in San Jose, so it was a great joy to see God's grace being expressed through them in such fruitful ways.

It was soon time for the return trip to Jakarta, and from there to make the journey of almost 2,500 miles to the east across the Indonesian archipelago of more than 17,000 islands. There were three stops, each time boarding a smaller plane than the one we exited. Our final destination was Sentani International Airport which we later learned had been a major part of the American facilities at Hollandia (now Jayapura) which was liberated from the Japanese during World War II – when I was only two years old!

Even with the uncertainty, Andrew and Ann were there to meet us, and we were off on the most adventurous days of our journey. Because of the large number of people groups on the large island of New Guinea who have no Scripture in their heart language, we met a number of linguists who had an identical ministry focus as the Sims. We were also able to witness the crucial role of missionary pilots, and met various ones with Jungle Aviation and Radio Service (JAARS), and others who served with Missionary Aviation Fellowship. Being able to fly with these extremely skilled and dedicated pilots in the small but amazing Helio Couriers was, without question, one of my most unique experiences ever. When we were ready to make the approximate one hour flight directly to the south, Andrew and Ann had not yet received any news about the status of their home, or even if the village would still be standing. As we flew over Lake Sentani, and began to increase in altitude through the Eastern Highlands of Irian Jaya, they had a familiar look, reminding me of the hills of Appalachia I dearly loved.

With Andrew and the pilot in the front seats, Clyde and I in the middle, and Ann and their young son, Brian, in the rear, Andrew was a wonderful guide, pointing out rivers and a few isolated huts along the way. We eventually were able to see where some of the burning had

162

occurred. When the village of Omban came into view, Clyde and I rejoiced with them that it was still there, and so was their home. Omban, their picturesque tribal village consisted of circular, bamboo

Andrew and Ann and their children, Brian and Elise

huts with thatched roofs. In the center was an airstrip on a steep incline, bordered by beautiful flowers. Mountains were on three sides, meaning the pilot had only one opportunity for a landing, but with his skill and the Helio Courier's ability to land and take off in a relatively short distance, there were no problems.

As we taxied to the top of the runway, it seemed that the entire village had surrounded the plane with tears of joy and gratitude, jumping up and down and waving their bows and arrows in the air. With the unrest in the area, some had wondered if they would ever see Andrew and Ann again. Before going to the village, I asked Andrew what Clyde and I should wear. His response was that whatever we wore, we would be the best dressed people in the village! When I saw the women dressed only in their grass skirts, and the men in their gourds, I understood what he meant. What captured our attention the most, however, was the joy and love they were expressing toward our dear friends. As we would later learn, this was only a small glimpse of their deep respect and appreciation for the Sims.

From the very beginning, the people had never expected Andrew and Ann to live like them. Because they were so eager to receive *God's talk,* as they referred to the New Testament, they insisted that the Sims build whatever type of home they needed to be comfortable. The result was a simple two story, wooden home located at the top of the runway, with the bedrooms upstairs. Our first night there consisted of attending a Bible study in one of the men's houses on a portion from the book of Acts which Andrew and his translation helpers had already completed. The singing of these Ketengban men, consisting of no more than three or fout notes, sounded strange to us. There was the smell of perspiration from this large group of men seated in cramped quarters with a small fire in the middle of the hut. When it was over, I asked Andrew what the study was about, and he explained that they were talking about caring for one another with a Christ-like love. Hearing his explanation took away some of the initial cultural stress I was experiencing. The return of the Sims was an occasion of great joy for the people, and some of the men painted their faces so we could see what they looked like when they worshiped evil spirits, and were bound by witchcraft. Many of them danced and chanted the entire night, even though there was a heavy rain. I kept a diary of our entire trip, and I occasionally open it even now to read about the cultural uneasiness I experienced that evening, being with people who had recently been bound by the fears and superstitions of their animistic way of thinking.

The Ketengban have a kinship culture, meaning that everyone is connected to someone else. In the case of Andrew and Ann, the people understood that the Sims had not come to their village by happenstance; someone had to send them, and Clyde and I were proof of that. The result was that the Ketengban constantly referred to us as their fathers, and we were shown great honor throughout our stay. One expression of this was the festive pig feast that was planned for us on the final day, a celebration normally held only once each year. For a people whose diet is made up of 80% sweet potatoes, to have any type of protein is a cause for celebration. But their pig feast was also an expression of great sacrifice, for the pigs they slaughtered had been family pets. As we observed the pigs being put to death with their bows and arrows, family members were standing nearby, weeping openly. While the Sims brought adequate food for our stay, I have to say that the Ketengban pork tasted mighty good, maybe not quite as tasty as the pork on our hog killing days in Kentucky, but still very delicious!

Helio couriers and those who fly them are of immense value in missions

Before our JAARS plane returned for us, I asked Andrew how much the people understood about the Gospel. Having only the book of Acts and a few selections from the Gospel of Luke in their language, I wondered if they knew about truths such as justification, reconciliation, atonement, mercy, forgiveness, and grace. Andrew's answer was that while they had a simple grasp of some of those truths, *"the most prominent thought in their minds when they become Christians is that they are committing themselves to follow God's Word...once they have it!"* That's like saying *yes* before you even know the questions! Months later I read of a similar example in words of the Apostle Paul to the church in Thessalonica: "For this reason we also constantly thank God that when you received the Word of God which you heard from us, you accepted it not as the word of men, but for what it really is, the Word of God, which also performs its work in you who believe" (I Thessalonians 2:13). Oh that we would have such respect and a heart for God's Word!

Andrew had planned for us to see other works in Irian, and we experienced additional memorable flights through the mountains, observing some remarkable ministries in the process. We were able to meet one of the missionaries Don Richardson tells about in his book, "Lords of the Earth", a book Andrew had recommended, along with "Peace Child." The culture described in both books is very similar to that of the Ketengban.

While we felt reluctant to leave, we knew we still had an exciting week ahead of us in Japan with Dick and Judy Amos. When we arrived at the Narita Airport in Tokyo, I remember standing in the line that said "Aliens", a solemn reminder that my true citizenship is in heaven, and that this world is not my true home. After having been in two very distinct cultures, one of them extremely primitive, Japan was an enormous change, and definitely not a third world country. With Judy being Linda's older sister, I knew we would be treated as royalty, and that was definitely the case.

Although Japan is impressively modern, it is a difficult culture to penetrate with the Gospel. Since Shinto is the ethnic religion of the people, the feeling is that to turn from it would be the equivalent of denying one's Japanese ethnicity. Around 35% of Japanese identify themselves as Buddhists. Many, however, are secular, with less than 40% identifying with an organized religion. Less than one half of one percent identify as Christian. Dick and Judy's ministry has been one of building relationships through English and cooking classes for all ages, most often in churches. Each class includes a devotional where seeds of the gospel are sown. While the process is slower, they have seen some miraculous conversions through their ministry.

Dick had a day of touring planned which would include a trip to Mt. Fuji, seeing the giant Buddha, and other points of interest. In the providence of God, Dr. Dennis Kinlaw, who had been our respected Old Testament professor at Asbury Seminary, had just completed a Bible conference in Tokyo, and was interested in being included in our day of sightseeing. Dick and I, along with Clyde, relished the opportunity to share three meals and have an entire day interacting with Dr. Kinlaw, with the privilege of asking him any question we wanted. It was memorable in every way and Dick and I have often reminisced about that treasured experience.

The other highlight from our week in Tokyo was being in the church of Matsumura Sensei, and meeting his lovely family. He had made such a positive impression when he spent six months with our church in Tyler some ten years earlier. He asked me to preach that morning, and then to meet with church leaders over lunch to describe more about our ministry in Tyler. Experiencing his gracious hospitality

Preaching in Japan

reminded me of an observation Judy Amos once made about Japanese people. Her comment was, *"Japanese people do not casually move in and out of each other's lives the way we Americans tend to do. When you show kindness toward someone from Japan, they consider you a friend for life."*

Interestingly, I often tell people that our final day in Japan was the longest Sunday of my life. We began the day by having a delicious buffet breakfast with Dick and Judy at a large hotel in Tokyo, then preaching in the church where Matsumura Sensei was the pastor, followed by lunch and visiting with his leaders in the afternoon, and dinner at the Narita Airport with the Amos and Matsumura families. We flew from Tokyo to Seattle, then on to Dallas, finally driving the two hours to Tyler, and it was still Sunday! We gained back that day we lost on our way to Bangkok! Clyde and I consider that month as one of the great highlights of our lives! Our missionary families were also encouraged by our visit, and the Lord gave His blessing each step of the way!

As we made our vacation trip the following summer to Kentucky, and then on to Indiana to visit family, the Lord had a challenging surprise waiting for us. When Sunday came, we were planning on going with Linda's mother to her church. But when the time came, she suggested that we go to Community Church of Greenwood, just south of Indianapolis. She knew that their church was similar in philosophy to ours in Tyler, and that we knew Charles Lake, the Senior Pastor, as well as Mike Henderson, one of his associates. As we were leaving, Pastor Charles said to me, *"It is amazing that you would be here today, for we have been talking about you. We're planning on beginning a new church in the Southport area, and we would like to talk to you about coming to be the pastor!"* Charles Lake was leaving the next morning, but he asked Mike Henderson to meet with me to share the details. While their church was already large, their philosophy was to plant additional churches rather than seeking to become a mega-church. I responded to the concept for I had been talking to our elders in Tyler about a similar idea, namely, planting a church in the Gresham/Flint area near our home where new subdivisions were being constructed. But Linda and I dearly loved our church in Tyler, and could not imagine leaving.

As we returned to Tyler, the time had finally arrived for us to move into our new, spacious multipurpose building. While we were packing out all three services with a total attendance around 1,000, we still had the feel of a smaller church, which I liked. There were definitely adjustments in having everyone together in a large group, and initial problems with our audio system added to the challenges. But there were also advantages in having the additional space, and we were beginning to adapt.

The way we left things with our friends in Indiana was that if we were interested after praying about it, we would let them know.

As the fall months passed, as much as I wanted to dismiss it, the idea of being involved in planting a new church continued to be part of my thoughts. Around that time, some friends in our church made their cabin in Angel Fire, New Mexico, available to us. In November Linda and I drove there for a few days, specifically to talk and pray more about Indiana. Our conclusion was that we would contact them to see if there was still interest. As it turned out, another pastor had agreed to come, but had changed his mind the week before my call. The result of our conversation was that the church in Indiana would fly Linda and me up for an exploratory weekend in January. We would discuss philosophy of ministry, meet with the elders, and I would preach in their two Sunday morning services. In my mind this was a good plan, for we could go to Indiana and get this wild idea out of our minds, and then return to our home at Grace Community, a place I never wanted to leave.

When we flew there for our January weekend, the temperature when we landed was 18 degrees – below zero! We stayed with Dr. and Mrs. Al Crumley, a lovely and gracious couple, and Al was Chairman of the Elders at Community Church of Greenwood. As I met Saturday morning to interact with the elders, and fielded their questions, I felt absolutely no pressure, and again that evening as we met with the elders, staff, and their wives. Even when I preached in both services the next morning, I was completely at ease, for I had no thought of trying to impress anyone and was not looking for a new position. As Linda and I met with Pastor Charles and his wife after church in the evening, he surprisingly informed me that the elders were unanimous in wanting us to come! Up to that point the gravity of the weekend had not become real, but suddenly it was, and I knew we had to give some type of response. In our conversation, Charles informed us that Linda's father, some years earlier, was one who planted in his mind the idea of a community church on the south side of Indianapolis. Whether that was to persuade us or not, we both were encouraged by his comment.

169

My response to Pastor Charles was that if we did agree to come, it would not be until the first of June, for we needed to give our children time to complete the school year. He said that was not a problem, but gave me until the first of April to respond. Those were agonizing months as we sought counsel from the elders, trusted friends, and family. We knew it would be difficult for our children, especially Scott because of his age, but our friends who knew him felt he would do well in making the adjustment, if we did move. Christy, our youngest, who was 10 at the time, wrote us a letter containing 10 reasons why it was a horrible idea to move to Indiana. But at the bottom of the letter was a P.S. which said, *"I don't mind Grandma!"* Yes, Christy and everyone in our family loved Grandma! If we did make the move, we would live in the same city as Linda's mother for the first time in our married life, and we would only be 325 miles from my mother in Southeastern Kentucky. After much agonizing prayer and discussion, Linda and I came to the conclusion that we could not say "no" to the invitation to move to Indiana, and the elders at Grace Community graciously allowed me to stay on until the end of May.

Interestingly, approximately one year before our move, I received a pay increase of $12,000 in one year, a wonderful blessing indeed! But as I looked back over our seventeen years at Grace Community, which included my year as a youth pastor and our four years in a *campus missionary* role where the majority of our support came from Grace Community, Linda and I feel nothing but gratitude for those years. I have often commented to others that God has always provided for us whether I made a little or a lot! But He always provided through His people, brothers and sisters who loved us and saw their gifts as investments in us, our family, our ministry, and our future. In those final twelve years in Tyler, we were given six vehicles, including two station wagons, three regular cars, and a custom van, which we were driving when we moved to Indiana. We were given a generous price on two rental houses, and were blessed by the extraordinary generosity of many who made it possible for us to build our first home. But beyond all the material gifts, of even greater value are the wonderful friendships we continue to treasure today, brothers and sisters we will enjoy even more throughout eternity! To us, the church in Tyler truly was and always will be a *Grace Community!*

Our family in front of our home just before our move to Indiana

CHAPTER NINE

When Hard Times Work for Our Good – Home Again in Indiana

"And we know that God causes all things to work together for good to those who love God, to those who are called according to His purpose."
Romans 8:28

One of the family blessings of moving to Indianapolis was being able to live in the same city as Linda's mother, and have her join us as one of the founding members of our new church. Linda would also be returning to the city of her birth, although she lived in the area only four months, just long enough for her parents to receive their visas for Medellin, Colombia, where they would begin their service as missionaries. Our move to Indiana also meant being closer to my mother in Southeastern, Kentucky, approximately five hours away, but making it possible for us to see her more frequently.

In early May, about a month before our move, we traveled to Indiana to look for a home, and were pleased to find an affordable tri-level in Colonial Meadows in Greenwood, not far from Linda's mother. We had no sense at the time of how our new church would progress, how long we would be in temporary quarters, and no knowledge of where our church would be located. With so much uncertainty, it seemed reasonable to find a home relatively close to Community Church of Greenwood, whose vision would enable our new church to become a reality.

In terms of ministry, I was keenly aware that our move would require a major adjustment on my part. I was leaving behind a church of 1,000, a staff of five other pastors who were my faithful coworkers, an efficient, full-time secretary, a spacious, comfortable office, and numerous supportive friendships that brought great joy to my life! Now at the age of 43, I was essentially starting over.

By this time in our lives and ministry, Linda and I were convinced that healthy relationships were at the very core of a biblical perspective on life. The directive of Jesus is unmistakably clear: "A new commandment I give to you, that you also love one another, even as I have loved you...by this all men will know that you are My disciples, if you love one another" (John 13:34-35). We were already making relationships a high priority in our lives, and were eager to become friends with the adventuresome believers who would be leaving their comfort zones to become involved in launching a new church. Some in that initial group were older, and we came to view many of them as spiritual fathers and mothers. Others were near our age, becoming fellow travelers and ministry partners in the church plant. Others were younger, and we considered them as our spiritual sons and daughters. While family ties are strong, friendships built around Jesus are for eternity, and this is what we would experience during our twenty plus years of serving our church in Indiana.

When we arrived, the plan was that I would preach in one of the three Sunday morning services at CCG, as we referred to it, on a rotating basis. The thinking of Pastor Charles was that this would enable the entire church to get to know the new pastor from Texas who had uprooted his family, moving to Indiana to begin the new church. Soon after we arrived, he also gave me a list of approximately 60 names of people who had expressed an interest in being part of the new church plant. Linda and I began to meet with these families, along with others who expressed interest, and the list continued to grow. The elders at CCG graciously communicated that those who were planning to be part of the church plant, scheduled to begin in September, could designate their giving accordingly, in order to provide us with a financial cushion when our church began. While CCG was responsible for my salary, the anticipation was that our new church would soon be healthy enough to rent temporary quarters, to provide curriculum for our Sunday school classes, as well as the pastor's salary and ministry expenses. CCG was no stranger to the church planting vision, as two other congregations were already under way, one on Brookville Road on the east side of Indy, and the other to the south in Franklin; ours would be the third.

For the first several months our church would remain under the authority and oversight of the CCG elders. Recognizing my need for support and encouragement, the elders appointed a Steering Committee of five men from among the families committed to our church plant. Their help was invaluable, and these men immediately became friends and a vital part of the decision making process. A point of gratitude as I write these words is that after more than three decades, two of those couples and their families, Jim and Kelly Hanson along with Mike and Carol Amos, remain faithfully involved in the life of the church. Two other couples, Dan and Wendy Kandel and Steve and Danelle Windle, have moved out of the area; the other, Jim Hall, is now in heaven, while his widow, Nancy, lives in Florida.

Scott before our move to Indiana

In terms of church activities, the summer months were slow paced and relaxed, with the exception of anticipating a return to Texas in August for Cheryl's wedding. But with regard to our family, we were beginning to experience some difficult challenges. Our son, Scott, 16 years old at the time, was struggling with the move, more so than we anticipated. He has his own story to tell about that difficult season of his life, and a part of his testimony is how he failed to trust in the loving and faithful character of God. The good news is that in spite of the waywardness of His children, our Heavenly Father has valuable lessons to teach us even when we go our own way. His discipline is often painful, but it is always purposeful, and carried out in love. God's words to His people in the days of Jeremiah, the prophet, are enormously instructive: "'Have you not done this to yourself by your forsaking the Lord your God when He led you in the way? But now, what are you doing on the road to Egypt, to drink the waters of the Nile? Or what are you doing on the road to Assyria, to drink the water of the Euphrates? Your own wickedness will correct you, and your apostasies will reprove you; know therefore and see that it is evil and bitter for you to forsake the Lord your God, and the dread of Me is not in you', says the Lord of hosts." (Jeremiah 2:17-19) Scott learned many valuable lessons through his season of rebellion that have enabled him to come along side numerous other strugglers over the years, lessons he is continuing to pass along. We could not be more thankful for where he is today with his beautiful family, and recognize it is all because of God's amazing grace!

But the Lord also had many instructive but painful lessons to teach me during that difficult season, and Linda as well. My primary thought during that distressing test was to reflect on God as our Heavenly Father, and to search His Word, seeking to learn how He parents His wayward children. One thing was certain; I could not let Scott go his own way without continuing to lovingly pursue him. A beneficial discovery I made at that time was that if our conversations became too emotional, as they often did, I would write Scott a letter, and include whatever warning or admonition I felt he needed, but state it in the context of my love for him as his father. Anytime I did that, without exception, the result was a constructive conversation where I went away knowing he at least heard me.   There were numerous times when I was wrong in my approach as his father, and had to humble myself and ask for forgiveness. One of the truths God has taught me over the years is this Biblical principle: "Before honor comes humility!" (Proverbs 15:33; 18:12) Years earlier I discovered this truth in my relationship with Linda. Before I could be honored in her eyes, I had to humble myself, confess my own sin, and ask for forgiveness. The same was true with Scott, and our other children; before I could be respected in their eyes, in humility I had to honestly deal with my part of the problem. Anytime we point the finger of blame at the other person, seeking to justify ourselves but fail, as Jesus said, to "take the log out of our own eye" (Matthew 7:5), there can be no reconciliation. And this is not a one-time act; it must be a way of life if our relationships are going to remain clear and healthy, without barriers.

As the years passed, the lessons I learned as a father through my relationship with Scott, I have been able to pass on to other struggling parents, another wonderful reminder that "God causes all things to work together for good to those who love God and are called according to His purpose" (Romans 8:28). Being a believer and having a Christian family does not mean we have it all together at all times, even if you happen to be a pastor! I am grateful for the way Jay Adams expresses this in one of his books about family life: *"The notion that a Christian home is a perfect or near perfect place is decidedly not biblical. The parents in the home often fail, and fail miserably. They fail one another, they fail their children, and they certainly fail God. The children fail, too...A truly Christian home is a place where sinners live; but it is also a place where the members of the home admit the fact, understand the problem, and know what to do about it, and as a result grow in grace."*[1] We have found this to be true in our family, and these same dynamics continue today.

As we sought a temporary meeting place for our church, we were able to work out an arrangement with the Parke Hotel, as it was called at that time, located at Emerson and I-465 in Beech Grove. We could use their conference center and adjacent rooms on Sunday morning, with the possibility of adding Sunday evening as well. Our first service was planned for September 8, 1985, the Sunday following Labor Day. By the first of August, our projected numbers were near 100, so we decided to have a *trial run* service, to get an idea for where we were. Bill Singleton, a funeral home director on South Madison Avenue gave us permission to use their chapel. A large group came, but it was the quietest church service I have ever attended, and certainly not typical of the outgoing family we would soon become.

On the Friday morning before our first service, we received the troubling word that our daughter, Cheryl, who had just returned to Tyler with her husband following their honeymoon, was seriously ill.

Dr. Dick Knarr, Cheryl's physician and one of our dear friends, was keeping us abreast of her status. While our first impulse was to immediately drive to Tyler, Dr. Knarr insisted that we remain where we were so he could stay in touch with us. This was long before cell  phones and texting. Cheryl's fever was extremely high, and nothing the doctors were doing could bring it down; it appeared that she was dying. Dr. Knarr missed his son's 18th birthday party that evening to remain by her side, calling in other physicians for consultation. Finally, a specialist in rare blood diseases, who had often been a referee at Scott's soccer games, made an educated guess, and began to give her large amounts of antibiotics. By Saturday morning, though still exceedingly weak, Cheryl was showing

Cheryl

signs that she would survive. Because of her *improvement,* however slight, Dr. Knarr encouraged us to go ahead with our first service, and then drive to Tyler afterwards.

As we met in that initial service with an encouraging crowd of well over 100, my heart was heavy. Before I began my sermon, I remember letting the people know that my hope and Linda's as well, was that in the years to come we would be able to help bear whatever burdens they might have to carry, and to pray with them about the deepest concerns of their heart. But from the depths of my heart as a father, I let them know that on this first Sunday of the church, Linda and I desperately needed their support and prayers because of Cheryl's needs. Afterwards, several came by to assure us of their prayers and support. It was on this extraordinary and extremely difficult Sunday for us, that *Community Church of Southport* began!

Immediately following the service, we departed for Tyler, a journey of 850 miles, driving straight through, arriving in Tyler early

Monday morning.   Dr. Knarr had said to us, *"I know you will be pleased, for she looks so much better!"*   But when we first saw Cheryl, my initial thought was of the photos I had seen of survivors from the German concentration camps following the war. She had lost weight, looked gaunt, and emaciated; it was clear that she had been through a war – a war for her very life. We didn't even try to imagine how she looked at her lowest. But the Lord, graciously working through His dedicated medical servants who were also our friends, answered our prayers and spared her life. We later learned that Cheryl had contracted a rare bacterial infection resulting in endocarditis that ultimately left the mitral valve of heart extremely damaged.   There was a concern that she would need to have valve replacement surgery due to the extent of the damage, a surgery with many potential adverse effects for someone her age. But by God's grace she began to improve and the doctors felt surgery could be delayed for a time. It would be more than a month before she would be dismissed from the hospital, and even then remained under the close supervision of her physicians.   Thankfully, Cheryl did much better than the doctors anticipated, living a fairly normal life, until the age of 37 when she began feeling fatigued from the slightest exertion. After meeting with her cardiologist, she learned that a surgeon in Houston was having good success with mitral valve repair, a far better answer than a replacement. Her surgery was successful, and since that time she has basically been as good as new!

Linda remained in Tyler for two weeks to assist in Cheryl's recovery, while Scott, Christy, and I made the return trip to Indianapolis. The plan was for Linda to fly home when it became clear that Cheryl had regained her strength. During that time, we received an unexpected and gracious offer from Rodger Hall, the Chairman of the Elders at CCG. He knew that I would love to see Cheryl again following her near death experience, so he offered to fly me, along with Scott and Christy, to Tyler in his private plane, and bring Linda home with us. We departed early on a Saturday morning, and Rodger rented a car to drive us to the hospital so we could visit with Cheryl for a couple of hours. During that time he and his pilot went to see Grace

Community, our former church, and take a brief tour of Tyler. Everything went according to plan, and we were even blessed with a gorgeous sunset from Rodger's comfortable plane just before we landed in Indianapolis. We will never forget his generosity!

The philosophy of ministry at CCG was built around the pyramid of worship, study and training. Pastor Charles would often say, *"We worship on Sunday morning, study on Sunday evening, and are trained for ministry on Wednesday evening."* Philosophy of ministry had been a major topic during our exploratory trip to Indiana on that freezing weekend in January, and we were in agreement. My only comment was that *fellowship* should be a high priority as well, and Pastor Charles did not disagree. CCG had small groups designed for mutual support which met monthly, and referred to them as *flocks;* our plan was to include these groups as well.

Another ministry of great importance at CCG was missions, and that was also our passion. If the Great Commission becomes the Great Omission, that church loses its reason to exist. Each fall, CCG held an annual missions' conference, and for logistical reasons, it worked well for us to have ours at the same time. So when our church, Community Church of Southport (CCS as we called it) was only six weeks old, we had our first conference. In the providence of God, Andrew and Ann Sims, our beloved friends, were in the States and able to come as our speakers. They had completed four years of ministry in their remote Indonesian village and had exciting stories of how God was honoring His Word. During that weekend, our people grew to love Andrew and Anne. Though only in our infancy, our church, like Grace Community in Tyler, *adopted them*, and became one of their supporting churches.

Our method of supporting missions was through what we referred to as a *faith promise.* We faithfully taught our people about the Biblical basis for missions, and introduced them to missionaries devoted to their calling. We then provided each family unit with a faith promise card where they could designate how much they would trust the Lord to channel through them in the year ahead to missions, over and above their regular giving to the church. The *faith promises are* done anonymously and without any pressure, and on the basis of that collective total, we set our missions budget for the year. It is a simple plan but one that worked well, and continues to be utilized by our Indiana church still today.

In those early weeks of the church, our people were progressively becoming acquainted with one another, and with what to expect in our services. Steve and Beth Dupree, who were newlyweds, became part of our church, and Steve directed the music in those beginning months, at times leading with his guitar. Larry and Peggy Trieb, at the urging of Pastor Charles, also came to be part of our church with the idea that Peggy would lead our choir, which she did with excellence. Our congregational music was a combination of traditional hymns and the praise and worship songs that were popular at that time. Linda often played the piano in those early years because she was familiar with the choruses I loved using, and could play them spontaneously without requiring the music.

During the fall of 1985, we only had a Sunday morning service, but our people continued to return to CCG on Sunday evening, to be involved in what was essentially Sunday school at night. But by January of 1986, the Steering Committee and I felt we were ready to add our own evening Study Hour from 6:00 to 7:30. We began with 30 minutes of *Body Life,* which included singing, testimonies, and prayer, followed by hour long classes for children, teens, and adults. We had a good working relationship with the Parke Hotel, and they had adequate space to accommodate our classes.

As the winter weeks progressed, however, the hotel recognized that because of their commitment to us, especially on Sunday evenings, they periodically had to say no to some profitable business opportunities. As a result, it was determined that Easter Sunday would be our final one at the hotel. It was time to find a new temporary meeting place, and from our earlier experience, we knew it would not be easy. One day I drove by a simple metal building on I-65 with a cross on the side, and discovered it was a church with the name, *Soul's Harbor Evangelistic Center*. What caught my attention was the time of the service – 3 o'clock on Sunday afternoon. I immediately wondered if we might be able to rent their building in the morning and evening when it was not in use. After contacting them, I learned that their pastor was a traveling evangelist who was away most weekends, but generally returned by midafternoon on Sunday, thus the unusual meeting time. They were open to my proposal, so we made arrangements for our Steering Committee and their wives to visit the building and see if it would meet our needs. While the space was adequate, the inside of the building was still under construction, and left much to be desired, and was even dangerous in places. While it was not ideal, because we were desperate, we worked out an arrangement, including being able to make some modifications inside the building, especially related to addressing our safety concerns.

Due to having met at the hotel, our people were already involved in the logistics of setting up and taking down chairs, and this continued to be a need at *Soul's Harbor*. We had some humorous experiences in that building, especially with the erratic audio system. As I was preaching one Sunday morning, a CB conversation between two truck drivers passing on I-65 came through the system with their typical *good buddy* slang, and we all stopped mid sermon to have a good laugh.

Amazingly, our church continued to grow during the approximately 20 months we met in a facility far less than ideal. I often commented that if anyone committed to be part of our church during those months, spiritual vision was required to look beyond the flaws of the building. One of the first couples who came during those months was Bob and Joan White, who had become disheartened in their main line denominational church. Anytime someone came to visit and expressed interest, my goal was to make an appointment and visit them in their home. When I approached Bob and Joan about the idea, they were interested, and I learned they were neighbors who lived on the other end of our street. As I sat in their living room, their

181

first comment was how good it was to hear the Bible again; they continued to come, and are still faithful members 30 plus years later.

Years earlier, when making my first feeble attempts at preaching in my home church in Kentucky, one of the men, Daunt Howard, routinely came up afterwards and said, *"You had a good subject today, Tommy!"* He never commented on how I did with the subject, only that it was a good one! While I have often laughed at his predictable remark, I have learned that as long as I'm preaching and teaching the Bible, *I have a good, even great subject, for it is the Word of God which He has promised to bless!* Sadly, our nation is in the midst of what the prophet, Amos, referred to as "a famine not for bread or a thirst for water, but rather for hearing the Word of the Lord" (Amos 8:11). This is what the Whites were expressing to me, and I am sorry to say that I have heard the same comment countless times from others who came from churches with a low view of God's Word.

Another family who came to visit, and stayed during our time at Soul's Harbor was Chic and Bets Wieting, along with their daughter and son-in-law, John and Cindy Bennett. They too had been in a traditional church but had developed a renewed love for the Scriptures through BSF (Bible Study Fellowship). Like the Whites, they were looking for a church where God's Word was faithfully taught. Bill and Audrey Bush also came during those months. On their first Sunday I shared my testimony of how I came to Christ. Afterwards they informed me that their previous pastor had recently stated that he did not have a testimony. Bill and Audrey continued with the church, and remain loyal friends to this day. The same was true of Terry and Nancy Moore. I remember introducing them to the Bushes, and suggesting that they ride together to Conner Prairie for a church outing, to enjoy their popular Christmas Candlelight tours. As a result, both couples began a long term friendship. Terry and Nancy invited us to their home for dinner, and had a long list of questions for me about the church, most of them inquiring about our commitment to Scripture. They too stayed and became special friends.

One of my greatest desires as a pastor, a passion I have shared countless times with individuals, families, and in newcomers' gatherings in our home is this: that we can meet people wherever they happen to be in their spiritual journey, and help them take the next steps toward Jesus Christ and greater spiritual maturity. God Himself is the model, for in His grace He meets us where we are, though He does not plan to leave us at that point; His plan is to take us on a life-long journey of spiritual transformation. When I think of the dear friends we have in the church all these years later, my mind often goes back to where they were spiritually when they first came into our lives and to the church, and I rejoice in where they are today in the life long process of sanctification and ongoing spiritual growth.

In hindsight, our difficulty in finding a temporary meeting place was used by the Lord to spur us on to find land where we could construct our own facility. While we considered several possibilities, some in excellent locations, each one was too small. Our thought was that we needed a minimum of 20 acres to allow room for future growth. In referring to the providence of God, R. C. Sproul uses the phrase, *His Invisible Hand.*[2] Though we could not see the scope of God's larger purpose at the time, several years later we would understand how *His Invisible Hand* had been clearly guiding our Steering Committee to 20 acres of farm land on East Stop 11 Road, on the west side of I-65, in Franklin Township. I will never forget our group standing on the bridge and praying over the 20 beautiful acres of farm land to the west, as the traffic passed by below. The land was owned by a Christian widow, Mrs. Florence Cole, who was still residing in the small farm house on the corner of the

Our first CCS office - the farm house

property. As I recall, the total asking price was $118,000, and we saw that as a good value. One immediate benefit was that we could establish a much needed church office in the farm house while the construction of our building was underway. Because our growing congregation had been generous, we were able to purchase the land. Our anticipation was that it would one day be surrounded by subdivisions.

With the land secured and plans underway for our own facility, Rodger Hall, Chairman of the CCG Elders, and Jim Hanson, who had been an elder at CCG prior to coming with us as a member of our Steering Committee, sensed it was time for us to dissolve the official ties with our mother church, and become autonomous. With Jim also being an attorney, he was able to complete the required paperwork for Community Church of Southport to become an official 501 C 3 non-profit organization. After some discussion, Pastor Charles and the CCG Elders agreed, and there was a formal commissioning as our church plant became official.

The plan Linda and I had all along was to relocate from Greenwood once we knew where our new church plant would be. Some friends from CCG had already informed us of their desire to purchase our home when we moved, and the sale went smoothly. We were able to find a lovely ranch style home in the Winchester Village subdivision, in the Southport area. The previous owners were Christians and loved the idea of selling their home to a pastor and his family.

In those early years we were following the ministry pattern which had already been established at CCG, and did the same in the formation of our elders. CCG had nine men with each one serving a three year term, and then three rotating off to make room for the three new elders. The plan allowed for a sense of continuity while also making room for new men to join the group, who were selected by a unanimous vote of the existing elders. In our case, we began with only six elders, but would add others as we continued to grow, and it seemed appropriate.

Once the land purchase was finalized, our people excitedly went to work on transforming the small farm house into an office, making needed repairs, and painting inside and out. By the time it was ready for occupancy, we had hired Chris Shepherd as our Youth Pastor, and Jan Channel as my part time secretary. Jan and her husband, Bob, were members of CCG at the time, but I liked the idea of having a secretary from outside the church. In Tyler my two secretaries had been from within the church, and I often felt sorry for them on Sundays, with people always asking for assistance that required them to be in the office. Jan was immediately a great blessing, and she was open to additional hours as the church continued to grow. From my years of pastoral experience, I have come to see the secretary as filling one of the most important positions in the church. Hers is generally the first voice outsiders hear, or the first face people see when they drop by the church. Jan was excellent in that regard for she consistently portrayed the grace I hoped we would communicate to everyone who came among us for any reason. She would serve in this capacity for 11 years, and we had a wonderful working relationship. Linda and I count Jan and Bob among our treasured friends still today.

In addition to the Steering Committee, most of whom moved on to become our initial elders; Hal and Pam Givens were also wonderful assets to our church that first year. Hal was a graduate of Philadelphia College of the Bible, and had considered going to seminary, but had placed the idea on hold. When they heard of our new church plant, the Givens volunteered to give leadership to our children's ministry, were very effective, and found great joy in serving. It was such a positive experience that Hal decided the Lord was leading him to enroll at Trinity Evangelical Divinity School in Deerfield, IL. Our church was able to assist in that process and they went on to have a fruitful ministry following graduation, first in Nebraska, later at Alaska Bible College, and are currently serving at Indian Bible College of Northern Arizona. Three decades later, our church is continuing to partner with them in ministry.

Hal was also instrumental in Bob Beaman's salvation. Bob's wife, Robin, was a new believer, and Bob had on occasion attended CCG with her and their children. Upon hearing about the beginning of our church, Bob was the one who suggested that they come and visit, and they stayed. Hal and Bob began to play tennis together, and it was not long before Bob responded to the Gospel and was saved. Nothing is more rewarding to me as a pastor than to see how God works in calling people to salvation and into His forever family, and then to see their lives transformed. Such was the case with Bob, for in time he would become one of our respected elders.

It was not long before a building committee was formed. Someone suggested Bob Beaman as the architect, but my concern was that if any criticism should come his way, it could be difficult for him as a new believer. After sharing my reservations, Bob assured me that he could handle whatever objections there might be. Jerry Martin, a builder in our church, was also part of the committee, along with Jim Hanson, Wood Hackenbracht, and Herm Tilly. The idea was to pattern our facility after the one at CCG which was decidedly multi-purpose. This enabled

Faithful men putting up our sign by I-65 on a snowy day

us to maximize the use of our space, using the larger part for worship but having sliding doors on the sides and rear which could double as classrooms and be used for overflow seating as our church grew.

It was an exciting time as we had our official ground breaking, and began construction. Having no mortgage on our land gave us greater freedom as we began to build. Once the slab was poured, we had a Sunday evening pitch-in on site. Bob Beaman had identified the names of the various rooms on the concrete to help us visualize the finished product. He delighted in telling me that my office was in the southernmost part of the building, knowing I would appreciate being closer to Kentucky! It was an exciting evening of rejoicing in what the Lord had already done, and affirming our faith in greater things yet to come. As construction began, Jerry Martin made it possible for us to work on various phases, especially clean up and painting. By the time the building was complete, more than 90% of our members had hands on experience; the others were elderly and unable to help physically, but faithfully prayed for the construction.

While our son, Scott, was still struggling, I remember how he came to me one evening to let me know that, contrary to what he felt in the beginning, moving to Indiana was actually the right thing, for he saw how God was obviously blessing the church. And we all recognized God's blessing as well, and were rejoicing to be part of our new CCS family!

An important question, but one not often asked is, *"Who pastors the pastor?"* Because my friendships in Tyler were established and strong, it was difficult for me during our first couple of years in Indiana. There were a number of men who were friends of the pastor, but my felt need was for men who were friends with Tom who happened to be the pastor. Jim Hanson was one who was a supportive, faithful friend from the beginning, and Jim Hall was another. He was a seminary graduate, had served as a pastor, but also had an engineering degree. We began to meet regularly, and even though he was a member of the Steering Committee, and then the first Chairman of the Elders, we had a relationship where I could freely share my life with him, including my struggles. Some months later, an opportunity came for Jim Hall to utilize his engineering degree with a group that provided architectural and engineering skills for ministries in third world countries. While I was rejoicing about his new opportunity, I knew I would miss our friendship. Before he and his family left Indy, he suggested that I begin meeting with Jim Young, who had recently begun attending CCS. Jim Hall's counsel was definitely from the Lord, for Jim Young and I began to meet weekly, and were able to develop a friendship I continue to treasure today. Jim, his wife, Sue, and the entire family, came to mean so much to

Lots of treasured memories from our first building on East Stop 11 Road

both Linda and me, but eventually moved to Columbus, Ohio. In time there would be countless other friendships I would come to treasure, but in those early years, these three men, all named Jim, were *pastors to this pastor*.

We were able to move into our own building in December of 1987, two years and three months after our church began. The blessing of being in our own facility made Christmas extra special that year. We had our first Christmas Eve candlelight service, which remains a tradition to this day. We had planned a baptismal service for our first Sunday evening, with Bob and Robin Beaman among those to be baptized. But there was one major problem; the heater for the baptistery did not work, and it was a cold winter night in December. We called and asked everyone to bring large containers of hot water with the hope that by adding them we could make the baptistry water a little more comfortable for those being baptized, but it was all to no avail.   Even so, we went ahead and had a memorable but cold baptismal service. That memory made me even more thankful for the many *warm* baptisms that would follow!

Because baptism is such a significant event, a time to publicly declare one's faith in Christ, we eventually moved our baptisms to Sunday mornings, and there were many cherished and unforgettable moments. I also designed an invitation so those to be baptized could invite family members and other special friends to attend. The power of the Gospel to transform lives is miraculous, and I never cease to be amazed in hearing testimonies of how God calls people out of darkness into His marvelous light!

Bob and Robin Beaman were baptized together.

As for our family, while Linda taught school while I was in seminary, she was able to stay at home while our children were in their growing up years. When Christy was beginning high school and Scott in college, we discussed the possibility of Linda returning to

189

teaching, knowing it could be a help to us financially. As we discussed it with Christy, she was comfortable with the idea. My thought was that if Linda found a job teaching in a subject that was an extension of who she was, I could be at peace with it. She sent out resumes but received only one response from Crispus Attucks Middle School, part of Indianapolis Public Schools, teaching first year Spanish. We were in agreement that it was a good fit, and though we had not settled on the length of her tenure, she would teach there for the next 16 years. At least 80% of her students were from the African American community, and Linda was able to have a significant impact on many lives. While those years were not easy, God used them to bring greater spiritual maturity to Linda's life than ever before, while also being a financial help to our family. As it turned out, her insurance was excellent, and I was able to be included for a very low cost, meaning the church did not have to cover that expense.

As our church was growing, we were able to support more and more missionaries, the majority of them with significant ties to our church. My concern was for us to also become involved in short term mission trips; by this time I had discovered that God often works through first hand involvement to forever capture people's hearts for the Great Commission. When Christy was 14, she was able to accompany me and a team from the church to the Dominican Republic where we served for ten days with Food for the Hungry. Our task was to build latrines in the western part of the country, along the Haitian border. It was a challenging time as we saw their feeding program for needy children in action, while also knowing our group was making a contribution to the overall health of the area.

Our church also made various trips to Haiti over the years, and Christy, while still in high school, was a member of one of those teams. I was later blessed to join a medical team from our church led by Dr. Kyley Wood, a highly skilled oral surgeon who was a member of our church before moving to establish his practice in Jasper, IN. What a joy it was to witness amazing surgeries as huge tumors were removed and other helpful procedures were performed. Our church also partnered with Children of the Promise Orphanage in Haiti, and the Woods soon adopted two boys from that wonderful ministry.

Our first work team to Laurel Mission near where I grew up in Kentucky

One of the greatest joys for me in missions was to lead a group from CCS to southeastern Kentucky, assisting in the ministry of Laurel Mission, directed by a longtime friend, Titus Boggs, in Harlan County where I was born. One of my aunts was part of the Little Laurel Bible Church where Titus was the pastor, and my mother and other relatives lived just across Pine Mountain in Baxter. As the years passed, more than 100 from CCS made that trip, and that number has multiplied many times over as the church is continuing even now to make an annual trip to share in this ministry whose purpose is to improve the spiritual and physical life of the people in Harlan County.

When Christy was only 15, our church walked through what was at the time our most difficult valley of sorrow. Christy's best friend, Christa Hillebrand, a year older, was killed in an automobile

With my mother and Aunt Ella Wilder after preaching in Kentucky

accident. Our youth group had been away for a weekend retreat, but Christa had remained at home with her parents. At the end of the Sunday morning service, in response to the message, Christa, along with her parents, expressed a renewed desire to have her life honor the Lord. She had no way of knowing that the next afternoon she would come face to face with her Savior. Only a day earlier, we had received word that the son of some close friends from Tyler had died. Tom and Shirley Porter were then living in Waycross, GA and asked me to come and speak at what would be a full military funeral for Tim. So after flying to GA for 22-year-old Tim's memorial service, I returned home to give the message at 16-year-old Christa's service, both extremely difficult sermons for me. The crowd of 600 who came filled every chair we could possibly get into our still relatively new building. While it was clear that God blessed the impact of Christa's life in that service, what I see in hindsight is how the work He did in so many of her friends, as a result of her influence, continues even today.

Not long afterwards, our church called Phil Jackson as our youth pastor. Phil was from the area and had been serving with his father in the inner city of Indianapolis. As he made his first trip to Kentucky with us, I was amazed at how well Phil related to people who were more disadvantaged than most of the teens in our youth group. As time passed, he was able to have a ministry that also impacted a number of teens in our church, and I know families today who are deeply grateful for his investment in their sons and daughters.

One of the most difficult and bewildering times of my ministry occurred a few years later. I found myself not enjoying ministry activities I normally loved, while also seeing myself being abrupt and even rude to a few people in the church; I could not understand what was happening. It was as if I were standing outside myself looking at this person I did not recognize. I talked with Linda about it, with Jim Young, and with the Elders, but no one quite knew what to do with me. During that time I was already registered for a pastor's conference in Chicago, so I decided to proceed with my plans. Several hundred pastors were in attendance, and everyone went to the main sessions, but there were also elective seminars. One that caught my eye was being offered in a small room in the basement that first afternoon with the title *Pastoral Burnout*, so I decided I would check it out. As I was making my way down the stairs, they were jam packed, like a freeway when an accident has occurred; my thought was that perhaps someone had fallen. As it turned out, all of these pastors had chosen to go to the *Pastoral Burnout* seminar as well! Because of the overwhelming interest, the seminar was moved to the large auditorium. While the seminar brought no immediate help, it was clear that I was not alone in my struggles.

In the weeks that followed, I came across an article in Leadership Journal with the title, *Checking Your Gauges.*[3] The gist of it was that anytime we experience feelings similar to what I had been facing, it is important to take a look at our spiritual gauge and see if we are regularly meeting with the Lord, drawing nourishment from Him. Second, we should check our physical gauge, to see if we are eating properly and getting sufficient exercise. As I examined my life at the time, my assessment was that both gauges were normal and healthy. But the article also mentioned your emotional gauge, and this is what caught my attention. In the weeks leading up to this bewildering season, I had been meeting almost daily with a young couple I loved like my own son and daughter who were in deep trouble in their marriage, and my emotional energy had become depleted. There were other highly intense church issues I was also facing, and I could see that my emotional gauge was running on fumes. Thankfully, the Lord graciously enabled me in time to walk out of that distressing valley of discouragement, and I was thankfully able to get back to normal.

Sometime later we began searching for a Pastor of Worship and Music, and I contacted my friend and former coworker, Larry Kent, from Texas. While he came for a visit and our people loved him, Larry and his wife, Mary, sensed they should remain in Texas because of needs within their respective families. While I was disappointed, our elders continued to pray and trust the Lord.

A few months later, Hal Givens gave me the name of Michael Mercer, who was the pastor at Waukegan Bible Church, north of Chicago, where Hal and Pam were members. Hal and Mike had met at Trinity Evangelical Divinity School, and both were graduates. Hal's thought was that Mike and I would work well together and that Mike, as well as his wife, Gail, had strong musical gifts, Mike also being a gifted teacher. Sometime later I made a trip and had a good visit with the Mercers, which led to inviting them to come and meet with our elders. We recognized that while Mike was not exactly what we were looking for, in some ways he was actually more. We invited them to join us at CCS and they accepted; we would be partners in ministry for the next ten years. While Gail led the choir, Mike was a gifted worship leader, song writer, and played the guitar. Because of his teaching gift, I asked him to share the pulpit ministry with me, preaching once each month. He also regularly taught one of our adult classes, and our people always responded well to his teaching, especially his classes from the Old Testament.

With our staff: Mike, Becki, Jan, and Phil

Within a two year span, Linda and I were blessed to become grandparents for the first time to Lauren and Nathan, both adopted. Cheryl was unable to have children, so she and her husband, Eric, made plans to adopt, and we were thrilled at the wonderful way the Lord answered. Though many fail to understand and appreciate this truth, adoption is a major part of our salvation. God has no natural born children. "But when the fullness of time came, God sent forth His Son...that we might receive the adoption as sons" (Galatians 4:4-5). "Blessed be the God and Father of our Lord Jesus Christ, who has blessed us with every spiritual blessing in the heavenly places in Christ, just as He chose us in Him before the foundation of the world, that we should be holy and blameless before Him. In love He predestined us to adoption as sons through Jesus Christ to Himself, according to the kind intention of His will, to the praise of the glory of His grace" (Ephesians 1:3-6a). Even as adopted believers are to the praise of God's glorious grace, Lauren and Nathan have been this to our family, and we love them dearly!

Dating back to my student pastor days, though I have not always understood the reasons, I have always loved preaching on Mother's Day and Father's Day. The congregation always seemed especially responsive toward those sermons. As we were on vacation one summer, Linda and I visited a church in Southern California, and the pastor was in the midst of a six week sermon series on the family, one that began on Mother's Day and would conclude on Father's Day. I immediately embraced that idea, and made plans to incorporate this same concept into our church. In addition to the sermons, we also sought to include songs about family life. We even began to develop family musicals to introduce the theme, often transforming the platform temporarily into an attractive living room scene with the musicians seated in couches, chairs, and around the dining room table. We did this for a number of years; our people were always responsive and appreciative. Mike and Gail Mercer became significant parts of these musicals, sometimes using the choir, but always helping to put the music together. My underlying passion was to teach our people what the Bible has to say about marriage and family life.

After eleven years of serving in our office, Jan Channel sensed it was time to move into another position. She had been a wonderful blessing to me, to our other staff, and to the entire church. During her years with us, Jan had been diagnosed with breast cancer, and remains a survivor to this day. She and Laura Denny, a friend of Jan's and member of our church, formed what they referred to as a FAITH group, FAITH being an acronym for "Friends Abiding in the Hope". The group which began with seven, growing to a high of thirty, met regularly for 20 years, and occasionally comes together still today. The Lord used this ministry to give hope to numerous women, some who are now with the Lord, while others remain here.

When Jan informed me she was moving to another position, I was basically in denial that she was actually leaving, and doing little to search for another secretary. Thankfully, Jan had compassion on me and helped me find her replacement. She contacted a friend she thought might be interested. Brenda Harbert soon came for an interview, and it was immediately clear to me that the Lord had answered. Though different in personality and gifting, Brenda brought the same grace to the positon Jan had exhibited, and we went on to have a wonderful working relationship for the next ten years.

Wood and Marge Hackenbracht

As the years passed, some of the men from CCS began going to Myrtle Beach, SC, in the winter months, taking advantage of some very affordable golf packages. The weather could be rainy and freezing, or sunny and in the 60's or even 70's. Scott and I were often able to be part of these groups, and have great memories of those trips. Most included four days of golf, 36 holes each day, with a long day's drive both ways. Some wonderful relationships were established during those trips, and other friendships grew deeper. On one outing Scott and I were riding in the cart together when Brian Hays, one of the men in our foursome, came toward us with a troubled look on his face. He had his large mobile phone in his hand, one of the first of its kind. The news was that a highly respected woman in the church, Marge Hackenbracht, who was a spiritual mother to me, had fallen down their basement steps, and died. As we drove toward the next hole, I still remember Scott putting his arm around me as we grieved and prayed together for her husband, Wood, their children, and for ourselves. I made arrangements to fly home to be with Wood and his family, and for Marge's memorial service. In my absence, Mike Mercer had been a wonderful comfort to the family, and had played a similar role with other grieving families at other times when I had been away. In the providence of God, while Mike would leave after ten years to become the Senior Pastor of another community church, he would eventually go on to have an effective ministry as a beloved hospice chaplain. He later authored an insightful book on death and dying called *Walking Home Together*.

CHAPTER TEN

When CCS Became LifePoint – God's Generous Miracle

"Now to Him who is able to do far more abundantly beyond all that we ask or think, according to the power that works within us, to Him be the glory in the church and in Christ Jesus to all generations forever and ever." Ephesians 3:20-21

One of the greatest highlights of our lives and ministry occurred in the summer of 1998. Linda and I, along with a friend from CCS, Mark Seaman, had the distinguished honor of traveling to Indonesia and the eastern highlands of Irian Jaya to join Andrew and Ann Sims for the dedication of the Ketengban New Testament. We would be able to witness with our own eyes the extraordinary impact of God's Word on this precious tribal group as a result of having Scripture in their heart language. After eighteen years of loving, faithful service by the Sims, the Ketengban way of life had changed dramatically. While many beneficial advances had been made in literacy, healthcare, agriculture, and community development, the most stunning difference was in their personal lives. Their formerly animistic culture which kept them bound by witchcraft, superstition, and fear, had been replaced by the faith, hope, and love of the Gospel of the Grace of God.

After my unforgettable trip to visit the Sims in 1984, my dream had been to join them and the Ketengban people for this very occasion, and to have Linda with me; now my dream was becoming a reality! Andrew had suggested that we enter and depart Indonesia through Bali instead of Jakarta as we had done on our earlier trip. He had arranged overnight lodging for us in one of the most uniquely beautiful, yet affordable accommodations we have ever experienced. The next day we left Bali for the Sentani International Airport, a trip of 1,800 miles, where we would connect with Andrew, Ann, and others from the U.S. coming for the dedication. Among them would be John and Kay Prestridge; Linda and I were looking forward to experiencing the dedication with them because of our long friendship and shared history with the Sims, and common commitment to their ministry. The pastor at Grace Community would also be attending, along with

With Linda on Main Street in Omban

several others, including a good friend and former next door neighbor from Tyler.

Dedications of the New Testament in tribal groups are celebrations unlike any other! From the time we arrived in Sentani, everyone connected to the translation community was overjoyed, especially the pilots who had faithfully served the Sims throughout their years of service. Flying over the dense jungles in those small, skillfully engineered planes, and landing on the diminutive airstrips in the villages, while common to the pilots and translators, would be a unique and unforgettable experience for us.

During our ten days with the Ketengban people, we participated in two dedications, the official one in Omban, where the Sims lived, and another in Okbap, a ten minute flight away. When the numerous cardboard boxes were opened and the New Testaments distributed, there were tears of joy as these grateful men and women received a personal copy of God's Word, many embracing the Scripture to their heart. As we walked through the villages in the days following, a common sight was to see family groups gathered outside their bamboo huts, their faces filled with joy, as they responded to having God's Word read in their heart language.

A crowd was always gathered around the front porch of Andrew and Anne's home where we stayed. When Andrew was present to interpret, the older people loved to reminisce about how life was before, and then tell, often with tears, of the miraculous changes that came once they received *God's talk* for themselves. Because of the magnitude of the celebration, and because we (*their fathers*) had joined them, we enjoyed celebratory pig feasts in both villages.

With John Prestridge and a Ketengban church leader

As I write these words more than twenty years later, I continue to incorporate memories of that dedication into my sermons and Sunday school classes. While there are countless enduring impressions from those days, the strongest is the love and respect we observed in the Ketengban people for Andrew and Ann, and appropriately so. The Sims were the ones who responded to God's call to Bible translation work while in college, and have continued to maintain a lifelong obedience in following that call.

One of the greatest joys of my heart is how our church in Indiana, even though I am no longer their pastor, has maintained and

Andrew and a village pastor

progressively increased their support to the Sims and the ministry of Bible translation. Their work has now spread to other related language groups where the Ketengban people have traveled with the transforming power of the Gospel. One group, the Lik peoples, recently participated in their own celebration as they too received the New Testament in their heart language. Through the ongoing ministry of Andrew and his translation assistants, the Ketengban now have the Old Testament as well, with our church in Indiana playing a major role in making this possible. Following the Sims' visit to Indianapolis in September of 2018, one of our friends in the church wrote the following.

"If you were to ask me to name the human being I admire most on this planet next to Jesus Christ, I would not hesitate to tell you who that is. It is a couple, actually, and they're still alive, and there will be thousands upon thousands of people worshiping with me in heaven who are there because of what God has done through this couple. They have been supported in missions by my church for over 30 years, and every time they come to visit us I cry tears of joy the entire time they're here. What's so special about them? They are simply vessels God could use because they answered His call and surrendered their bodies to him, as Romans 12 calls us to do. That's all. Thank you, Pastor Tom and Linda Madon, for bringing the Sims to our church - we're still being blessed like crazy in this partnership!" Kristin Morris

On our return trip from Indonesia in 1998, Mark, Linda, and I, at Andrew's urging, spent two additional nights in Bali, to tour parts of the island. While Indonesia is the largest Muslim nation in the world, the island of Bali is predominately Hindu. The guide Andrew had arranged for the day was a Hindu by the name of *Paul Newman*, and his daily offering was displayed on the dash of his minivan. We also witnessed women walking through the streets with their offerings of beautiful, freshly-cut flowers on their way to the Hindu temple. We had lunch across the street from the famous Mount Agung volcano. Throughout the day I had prayed for what the Apostle Paul refers to as "a door for the Word" (Colossians 4:3), and it came when Paul was describing the caste system in which he and all other Hindus are bound. He was fascinated as I described that in Christianity all peoples, regardless of their differences, are one in Christ, and on equal footing. "There is neither Jew nor Greek, there is neither slave nor free man, there is neither male nor female; for you are all one in Christ Jesus" (Galatians 3:28).

After departing from Bali, we also stopped in Tokyo to visit Dick and Judy Amos. We again saw the giant Buddha, and observed the various ceremonies and rituals of Shintoism. With the unforgettable celebration of the Ketengban people coming out of an animistic culture fresh on our minds, and then adding our exposure to Islam, Hinduism, Buddhism, and Shintoism, we had essentially taken a tour of the majority of the world religions. Before we went to church that Sunday morning, I was having my quiet time in John 17 and was struck by these words in Jesus' prayer: "This is eternal life, that they might know You, the only true God, and Jesus Christ whom You have sent." (John 17:3) We were blessed to worship that morning in a relatively small but beautiful Japanese church surrounded by fields of rice patties, and were warmly welcomed by a loving church family. While all communication was in Japanese, some of the songs were ones we knew in English about the joy of worshiping the one true God who has revealed Himself in a variety of ways, supremely through the Living Word – Jesus Christ, and through His written Word, the Bible. I could not hold back the tears of joy for the astonishing, undeserved grace we and these joyful Japanese believers had been shown.

Soon after returning home to Indianapolis, Michael Mercer was asked to become the senior pastor of a neighboring community church, and he accepted with my recommendation and blessing. I was grateful for our ten years of shared ministry, for I had learned much from Mike, and he had made a significant contribution to our ministry. What this meant for CCS was that we needed additional staff, namely, a Pastor of Worship and Music, someone with strong musical gifts, but one who also shared our philosophy of ministry. As we followed up on various resumes, and invited promising candidates in for visits over a period of several months, we could never reach the point of being at complete peace, until we met David and Mary Harris! Their weekend visit with us went extremely well. While we were impressed with David and Mary's gifts, I appreciated their gracious spirit, and sensed

David and Mary Harris

that David was someone with whom I could easily work and share the ministry. We offered him the position, and his response was that they wanted to pray about it. Surprisingly, on their return trip home to Florida, they called from their layover in Charlotte to say that they had already been praying about it, and knew that we were the answer to their prayers. David and I would work together for my final seven years in Indy, and those are among my most rewarding years of ministry. And the even greater news is that David is faithfully continuing in this same ministry a decade later, working alongside the senior pastor and the current ministry team.

One of my desires in writing these personal and pastoral memoirs is that I would not tell anyone else's story, especially those of our three adult children; each one has compelling life-changing messages to tell. Anything I have written about them is done with their permission.

In 2002 our family went through another extremely difficult time as our oldest daughter, Cheryl, experienced the anguishing pain of a divorce. God's Word commands us to "let marriage be held in honor among all" (Hebrews 13:4), and this has long been one of the passions of my heart, especially since that summer of 1970 when the Lord transformed our troubled marriage into one that has been a delight to us, and where our desire is to honor Him. As a pastor, one of my favorite activities is pre-marital counseling and officiating at weddings. My favorite weddings, of course, were those of our children, walking our daughters down the aisle, and also officiating at the ceremony. In the case of Scott and his wife, Wendy, of course I only officiated at their wedding. While the Bible clearly describes the grounds for divorce, and provides other guidelines in working through that agonizing process, it is nevertheless, one of the most painful of life experiences, and for families and friends as well. There is hardly a home today that has not been touched in some way by the heartache of divorce. And while the Bible is clear that God hates divorce (Malachi 2:16), He does not hate divorced people. Because of His grace, there are lessons to be learned and new chapters to be written. A couple of years after Cheryl went through that experience, the Lord brought into her life and to our family, James Helliwell, a man who dearly loves Cheryl and provides and protects her as his own; we are deeply thankful for him. They live near us in California, are members of our church family, and we are blessed to share life together.

Our youngest daughter Christy met her husband, Scott Mabs, at the Master's University in Santa Clarita, CA, and they were married

Our family at Christy's wedding

at CCS in December of 1995. Though Scott was born and grew up in the San Joaquin Valley, where we all now reside, they spent the first five years of their marriage in Indianapolis, and their two oldest children, Ashlyn and Trent (our third and fourth grandchildren), were born at St. Francis Hospital. It was wonderful to have them as part of our church for that time. It was a sad day, however, when we saw their moving truck pull away with two of our beloved grandchildren relocating to CA. Christy and Scott would later have two additional daughters, Ainsley and Allyse. We are thankful that they too live nearby and are also part of our church family in California.

Our son, Scott, met his wife Wendy when they were co-workers at Kroger in Indianapolis. Wendy was from Tennessee and grew up in a culture similar to the one I knew in Southeastern Kentucky. They also were married at CCS in March of 1999. The Lord has blessed them with two children, Brooke and Seth. Brooke is scheduled to graduate with honors from Southport High School in the spring of 2019. Seth is two years younger and is our favorite ASD young man. The spectrum of autism is extremely broad, but Seth is a complete delight, never argues with his sister, or complains, and loves life and his family. Brooke has been and continues to be a great blessing to him as his older sister. Statistics reveal that the divorce rate is much higher for parents of autistic children, but Scott and Wendy's testimony is that Seth has helped to bring them closer. Scott and his family are benefitting and enjoying being part of our former church in Indianapolis.

The time came for us to again search for a youth pastor, and the Lord brought to us Seth Bartal, a graduate of Taylor University. Though he was young and with limited experience, our elders sensed that he was the one for us. Seth had a set of computer and electronic skills unlike anything I had witnessed, and was a gifted communicator. He had a number of fruitful years with us before leaving to serve in another community church in Eastern Indiana where he is now the senior pastor. He met and married Kari Trieb, one of the young ladies who had grown up in our church, and they now have three lovely children.

The Lord was blessing our church in many ways, and we had a good measure of health. We accelerated the payments on our initial mortgage and paid it off in approximately twelve years. Numerically, we were always growing and adding new families, but we were not always able to keep them, especially in the early years. While an occasional family went away disillusioned, it was extremely common, especially with our young couples, to have them move out of the area. Our average attendance in two services was in the 350 to 425 range. When we purchased the land on East Stop 11 Road, our hope had been that subdivisions would grow up around the church, but this was not to be, as the Lord had a different plan. St. Francis Hospital in Beech Grove, one of the largest in Indianapolis, chose to relocate, and purchased the acreage directly across from us. Instead of CCS being surrounded by homes, we were suddenly at the epicenter of a major medical development. While it took some time for our elders to discern what this meant for our church, we eventually learned that the value of our land had increased exponentially, just how much we could not be sure. Though some attempts were made, it was impossible for an appraiser to find a comparable piece of land, since our location was completely unique. We were in a position where our facilities needed to be expanded and improved, but were now faced with the very real possibility that God's plan could be for us to sell our land and relocate.

Through prayer, research, and ongoing discussions, we eventually reached the point where we were at peace and in complete unity that it was God's will for us to sell the land. After additional research, we chose to sell it in two phases. As people in real estate often say, your land is worth what people are willing to pay. In our case, because it was in a highly desirable location for those in the medical community, we were blessed to receive a significant amount, *as in a few million,* for both transactions. We sometimes commented that if any one of us had demonstrated the wisdom and foresight to purchase those 20 acres of land in 1986, being confident that we would some years later make such a major profit, we would have forever congratulated ourselves! In the case of CCS, there was one with infinite wisdom who saw the future perfectly, our Omniscient Heavenly Father, and He had the future of our church on His heart. Though it was impossible for our Steering Committee to grasp the magnitude of our decision nearly twenty years earlier, *God's invisible hand* had been guiding us. Our church was blessed to experience the miraculous abundance described by the Apostle Paul, "Now to Him who is able to do far more abundantly beyond all that we ask or think, according to the power that works within us, to Him be the glory in the church and in Christ Jesus to all generations forever and ever" (Ephesians 3:20-21).

Even though the decision had been made, we understood that relocation would be a lengthy process, beginning with finding the right parcel of land. As time passed, one of the physicians in our church, Dr. Gary Creed, informed us that he had a patient with land for sale on Combs Road in Franklin Township, and it had a major subdivision directly across the street. While there was some initial hesitation, we soon came to see this as the location. We were able to purchase 20 acres of a 40 acre tract, and it has become the ideal place for the church. While it was less than two miles from our initial location, it was not in Southport, so this necessitated a name change. Though this too was a lengthy process, we agreed that our new name would be LifePoint Church.

Our LifePoint Staff

While we were wonderfully blessed by the sale of our land which gave us an enormous head start in relocating, we still had a need for additional funds. For the first time ever, we decided to conduct a capital campaign. The heart of it was a series of messages I would give on the Biblical principles of giving, and we would ask our people to pray about what the Lord would have them give, over and above their other giving to the church. All this was done without any pressure or personal appeals, and the commitments would be anonymous. Amazingly, our congregation of approximately 400 committed to approximately 1.6 million dollars, and faithfully gave that during the specified time frame, over and above their other giving to the church. The result is a uniquely beautiful, highly functional facility, one for which we are deeply thankful!

Linda's mother was a positive asset to our church from the beginning, and a wonderful example of a godly woman. I often told people that none of the typical mother-in-law jokes applied to her. When she gave me a card for my birthday, Christmas, or during pastor appreciation month in October, she always let me know that she was not only thankful to have me as her son-in-law, but also as her pastor. If all of the parishioners were like her, my ministry would have been problem free! In the winter of 2004, however, Mother suffered a stroke. As the entire family gathered by her hospital bed that evening, one of the doctors said to her, *"Mrs. Gillam, you have suffered a major stroke, and you will not survive the night."* Her immediate, peaceful response was, *"Is that right? Well, I am a Christian, and Jesus is my Lord and Savior. I don't want heroics; I want to go to heaven, so will you let me?"* In the providence of God, she was still alive the next morning, and the Lord kept her with us two additional years, with Linda, her sisters, and sister-in-law sharing the responsibility for her care. Our new building was under construction during that time, and Linda would often bring her mother in her wheelchair where they would join other ladies as they went through the building praying for the ministries that would soon be taking place in each room.

In the summer of 2005, the church made plans to surprise me with a celebration of our twenty years of ministry. The church was always generous during our years there, including salary, vacation time, and other benefits. When we celebrated our 30th wedding anniversary, for example, they surprised us with a fall trip to New England, setting up in advance charming bed and breakfast spots in the different states, even two nights in Plymouth, a place we had long desired to visit. Now, for my twenty years of ministry, working with Linda behind the scenes, they paid the airfares for our California children and grandchildren to fly to Indianapolis and also arranged housing for them. My family will tell you that it is hard to keep a secret from me. Some have suggested that I would have made a good detective had the Lord not called me to be a pastor. But in this case, it was my wife, who is *the most without guile person I have ever known,* who slipped and gave away the secret. I went along with everything, of course, and there was an element of surprise for me. My mother, who had experienced successful bypass surgery only six weeks earlier, was able to come from Kentucky with my sister Ella, making the celebration even more meaningful. When I first began to talk about the ministry in high school, my mother was not so sure about it because of the high expectations she knew that churches had for pastors. But my mother had visited us at Grace Community in Texas, and this would be her third visit to CCS; in both churches she had witnessed the love and affirmation the people had given to me, along with the health of the church, and I knew she was blessed by what she saw. It was a great weekend, one for which I was deeply thankful, and the church insisted that I take a few days off to spend with my family.

Foundational to the pastoral ministry is a belief in the transforming power of the Gospel. Regardless of a person's past, no one is beyond the reach of the gospel, for it is "the power of God unto salvation to everyone who believes" (Romans 1:16). The truth of God's Word, however, is that without Christ we are all spiritually dead in our trespasses and sins, and dead means dead - without life! One day the Lord brought into my life a young husband and father who had been on cocaine and was experiencing other troubling issues. He was alienated from his wife and children when I met him, his life reflecting the spiritual darkness he was in. While in jail, he had picked up a Bible and began to read, and had just been released when he called and asked if he could see me. During that initial hour we were together, I shared with him the Gospel of the Grace of God. We then prayed, and in the days and weeks that followed, his life began to change. While there were definitely rough spots along the way, he was eventually reunited with his wife and children, and they were all baptized in our church. As I was regularly spending time encouraging him in his faith, two men in the church whom I respected cautioned me about getting my hopes up too much, and to be aware that statistics indicate that the majority of people from that background end up back where they were. While I listened to their caution, my response was that if I did not believe that God could change even people like him, I was in the wrong vocation! Salvation, after all, is not a human work. Jesus is described as *"the Author (Source, Originator) and Finisher (Completer) of our faith."* (Hebrews 12:2) The Apostle Paul beautifully affirmed this in his letter to the church in Philippi: "Being confident of this very thing that He who began a good work in you will continue to perfect it until the day of Jesus Christ" (Philippians 1:6). All these years later, I am grateful to report that the same ongoing sanctification process that is taking place in me, and in each one of God's children, is also continuing in him and his beautiful family!

Wednesday Night Men's Bible Study

One of my favorite ministries during my tenure at the church was our Wednesday night Men's Bible Study that continued for many years. This informal gathering gave me an opportunity to share my heart and interact with the men in a way that was not possible on Sunday mornings. Even now I can visualize the faces of men whose lives were progressively transformed as we studied God's Word together, always with a view toward life application. Numerous friendships were also formed which will continue in eternity.

Because Scott and I both enjoyed golf, we had often talked about how great it could be to attend a practice round at the Master's in Augusta, Georgia. In 2008, one of our friends was able to purchase tickets, and we made a memorable trip there together. Playing golf at a couple of courses along the way, we also spent a wonderful night with my mother in Kentucky. On a course in Greenwood, South Carolina, I even had my first and only *hole in one*. The next day we enjoyed walking the stunningly beautiful course at the Master's, covering most of it twice, and had an unforgettable time. As we were

Lots of great memories!

driving home, Scott commented, *"Dad, I believe your hole in one was God's way of saying that He was pleased with our trip!"* Another blessing came three months later when Scott had his first and only *hole in one* at Purgatory Golf Course in Indianapolis, and I was there to share in his joy even as he had shared in mine.

While there are countless joys and blessings of being a pastor, there are also challenges. Many are relational, but our call to peacemaking and unity never changes: "Be diligent to maintain the unity of the Spirit in the bonds of peace" (Ephesians 4:3). "If possible, in as much as it depends on you, be at peace with all men" (Romans 12:18). Even on rare occasions when people would leave the church, regardless of the reason, my goal was to preserve the friendship. With staff, where the working relationships are closer and more intense, I am thankful for the friendships that were forged through our shared ministry partnerships, and I continue to value each one today.

Another challenge is when people have expectations for their pastor that are unrealistic, whether that is in how he preaches, his leadership style, spiritual gifts, how he cares for them, or even his personality. While there is always room to grow and be enlarged within the gifts and ministry sphere God has entrusted to us, each pastor is unique. It is difficult for anyone to function if you are a prisoner of another person's expectations. For several years I have said to the church, *"If you say 'Tom Madon is my shepherd,' you cannot say, 'I shall not want.'"* Only Jesus Himself can meet the deepest needs of our lives. What has helped me when I sense expectations in others beyond what I can meet is to remember that each one of us, pastors and all Christians, are called to live our lives to an audience of one – our Lord! Yes, we have accountability to one another in the body of Christ, and to those over us in authority, but our foremost inner motivation must be to please the Lord and follow His Word.

A popular model in some of the mega churches is to view the pastor as a CEO, and God clearly calls some with leadership gifts of this nature. For me, however, I was simply a pastor with a motivation to get to know and then build a friendship with each person and/or family who came through our doors. Throughout my ministry, I followed the old-fashioned method of going to the back of the church and saying goodbye as the people were leaving. This gave me the opportunity to meet any who were new that I had missed before the service, but it also gave me a chance to hear from those I already knew, gaining information I could follow up on during the week. My desire was to graciously connect with as many people as possible each time I was in church, and that continues to be my passion today. One of my greatest desires was for our church to be known as a place where everyone who comes among us feels welcome, is shown grace, and senses that our church, the body of Christ, truly cares about them.

While enrolled in seminary preaching classes in the '60's, some of my classmates attempted to preach like Billy Graham. In my earliest attempts, I sought to mimic some of my favorite camp meeting preachers, but quickly learned that was to no avail. On the other hand, because I loved the way the camp meeting preachers included personal stories to illustrate the truths in their sermons, it came naturally for me to do the same. In fact, the friends who admonished me most strongly to write this book did so because they believed the life experiences they had heard me share in my sermons needed to be passed along! The preaching style I eventually settled on came from a desire to be no different in the pulpit than in a one on one relationship. My even greater passion was to heed the admonition the Apostle Paul gave to Timothy: "Be diligent to present yourself approved unto God, a workman who does not need to be ashamed, accurately handling the word of truth" (II Timothy 2:13). It is God's Word He has promised to bless, not my ideas and experiences. Outlines seemed to easily emerge from my inductive Bible study.   A friend at CCS who liked my outlines, which always had Biblical support, suggested that my style would lend itself well to PowerPoint, and this is what I began to do my last few years at CCS; I continue to utilize it today when I am able.

When I reflect on my ministry, as I am doing in this writing project, I often think back to an unforgettable experience Linda and I had with Andrew and Ann Sims in the late 1970's when we accompanied them to the Wycliffe Bible Translator offices in Duncanville, near Dallas. As we were ready to leave the compound, Andrew exclaimed, *"There's Rachel Saint! Would you like to meet her?"* Rachel, by this time an elderly woman, was the sister of Nate Saint, the pilot among the five missionaries killed by the Auca Indians in 1956. Numerous books have been written about that event and the amazing miracles that eventually came out of that experience, not to mention the hundreds of missionaries and pastors (like me) who were influenced by their lives. Of course we wanted to meet her! In our brief exchange, I commented positively on the impact of that ministry in Ecuador, and what a well-known, influential work it was. She then responded with a profound observation that has never left me: *"As part of His sovereign purposes, God chose to shine a bright light on our work, and we are thankful. But there are other ministries all around the world that are far more significant that only God and a handful of people know anything about."*

As the years have passed, my appreciation for the truth in her brief comment has only increased. Linda and I have been blessed to witness and participate in some of those lesser known ministries, and meet the faithful servants who are involved. Some are missionaries, while many others are pastors. Within Christian circles we know the names of pastors of mega churches, those who are prolific authors, and have radio and television ministries. But by and large, the vast majority of pastors around the world are known only by those in the flock where they serve. Over the years I have come to have the highest respect for the countless bi-vocational pastors who labor at another job during the week, while giving of their time and gifts to serve a small group of believers each Lord's Day. Many of them are here in our nation, some in the inner city, others in remote rural areas, with countless others serving in third world countries around the world. While they are not in the spotlight, the Lord knows who they are; they are the faithful men and women being used in a variety of ministries as He continues to build His church. While the ministry Linda and I have been blessed to share has not been in the bright lights, we have felt loved and appreciated everywhere we have been, our longest stint being our 24 years in Indianapolis. While I have been blessed as a pastor to be generously compensated, the health of any church is always inseparably linked to the faithful volunteers who partner with their pastors, unselfishly investing their gifts, their time, and their finances in the church they love, seeking to do all to the glory of God!

On the first weekend of June of 2007, the time came for us to make the transition from Community Church of Southport at 5250 East Stop 11 Road in Perry Township, to LifePoint Church at 8540 Combs Road, less than two miles away in Franklin Township. We planned an open house that Saturday for the people of the community, giving an opportunity for all who desired to walk through the building they had witnessed being constructed. In the weeks and months that followed, several returned to visit, and some eventually became part of the church. Numerous friends from other churches came to celebrate with us that Sunday as we dedicated our beautiful new facilities to the Lord. Linda's mother was overjoyed to be part of that first service, and we have a cherished photo of the three of us from that day. As it turned out, the Lord called her home that next week, so her memorial service was the first one in our new building. As her *pastor* and son-in-law, it was my honor to give the message, and my text depicted her character: "For me to live is Christ, and to die is gain!" (Philippians 1:21)

LifePoint Church - 8540 Combs Road

Though we had chosen to have one crowded service for the dedication, we had planned to return to our pattern of having two in the weeks that followed so as to allow room for growth. Linda and I had opened our home for periodic newcomers' gatherings over the years, any time it seemed appropriate, but once we were in our new building, it became necessary to have them one Sunday evening each month. By this time we had moved into our third Indianapolis home, this one less than a mile north of the church, and it was an ideal place for our gatherings. With the assistance of others in the church, we provided a meal before assembling in the family room. I loved to explain that even as God in His grace meets us wherever we are, not to leave us there, but to take us on a life-long journey of spiritual transformation, so my desire as a pastor was that our church could also meet each one where they were, and help them take their next steps toward Christ and greater Christian maturity. I also explained to them the five priorities of our church: worship, study, training, fellowship, and outreach. Over the next two years, 90% of those who came to our newcomers' gatherings became part of our church family. During that period of nearly two years, we grew from approximately 425 to where we were averaging 750 each Sunday. We even had to increase our parking lot space about a year into the building to assure that we would have adequate room for those who were coming.

All through this process the elders and I were praying, discussing, and working toward the time when we would transition to a new senior pastor. Our prayer was that our leaders would be in unity about who he would be, and also that it would be a smooth transition. While retirement from ministry was not my goal, I did not want to stay so long that my health could become an issue and place the church in a difficult position. Linda and I were confident that when that time came, the Lord would give us wisdom as to what He had next for us.

Once the search for a new senior pastor was made known through appropriate sites on the internet, we received more than 600 resumes. It was obvious that there were many pastors who wanted my job, and for good reason; we were a healthy, growing church with beautiful new facilities, and in one of the most desirable cities in the nation. We had a search team which consisted of a few elders, a staff member, and people from different age groups in the church. While the elders would make the final decision, they would rely heavily on the research and recommendation of the search team, and I would give my input as well. During this time, a few people approached me, fearing that the church might move in an entirely new direction with a different philosophy, and there were some who had voiced this desire. My response was that we needed to trust the process. The practice our elders had followed for our first 24 years was that all decisions would be unanimous. We had a provision in our policy of how to proceed if we were not, and there had only been two instances when we were not unanimous, and in both cases things worked out smoothly without any division. This is the protection that comes with having multiple elders, in our case nine men, which prevents a small group from promoting their own agenda to the exclusion of others. In the ultimate sense of the word, as shepherds of the church, elders are called to prayerfully discern God's will for every matter that comes before them. While the level of spiritual maturity of one group of elders will vary from another, I had confidence in our men and the process they would follow in selecting the new pastor.

After a considerable amount of work on the part of the search team, including listening to sermons, phone interviews, visiting appealing candidates in their setting, looking at websites, etc., they asked a few men to submit formal applications. One day our search team brought to my office the top five. They were given to me at an extremely busy time, and it was at least two days before I could even begin to examine them. When I finally had a few minutes, I picked up one from the group, an application from a man named Jym Gregory who was at that time serving as an administrative pastor at a Baptist church in Springfield, Illinois. When I finished, I was absolutely delighted with everything I read, so much so that I bowed my head and thanked God for such a high quality candidate. While I had not heard Jym Gregory preach, or met him face to face, my initial thought was that if the other applicants were this strong, LifePoint Church would be in a good position. As I read through the others in the days ahead, while I observed positive qualities in each one, I also had cautions and reservations about the others.

In the weeks ahead, we invited Jym and his wife, Dedra, to come for a visit to interview with our elders and staff. They stayed with us in our home; we had a delightful time, and the interview went very well. A couple of weeks later, Linda and I drove to Springfield for the day to have lunch with them and to see Jym in his setting. They later came for another visit, again staying with us; the church offered him the position, and he accepted. While Jym had the administrative gifts our growing church needed, his passion was to preach and teach God's Word regularly, as a pastor/teacher.

In the weeks leading up to Pastor Jym's arrival, I had two difficult but tender funerals for young children. The first was a precious little girl from Haiti, Nallie, brought to the U.S. by Matt and Heidi Pierce, with the hope that her physical needs could be met by having her receive treatment at Riley Children's Hospital. While she forever captured our hearts, God in His sovereignty called her home. The other was a beautiful little boy, Max, whose parents were Jamie and Nancy Ferguson, but he did not live beyond birth. In back to back weeks, our church walked through the valley of sorrow with two grieving families. After the second one, Pastor David Harris commented to me, *"I hope our new pastor will be ready for challenges like this!"* Pastor Jym would be, of course, because God gives us the grace and wisdom as we need it in following His call.

With Pastor Jym and his wife, Dedra

As we discussed the timing of the transition, it was decided that I would preach on Easter Sunday and then have my *farewell sermon* the following week, but that Pastor Jym would already be in the church. It all worked very smoothly, and I was able to share my perspective on the transition, affirm my strong belief that Pastor Jym was the right choice, and express my support to him, even remaining for a time as a member in the congregation. Pastor Jym was extremely gracious toward me from the beginning, and the Lord has blessed us with a good friendship. In the years since, each time we return to LifePoint, he gives me the opportunity to preach and is always so affirming in his comments. People give me a lot of credit for the smooth transition, but Pastor Jym had at least an equal part, though it was ultimately God's blessing on our church, and answering our prayers.

On my final Sunday, the church surprised Linda and me with the news that they had arranged a summer cruise for us that would depart from Boston, with stops at Acadia National Park in Maine, in Nova Scotia, and Prince Edward Island, before traveling down the St. Lawrence Seaway, ending in Montreal. We would be with Dr. David Jeremiah, a pastor and author in San Diego the church knew I respected. We would have the opportunity to hear him preach each morning and evening, and to interact with members of his staff.

The church also gave us two large photo books of our church family which included individual notes of appreciation. While the cruise was wonderful, the photos and notes from our loyal friends remain. The common theme was an appreciation for how we were there to share special moments in their lives: births and dedications of children, baptisms, weddings, graduations, and anniversaries. Many also mentioned how we walked with them through difficult times: hospital visits, death of loved ones, and funeral messages. Others spoke of how we were the ones to share the Gospel and help them trust Christ, or how our Biblical counsel gave them wisdom and encouragement at a difficult time. Some parents spoke of how we helped them when they had difficult issues with struggling marriages and rebellious children. Others reflected on how I greeted and introduced myself to them before church, or how I remembered their names. Many commented on how they came and stayed at the church because I was faithful to teach and preach directly from the Bible, along with my stories of how the truth applies in everyday life. After reading all of the comments, my impression was all those things they appreciated were simply those ministries which were at the heart of my calling as a pastor as I understood it and who God has made Linda and me to be as a couple.

What especially caught my attention was how several said that it was through our ministry that they first came to understand the grace of God in truth, more than one saying that I was the first pastor to introduce them to the Gospel of Grace. While that was encouraging, it made me question what others are teaching and displaying. Though I have not always preached or modeled grace consistently, my ever-increasing desire has been to embrace the calling expressed by the Apostle Paul: "I do not consider my life of any account as dear to myself, so that I may finish my course with joy, and the ministry which I have received from the Lord, *to testify solemnly of the gospel of the grace of God*" (Acts 20:24).

Over these many years as a pastor, I have periodically been evaluated by the elders with whom I served, as was specified in our constitution and bylaws. Though more informally, the people in the church have also evaluated me, sometimes with their words, but always in their minds. In addition, I have regularly sought to assess myself and my ministry. In the final analysis, however, it will only be the Lord's evaluation that ultimately matters. During my years at Grace Community in Tyler, Texas, while in a sermon series from I Corinthians, I came across a passage that helped me immeasurably in this regard: "To me it is a very small thing that I may be examined by you, or by any human court; in fact, I do not even examine myself. For I am conscious of nothing against myself, yet I am not by this acquitted; but the one who examines me is the Lord. Therefore, do not go on passing judgment before the time, but wait until the Lord comes who will both bring to light the things hidden in darkness and disclose the motives of men's hearts; and then each man's praise will come to him from God (I Corinthians 4:3-5). While I have been richly blessed as a pastor, I am fully aware that anything of eternal value coming from my ministry will only be because of the One who called me, being pleased to work through me. Again, I embrace the perspective of the Apostle Paul: "Because of the grace that was given me from God...I will not presume to speak of anything except that which Christ has accomplished through me" (Romans 15:15, 18).

CHAPTER ELEVEN

When the Lord Surprised Us with New Ministries – Coming Off the Bench

"They will still yield fruit in old age; they will be full of sap, and very green." Psalm 92:14

While Linda and I had experienced several new beginnings throughout our marriage, transitioning into the season called *retirement* brought a unique sense of uncertainty. I was completely at peace about stepping aside as the pastor at LifePoint after 24 years, and over flowing with gratitude for how the Lord brought Jym Gregory and his family to LifePoint, and especially thankful for our smooth transition. My belief was that the church would thrive, and that Pastor Jym and I would continue to grow in our friendship. Though I could not yet see what the Lord had next, *retirement from the ministry* was not part of my thinking.

One of my immediate concerns was Brenda Harbert, who had served as my faithful secretary for ten years, but was in the final stages of aggressive breast cancer. She had been unable to work for some time, and had been in and out of the hospital as her doctors sought to prolong her life and manage her pain. During the years we served together, Brenda and I were not only co-workers but friends, and she often told me that I was her pastor, even though she and her husband, Bill, were members of CCG. Each time she was in the hospital, I went to visit, and we had edifying conversations about God's love and grace, and the future that awaited her in heaven. We always concluded with prayer, affirming that our lives were in His hands. After Brenda left the hospital, we were emailing each day, and she would share Bible verses the Lord was using to give her encouragement. One day the emails stopped, and I sensed the end was near. When we went to church that Sunday, my heart was heavy, and I voiced my concern to Linda. Just as we arrived home, Brenda's sister called and asked me to come. When I entered the room where her family had gathered around her bed, her husband, Bill said

"Brenda, Tom's here!" Her head began to move and her eyes attempted to focus on where I was, but suddenly she stopped moving,

and she was gone. *"To be absent from the body, is to be at home with the Lord"* (II Corinthians 5:8). Her sister informed me that a few minutes earlier, Brenda had whispered to her, *"I can already hear the angels singing!"*

Brenda Harbert

Brenda's memorial service was at CCG, but I had a significant part as Brenda had requested. She had responded to God's call in her teens, had sought to serve Him throughout her life, and was now in the presence of the One who redeemed her. Saying goodbye to friends and loved ones is never easy, but when they are believers, we know we will soon see them again.

Around this same time my sister, Linda, in Kentucky, had a massive heart attack and had to be airlifted by helicopter from Harlan to a hospital in Hazard to save her life. She had always been adamant that she would never fly, but on this occasion her brief but adventuresome flight across the mountains made the difference, though bypass surgery in Lexington became necessary soon afterwards. We were able to be at the hospital with Linda, her devoted husband, Paul, and our other sister, Ella. Our mother was there as well, and we all reminisced about how she had gone through the identical procedure in the same hospital four years earlier. It was a tender time for us all, and it was a new experience to fully support my family without thinking of responsibilities waiting for me at the church.

During these weeks Linda and I were continuing to talk and pray about a move to California, and the Lord used two factors to give us peace that this was His plan. The first had occurred on New Year's Day more than two years earlier when we were in California visiting our daughters. Cheryl and James were already taking steps to move

223

from their home in Southern California to Porterville where Christy and her family had been residing for some time. After returning from viewing a home they were considering, Cheryl asked her mother and me to sit down at Christy's kitchen table, and proceeded to challenge us to prayerfully consider moving to California ourselves, once our new pastor was in place. She gave several reasons, being passionate in her appeal, and her words had remained in our thoughts. The second factor was the challenge Christy was facing in homeschooling her four children, one she expressed in varying degrees of desperation, especially to her mother. In the two years following Linda's mother's death, her desire to assist Christy became increasingly apparent, and rightly so. The move would involve leaving Scott, Wendy, Brooke, and Seth in Indianapolis, which would be difficult. We were thankful, however, that Wendy's mother and step-father lived nearby, and were regularly involved with Scott, Wendy, and the children. The most important factor, of course, was God's will, and we gradually reached a point of peace that He wanted us in California.

The next step was to put our home on the market. Because we had numerous friends who were realtors, selecting one was not an easy task. We eventually settled on Karen Rumba, whose parents had become dear friends while they were part of our church, before their departure for heaven. Karen did an excellent job, enabling us to get a top price, and the sale was done in a timely fashion. Linda remembers all the dates; she likes to say, *"We put our house on the market on June 23rd, sold it on August 23rd, moved out September 23rd, and moved into our new home in Porterville on October 19th, exactly six months after Tom's final Sunday at LifePoint, which was on April 19th!"*

While our home was on the market, we were enjoying the one week cruise the church had graciously arranged for us. It was our first, and still our only cruise, but memorable in every way. There was an abundance of delicious food, of course, but we also made new friends, enjoyed various stops along the way, especially Prince Edward Island,

and were encouraged by being able to hear Dr. David Jeremiah teach twice each day.

Once we accepted a reliable offer on our home, our plan was to drive our little Honda Civic to California to search for a new place to live. For several weeks I had been looking online and had a good understanding of the housing market in the Porterville area. The ones with tile roofs and palm trees captured my attention, for they were so characteristically California! The morning we were to leave, we awoke earlier than planned and decided to get ready and go. We always pray before departing on a trip so as we sat in the driveway at 4:30 a.m., I asked God's blessing on our journey, and then spontaneously added, *"Father, there are a number of houses we would like to see, but perhaps there is a home not yet on the market that You have been saving just for us; but either way, we trust You to provide."*

We had an enjoyable journey driving across country, making even better time than anticipated. We loved the quaint, little town of Exeter, north of Porterville, and looked at houses there the first day without any success, but our realtor had arranged for us to view and consider six homes the next day in Porterville. When we returned to Cheryl and James's home where we were staying, Christy called and said, *"Dad, you and mom need to get online and look at this house on Nancy Ave. It just came on the market today, and it looks really nice!"* As she spoke, I immediately recognized that her words were almost identical to my brief prayer in our driveway before we left Indianapolis. As we looked online we were impressed, noting that *it had a tile roof and two palm trees in the front!* The square footage was greater than we were expecting for our price range, and it also had an attractive back porch, completely covered. I called our realtor, asking if she could add it to our list. Though it was the final one we saw, we immediately loved it, and so did our daughters. Their comment was that our furniture would fit very well. While we saw the tile roof and palm trees as extra expressions of God's grace, what mattered most to us was that it be conducive to hosting our family and friends, and have room for guests who would visit. We made an offer, and by noon the next day received word that it was accepted; 2156 West Nancy Avenue would be our Porterville home!

Thankful for God's gracious provision

When people ask where we live in California, my initial response is to say that we live in the affordable, conservative section. House prices fluctuate in Porterville, of course, but when we purchased our home, the market was comparable to Indianapolis. The political landscape was also similar to Central Indiana, for those who live in our San Joaquin valley are generally much more conservative than those in the larger cities of our state.

California's Central Valley, [1] which is actually two valleys, the Sacramento to the north, and the San Joaquin to the south, is approximately 450 miles long, running from Bakersfield to Redding. It is 60 miles at its widest, between the Sierra Nevada Mountains to the east and the Coastal Ranges to the West. Our town of Porterville is approximately 50 miles north of Bakersfield, placing us in the southern part of the San Joaquin Valley. Our realtor informed us that more than 150 different varieties of fruit, nuts, and vegetables are grown here, more than half of all that are grown in the U.S. Tulare County, where we live, is also the number one dairy county in the U.S. Some of our close friends, Andy and Vikki Rynsburger, are third generation dairy farmers, and when we arrived their company was milking 2,500 cows every day. Tulare County is also the number two agricultural county in the U.S. with Fresno, our adjoining county to our north, number one. The Central Valley is the world's largest patch of Class 1 soil, the best there is.[2] The 25-degree (or so) temperature variation from day to night is the ideal growing range for plants, and the sun shines nearly 300 days a year. We are dependent, however, on the snow melt from the Sierras which flows into various reservoirs before being channeled through a network of canals to bring water to our otherwise desert-like valley. With the winters being cool, this provides an entirely different growing season for plants that cannot tolerate the summer heat.[3] When there is relatively little snowfall in the mountains, especially for successive years, our entire economy suffers. We have no snow in the valley, except on extremely rare occasions, but can easily see it in the Sierras, which is perfectly fine for us!

Demographically, the 2010 census[4] revealed a population in Porterville of approximately 55,000. Soon after we moved, our grandson, Trent, 10 at the time, said, *"Grandpa, you're going to love living here; we have absolutely no traffic!"* He was correct, and this is one of the benefits of small town living. Our home is only ten minutes from our daughters and their families, and they are also ten minutes from each other. In going to their homes, we only have to navigate one stoplight. One notable feature of the census is that nearly 62% of the people are of Hispanic or Latino origin. While many are third and fourth generation, it is common for grocery store clerks, bank tellers, and others who serve the public, to transition effortlessly between English and Spanish, depending on who they are serving. Having a wife who is fluent in Spanish has proven beneficial on numerous occasions. Soon after we moved in, our next door neighbor commented, *"We can't talk about them, for she will know what we are saying!"* The majority of those on our end of West Nancy Avenue trace their roots to Mexico, a joy to Linda and me as we share a strong affinity for the Hispanic culture. We could not be more thankful for our neighbors who have also become our friends.

Because we live close to Sequoia and Yosemite National Parks, and live only two hours from the coast, we have been able to take advantage of the beauty of California, and love sharing it with others. We have been blessed with visits from numerous friends, especially from Indiana, and I have become reasonably proficient as a tour guide, especially in Sequoia which is closest to us. But I often comment that we did not move to California because of geography, but rather, sociology - family relationships.

Even before we were fully settled into our home, Linda began going to Christy's each morning to assist her in homeschooling, and this has been the pattern since late fall of 2009. Linda is not only a gifted, experienced teacher, but a consistent, spiritual mentor worthy of imitation. It has been such a joy to see our grandchildren thrive in their homeschooling, and also develop in a balanced way, even as

Allyse and Ainsley with Linda

"Jesus increased in wisdom and stature and in favor with God and men." (Luke 2:52) Our ongoing prayer is that our eight grandchildren, along with those in future generations, will come to know the Lord and have a heart to pursue His purpose for their lives.

With Cheryl, Christy, and their families already being members at Living Word Fellowship, there was no question as to the church where we would become involved. Having attended LWF on several occasions while visiting Christy and her family, we already knew some of the people and were to some degree familiar with the ministry of the church. We were also aware that the congregation had gone through a difficult period a couple of years earlier, and understood that the people were still in the process of healing. The pastor was Ken Rollans, who was enrolled at the time in his fourth year at the Master's Seminary, located two hours to the south. Already a member of the congregation, he was asked to step in as pastor during the struggles after the previous pastor had resigned, certainly not an easy task. Though I had met Pastor Ken, I did not know him well. What I did know was that it was in my heart to do everything I could to become his friend and encourager. We were also anticipating worshiping and serving in the same church with our daughters, sons-in-law, grandchildren, and even some nieces and nephews. All this would be a new experience, especially with my not being the pastor but simply a member of the congregation.

While there were numerous unknowns as to the ministry the Lord had for us in Porterville, we did have two exciting trips on our schedule for 2010. We would travel to Cuba at the invitation of Rich Yoder, who along with his wife, Anita, came to be part of our church family two years before my *retirement* from LifePoint. Rich had already been making periodic ministry trips to Cuba for a number of years. After hearing me speak on marriage during our annual family series, he asked if Linda and I would join him and Anita, sharing some of that same teaching to Nazarene pastors and their wives in three different locations across the island, and we enthusiastically accepted.

When the time came in spring of 2010 for us to make our trip, we flew from LAX to Cancun, Mexico and from there a short flight over to Havana. After going through customs and immigration, we were met by Leonel and Caleb, two of the dedicated leaders of the Nazarene ministry in Cuba who drove us to the seminary, the site of our first retreat. Linda's Spanish is invaluable in situations such as this, and during our two weeks in Cuba she was my ears and my voice! We later met Leonel's wife, Migdalis, and Caleb's wife, Vivian, along with Yaima, the executive secretary for the denomination, also a winsome worship leader with a beautiful voice. We also met another young lady, Alysney, who would be my interpreter during our stay in Cuba. When Linda and I met her, my first words were these: *"You and I are going to get to know one another very well over the next two weeks!"* Through Alysney I would be able to open my heart to these pastoral couples, sharing the important Biblical truths about marriage, along with lessons Linda and I had learned in our journey as husband and wife.

With Rich, Anita, Leonel and Migdalis

Our theme at all three locations was Hebrews 13:4 which states, "Let marriage be held in honor among all!" Each couple was given a commemorative marker of the verse in Spanish to place in their Bibles. With Alysney's skilled assistance, I would explain marriage as God designed it before sin entered the world. We would talk about how sin destroyed the God-given intimacy of that first relationship, but how He works through His grace and by His Spirit to restore what sin destroyed. We would teach about the important place of communication, of physical intimacy, conflict resolution, and the joy of sharing life together as covenant companions. Alysney was an effective interpreter for each session, communicating not only my words, but my emotions. Linda and I came to treasure our friendship with her, one we are blessed to sustain these years later.

During our retreat, which also included lots of fun activities led by some of the young couples, I shared with these pastors (most o them near the ages of our children) that we would conclude the retreat with what would essentially be a wedding ceremony, a time when I would lead them through a renewal of their marriage vows. When that session came, I carefully explained what the marriage covenant involves, and how it is meant to be a portrayal of the committed relationship Christ has with His church. As I led them through an exchange of the vows, I was not prepared for their open and tender displays of emotion, including many tears. Later I learned the reason; most of the couples had not experienced an actual wedding or ceremony of any type; they had only obtained a document from the government, certifying that their marriage was legal.

Rich rented a large van for our adventurous journey from Havana to Holguin and then to Baracoa, with Caleb as the driver. In

Caleb and Vivian

addition to the four of us from the U.S, were Leonel, Caleb, Vivian, Yaima, and Alysney. While Cuba has experienced numerous challenges over the years, it remains a beautiful island with friendly, attractive people. Each place we stopped to eat was a delightful culinary experience, one we will always remember. The most treasured part, however, was the rich fellowship our team shared on our journey, and with faithful pastors and many in their congregations. In addition to teaching on marriage, I was given the opportunity to preach in one or more churches in all three locations. It was one of the unique ministry trips of our lives, and the good news was that we had the opportunity to repeat it in the fall.

When we returned and shared about Cuba with our church in Porterville, the Lord surprised us by opening new doors of ministry which are continuing today. Though we were unaware of this when we first moved to Porterville, Living Word Fellowship had two sister

231

churches in Mexico, one in La Mision on the Baja Peninsula, located approximately one hour south of Tijuana, and the other in the mountains of Oaxaca, south of Mexico City, among the Mixteco people. Bill Beech, one of the deacons overseeing the mission ministry of our church, approached me with the news that both Mexican churches had been requesting teaching on marriage. He asked if Linda and I would join them and present the marriage material I had shared in Cuba. Accepting Bill's invitation meant that before 2010 was over we

Bill and Bobbi Beech

would have three additional opportunities for mission involvement: a June trip to La Mision, a return trip to Cuba in September, and a November trip into the mountains of Oaxaca.

A few weeks prior to our initial trip to Cuba, Faith Baptist Church in Strathmore, just north of us, approached me to see if I could fill their pulpit periodically. Their pastor had retired at the end of 2009 and moved to Iowa to be near family. Before their move, the pastor's wife had been at a women's retreat where Linda was the speaker. Upon learning we had just moved to the area, she asked Linda if it would be okay to pass my name along to the deacons of the church. After being interviewed by two of them, I began to preach there quite often. I later determined that I was there twenty Sundays during 2010. They had Sunday morning and evening services, and the church loved to sing, especially the old songs of the faith that Linda and I knew and loved. We enjoyed the new friendships we were establishing and were thankful for this exciting opportunity. In the fall their leaders approached me about the possibility of becoming their interim pastor, and we had an interview. Before voting, they asked me to speak to their Spanish congregation which had their own pastor, Victor Ordonez. When we met with them, Linda looked at their hymnal, and said, *"This is the hymnal my mother loved, and I believe*

232

some of my dad's songs are in it." When we looked at the index, we found at least two of his songs, and we enjoyed sharing this information with the church.

The very same week the Faith Baptist leaders asked me to become their interim pastor, the elders at Living Word Fellowship asked if I would come and meet with them. Their reason was to invite me to come on staff part-time to assist Pastor Ken in the ministry. As much as we had grown to love the people at Faith Baptist, as Linda and I discussed and prayed about the opportunities before us, we knew that LWF was our church, and where we would be long-term. Especially appealing was that I would be in a position to do what the Lord had put in my heart even before we moved to Porterville, and that was, as an older pastor, to be an encouragement to Pastor Ken. I had no other goal than to be his friend, his partner in ministry, and help him become all that God intended him to be. On a considerably smaller scale, I saw my role as similar to that of John the Baptist when he said of Jesus, "He must increase; I must decrease." (John 3:30) My days of being a senior pastor were deeply rewarding, but they were behind me. Now it was time for me *"to come off the bench!"* as a newer member of the church recently put it. In terms of ministry involvement, this is what I have been doing: preaching when called upon, averaging 12 to 15 times each year, leading worship, teaching adult Sunday school, coordinating our Shepherding Groups, and leading one myself, meeting and counseling with various people, including pre-marital counseling and officiating at weddings. I am asked occasionally to speak at funerals, and am regularly involved in our missions ministry, not only teaching on all the trips, but helping Bill Beech and his wife, Bobbi, through my hobby of photography, seeking to better communicate what our ministry in Mexico is all about. I am also blessed to be one of the elders; one of my great joys is serving alongside these dedicated men who deeply love our church. Pastor Ken and the elders have also given me the freedom to fill in at various churches in the area when I am asked to preach. Their belief is that this is a way of supporting the larger body of Christ in our valley. It has been a rich blessing to me and to Linda, for it has given us the opportunity to become acquainted with other believers in and around Porterville. It is rare for us to go out to eat or to the grocery without running into someone we know.   *Retirement* from the ministry is apparently not what the Lord had in mind!

Our first trip to La Mision, a drive of approximately eight hours, was in June of 2010. The pattern of our church is to go for a long weekend. My role is to preach on Friday and Saturday nights, and again on Sunday morning.   During the services, the children are dismissed to attend VBS type classes and activities, where Linda's fluency in Spanish and passion for teaching children is put to good use. There is an additional children's teaching opportunity on Saturday morning, as well as a gathering for ladies where one of the women from our church provides the teaching. Our church also provides snacks and/or a light meal for the church after each service, giving the people a reason to stay afterwards to visit with our group.   Until recently, this was organized by Bill Stevenson, another of our deacons in missions before he and his wife moved out of the area. He is always assisted by members of our team from LWF, primarily our teens.

In our initial trip, the people in the church were responsive to the teaching on marriage, and it was a fruitful time. One of the most enthusiastic couples, however, said to us after the final session, *"By the way, we are not married, but after hearing this teaching, we plan to be married soon."*   Pastor Tomas informed me during our trip a year later that they and three other couples in the church had married during that year, and their obedience to God's Word had become a positive example to the others in the church. He also explained that he had never heard any teaching on marriage in the church, and went on to say how pleased he was that his church could hear these life-changing truths from God's Word.

It was a delight to meet and work alongside Pastor Tomas and his lovely wife, Agustina. In the months prior to our initial visit, their youngest daughter, Melisa, age 5, had died, and their sorrow was still very apparent. All three children had chickenpox, but Melisa was not getting better, so they took her to a different doctor who mistakenly gave her the wrong medication. They have an older daughter, Elizabeth, and a son, Marcos, who has Down syndrome, and both are always a delight to our group.

Pastor Tomas and Agustina

Having now experienced more than ten trips to La Mision, we have come to dearly love Pastor Tomas and Agustina, and have high regard for the growing ministry the Lord has given to them. In 2016 our church provided the funds and much of the physical labor to build their family a much needed home. We also recently purchased a more reliable vehicle for Pastor Tomas, one he uses to transport people to and from the church each time they gather. A great joy for Linda and me is that three of our grandchildren, Lauren, Trent, and Ainsley, have experienced multiple trips to La Mision, and their lives have been deeply impacted.

Our return trip to Cuba in September of 2010 was equal to the first, except this time we were not going to strangers, but to couples we had grown to love. Several were eager to share with us the positive changes in their marriages, and it was deeply encouraging to hear their stories. We followed the identical schedule as before, with meetings in three locations. This time, however, they asked me, as an older pastor, to address specific areas of concern to them in their ministries. They wanted the answers to come from God's Word and my own experience. Interestingly, and the most demanding topic for me, was material wealth. While they had very little, they nevertheless wanted me to speak to this area. As I prayed and agonized over what I could say that would be instructive and encouraging, the answer came as I was having my daily quiet time in the book of Revelation. Jesus' message to the persecuted church of Smyrna seemed to leap off the page, "I know your tribulation and poverty, but you are rich." (Revelation 2:9) It was a joy to assure these dedicated but vulnerable pastors that Jesus fully understood the unique challenges they were facing just as surely as He knew about the church in Smyrna. It was

With Pastor Idel in Havana, and Alysney, my skilled interpreter

such an encouragement for them to see that in spite of their limited resources, because of Jesus, *they were rich!* As I look back on that trip, the area I felt least qualified to address was the one that seemed to minister to them the most; but that is how God works by His Word when we cry out to Him. We will never forget our two visits to Cuba, the brothers and sisters who are faithfully serving the Lord, and how God is blessing His church on that lovely island. We are also deeply thankful for the vital ministry God has given to Rich and Anita Yoder Through Facebook we are able to be in touch with numerous Cuban friends. Sadly, at least four of them were among the 20 pastors who were killed in the plane crash in Havana in May of 2018. While the church in Cuba needs our prayers, the ministry there is thriving!

Soon after our return from Cuba, it was time for our first trip to the mountains of Oaxaca in Southern Mexico, to the church among the Mixtec people. The founding pastor, Tiburcio, had a captivating conversion story, one I love to share with others. As a young husband and father, he was working in the farm labor camps of Northern Mexico. He and his wife, Josefina, had two daughters and a young son named Esteban. Theirs was a difficult life because of the poverty, but made even worse because of Tiburcio's drinking problem. While they were surviving, there was not a lot of joy in this poor Mexican family. One day Esteban heard of a Bible club for children in the labor camp, and he began to attend. Upon hearing the good news of the Gospel,

Tiburcio

the Holy Spirit opened his heart, and Esteban eagerly responded. Though he was only eight years old, his young life began to change, and he excitedly told his family about Jesus. Not long afterward, however, as a result of playing in unclean water, Esteban became extremely ill, and was diagnosed with hepatitis. Nothing could be done to make him well, and he and his family learned that he was going to die. A few days later, while speaking with his father, Esteban said, *"Papa, I'm going to have to say goodbye because you are not a Christian. If you knew Jesus, then I would say, 'I'll see you later,' but since you don't know Him, I'm going to have to say goodbye."* Not long afterward, Esteban died and went to be with Jesus; his words to his father, however, lived on, and they were used by the Holy Spirit to bring Tiburcio to faith in Christ.

It was not long before Tiburcio's wife and daughters were also saved. Even though he was far from home, Tiburcio's heart began to turn to his family in the mountains of Oaxaca. Tony Heredia, a missionary with Christians in Action, the man who had organized the Bible club where Esteban became a Christian, began to disciple

Tiburcio, and the two of them made the long, arduous journey by truck to the little Mixtec village of Yososcua, or San Pedro, as it is known in Spanish. That trip resulted in Tiburcio sensing God's call to return home to share the gospel with His people, and a church was soon established in their small adobe home.

Our church, Living Word Fellowship, learned about Tiburcio's ministry through Tony Heredia, affectionately known as *Brother Tony*, who resides just north of us. Bill Beech, with no experience of traveling in Mexico, made an exploratory trip with Brother Tony and two men from Alaska in January of 1996. The hope was that our church could come alongside Tiburcio's ministry and help provide a building for the new Mixtec church. At first Pastor Tiburcio was reluctant, concerned that we might begin a work but fail to see it through to completion. In time, however, Bill was able to convince him that our church was serious, and a lasting partnership was formed. Numerous men and a few women from LWF gave their vacation time to travel and help with the initial church building. In the years that followed, a two story building was added, along with a helpful expansion to Tiburcio and Josefina's home. Our church provided the finances and much of the labor, with the Mixtec people joining in. The second structure included a simple kitchen, meeting rooms, bathrooms, and two rooms upstairs where bunk beds could be placed. Whereas our earlier groups slept in tents and on the floor of the church, during our trip in 2010, and in subsequent ones that followed, we have slept in bunk beds upstairs, not having to *rough it* nearly as much as the deeply dedicated ones did in the beginning.

Getting to the small village of San Pedro requires considerable time and stamina. The journey from Porterville to the town of Tlaxiaco in the state of Oaxaca where we spend the night requires an overnight flight to Mexico City, an hour long flight to the city of Oaxaca, and two always adventurous rides in large taxis for three to four hours. Our hotel on the city square in Tlaxiaco is always a welcome oasis for our weary group. The tasty meals are attractively presented, the servers delightful, and the beds inviting! Across from

238

the hotel is a colorful, open air market where we shop the next morning, purchasing food for our week in the mountains. Linda's fluency in Spanish has enabled us to establish friendships in the market, and it is a delight to see some we know each trip we make. A group from the church comes to meet us in trucks or a van, depending on the size of our group, and they typically arrive in time to join us for breakfast. Once the food has been purchased, we begin the two hour trip over rough roads but scenic terrain to the church in picturesque San Pedro, our home for the week.

With three Mixtec boys

During our first trip, God worked to establish a bond with the Mixtec believers, enabling us to enter into an enduring friendship. My teaching on marriage was for three nights, with Brother Tony as my interpreter. Even though this was the first time the church had heard teaching on marriage, there was an enthusiastic response. Because of Brother Tony's history with the people, their pattern is to wait until he comes to have baby dedications, baptisms, and weddings. On our first trip there were no weddings, but we were fascinated with the dedications and how the parents dress their children to the hilt in beautiful white outfits. Friends and family from outside the church also view this as a major event, and come to give their blessing. The baptisms of teens and adults in a small outdoor baptistry in front of the church was a high moment, as it is in any culture when believers celebrate their new life in Christ.

Prior to our trip, we received the news that Pastor Tiburcio had an aggressive form of cancer and was undergoing treatments. The highlight of our initial trip was a special afternoon service to dedicate the new two-story building. Though he was weak, Pastor Tiburcio gave the entire history of his conversion, his call to return to his own people, and the work God had done over the years. The church was overflowing, with numerous people standing outside. Among the guests were some from the Trique tribe from the other side of the mountain, whose women are known for their bright red attire, a striking contrast to the more subdued black and gray rebozos worn by the older Mixtec women. Pastor Tiburcio first shared his message in Spanish with Brother Tony interpreting for us as English speaking guests. He gave the same message again in the Mixtec language so the older people who do not speak Spanish could hear it as well. Pastor Tiburcio was exhausted afterwards, but it was a service our team will never forget. Before leaving early the next morning for treatment in Mexico City, Pastor Tiburcio was deeply emotional in expressing his thanks for my teaching on marriage, indicating how much his people needed it. He also voiced his sincere hope that Linda and I would return and provide additional teaching from God's Word,

and this is what we are continuing to do. In the providence of God, that would be the last time any of us from LWF would see Tiburcio, for his death came the following February. God's purpose for him in his generation was complete, and a thriving congregation is the result. Two faithful elders, Faustino and Enrique, now give leadership to the church. Before coming to Christ, they were known as two of the

Faustino, Josefina, and Enrique

meanest men in the area. Some younger men are also assisting in the leadership, and Pastor Tiburcio's widow, Josefina, along with a daughter, Blanca, and a son, Josue, are also faithfully involved. Like the Ketengban tribe in Indonesia, people from the Mixtec tribe in the mountains of Oaxaca will be included in that group described in the song of Revelation: "Worthy are You to take the book and to break its seals; for You were slain, and purchased for God with Your blood men from every tribe and tongue and people and nation" (Revelation 5:9).

Since our move in 2009, we have been able to return to Indianapolis at least once each year to visit family and friends. With Scott and his family not quite having space for us, we have a standing arrangement to stay with Gary and Sandy Creed, members of the church who are exactly our age. While we have appreciated their friendship since they first came to the church, their gracious hospitality each time we return has given us the opportunity to share more of our lives together, and this has brought us even closer. The Creeds came and spent a week with us in February several years back, and we made more wonderful memories together.

An unexpected trip became necessary in January of 2012 when my beloved mother went home to be with the Lord. Her granddaughter, Faith, thankfully, was with her, and after 90 years, 2 months, and 28 days, it was God's time. "In Your book were all written the days that were ordained for me, when as yet there was none of them." (Psalm 139:16) My mother and I had enjoyed a tender conversation just hours before she died, and while the news was difficult, the Lord gave me peace about her death. Even though it was Super Bowl weekend in Indianapolis, it nevertheless worked best for us to fly there, and a friend graciously made a car available for our drive to Harlan, Kentucky. Cheryl was able to join us, while Christy felt sorrowful that she was unable to leave at that time. Through his bereavement leave with Amtrak, Scott was able to join us in Harlan for what was a warm and unforgettable family gathering.

Memories of my mother flooded my mind in the hours and days that followed, far more than there is space to record. She was born and raised on Sugar Run near Jonesville, in Lee County, Virginia. We were able to take her there on her 89th birthday, a day we loved as Mom shared many treasured memories from her early years. She was the oldest of six children born to Henry and Flossie Pendleton, though one of her sisters died at a young age. My mother loved her parents, especially her daddy, but was not as close to her mother, who kept her home from the school she dearly loved after the 6th grade to help with her younger siblings. When my mother was in her early teens, her

241

father acquired a job with the L & N railroad, which required a move from Sugar Run to Baxter, Kentucky, another state, but only 40 miles away. My mother lived with her family in *a section house* provided for employees of the railroad. As I mentioned in an earlier chapter, it was here that she met the man who would become my father, the milkman who delivered milk each day to the Pendleton home.

A rare photo of Ella, David, Linda and me together

As their first born, I was blessed to enjoy my mother for 7 decades. When the Lord called her home, I recalled the words of the Psalmist: "For You formed my inward parts; You wove me in my mother's womb" (Psalm 139:13). My mother was intensely loyal to her children and grandchildren, but also to my dad, even though it was difficult at times due to his battle with alcohol. Though she was not a believer when I came to faith in Christ, she was nevertheless fully supportive of my new faith. She was saved just over a year later, two weeks after my dad, and they were baptized together in the Poor Fork River. My mother was always gracious and hospitable toward my friends, and many of them have affirmed over the years how kind and courteous she was. When Linda came home with me the first time my mother loved and accepted her, and I am so grateful for the affectionate relationship they shared. My mother's deepest grie came when my brother, David, died at the age of sixteen. She often said that if she made it through that, she could endure anything. She was able to continue on by receiving God's comfort and trusting in His plan, even when she could not understand.

While my sisters and I assisted her from time to time when she had special needs, my mother lived simply. She was deeply thankful for my father's modest Social Security check she received in the years following his death in 1979. Though she lived as a widow for 33 years, Mom was content and grateful. It was always difficult to know what to get her for Christmas or other special occasions, but on her 85th birthday I asked Cheryl, Scott, and Christy to write a letter to their grandmother, expressing what they remembered and appreciated about her; Linda and I did the same, and we gave them to her in an attractive folder. While each letter was unique, a common theme was how we all looked forward to Grannie's cooking, an area where

I was blessed to enjoy my mother for 70 years!

she excelled. All three mentioned how she always remembered their birthdays, faithfully sending a card. In my reflections I also recalled her initial resistance when I spoke of the possibility of being a missionary, but then saw her attitude change. When I asked her about it, her response was this: *"I realized that my attitude was wrong, for I know in my heart that you don't belong to me anymore; you belong to the Lord."*

Our family loved the two occasions when she flew to visit us in Texas, a special treat for her, and for us! After we moved to Indiana, we were able to see her more frequently. I loved driving the five hours to Baxter, being able to have a leisurely visit over dinner, and then share Mom's breakfast, one unlike any other. Our daughter Christy often joined me while she and her husband Scott were still living in Indiana, also bringing Ashlyn and Trent when they were very young. When Mom was no longer strong enough to prepare something for us to eat, except a blackberry cobbler that seemed to miraculously appear, I would stop and pick up something for us along the way. In her later years I introduced her to Mexican food, my favorite, and was pleased at how she learned to enjoy it, and even prefer it on those occasions when we would go out to eat in Harlan.

In addition to her numerous photo albums we all loved, in later years my mom kept pulling out boxes with old report cards, clippings from my Little League days, cards from old girl friends, and letters I had written to her and Dad when I was in college. On her 90th birthday, less than three months before she died, I put together a photo book of her life, including some pictures she had never seen that I was graciously given by my cousin, Stephen Pendleton, which he had printed from old negatives in our grandfather's dark room. She was so excited about it and called it *"a book of my entire life!"* She looked at it again and again during her final weeks, and her joy brought me great delight as well. Like Linda's mother, my Mom also prayed for us faithfully. One time she said to me, *"Sometimes I don' know if my old prayers do any good or not, but I keep on praying!"* assured her that they did, and that only eternity will reveal the ful impact of how God sovereignly works through the prayers of His people to accomplish His purpose in our lives.

In the years before my mother died, we agreed that if I were still living, I would speak at her memorial service, and for some time I knew the approach I would take. On my mother's refrigerator were a number of "Thoughts for the Day" she had carefully clipped from the *Harlan Daily Enterprise*. In addition to each brief thought was a corresponding Bible verse. When I asked her about them, she explained that while she read them every day, she only cut out the ones that especially encouraged her or challenged her to grow stronger in the quality being described. She went on to say, *"Some people may think it's silly, but I enjoy doing it!"* She said she had some others, but had not felt strong enough to put them up. Linda volunteered to do it for her, so they too could be on the refrigerator. After the new ones were in place, I took a picture so I would have them when the time came for her memorial service; now that moment had arrived.

As I reflected on these concise but profound Biblical truths she had painstakingly clipped from the Harlan newspaper, when viewed all together, I was impressed with how they painted a compelling portrait of my mother's faith and what she had come to value most. As I organized them in preparation for her service, the themes easily emerged: God's protection, God's faithfulness, God's sovereignty, and God's plan for our lives. Included under God's plan were these truths: to serve others, to be content, to not complain, to rely on God's strength as we grow older, to forgive others, to have the right attitude toward your family, to accept God's gift of salvation, to always show love, and to trust God's timing in bringing us to heaven. I found great joy in talking about my mother and her simple but genuine faith with our family, and numerous Harlan County friends who came to express their love and support. God worked by His Spirit and through His Word to give us closure to a 90 year life well- lived, that of my devoted mother, Eula Pendleton Madon.

With Ava and Howard, two lifelong Baxter friends who dearly loved our family

Among the many friends who came to Mom's service was Peggy Bianchi Byrd, a long time Baxter friend of our family. She and I talked about how great it would be if we could have a *Baxter reunion.* Peggy then said, *"If you will tell me when you can come, since you live the farthest away, I'll organize it!"* That brief conversation sparked the first of three memorable reunions of dear friends who trace their roots back to our unique and beloved Appalachian community!

One of our memorable highlights of 2013 was our golden wedding anniversary, planned by Cheryl, Scott, and Christy. They invited everyone in the church, friends from Faith Baptist, our neighbors, and others we knew in the area. Jim and Kelly Hanson, friends from the time our church began in Indiana in 1985, also came. As we met at LWF on a Friday evening, Cheryl, Scott, and Christy all gave tributes, as did our eight grandchildren. They also prepared a slide presentation with music which spoke of the heritage we pass on to future generations. While Linda grew up with a strong Christian legacy, I am a first generation Christian. When the Lord called me to Himself as a 16-year old, I could not have fathomed the extraordinary plan He had for me as a pastor, but especially with regard to His blessing on my family, and much of this was highlighted by our children on our 50th anniversary.

With Wendy, Brooke, Seth, and Ainsley at our 50th anniversary

In March of 2014, we were able to fulfil a dream that had been in my heart for several years, and that was for Linda to return to Medellin, Colombia, where she spent the first thirteen years of her life with her missionary parents. Having heard all her favorite memories from those years, I longed for Linda to walk again on the grounds of the missionary compound she so loved as a child. The occasion that made this a reality was an invitation to attend the 70th anniversary of the Biblical Seminary of Colombia, cofounded by Linda's father, Bill Gillam, and Ben Pearson. Their vision was that the institution would be utilized by the larger body of Christ for the training of pastors throughout Latin America, and this had become a reality. Several others from the U.S were also invited, so we were part of a delegation of approximately fifteen who attended. Linda's sister, Judy, was there as well, along with at least ten other adults who had grown up as missionary children on the seminary compound. While there we were blessed to worship in the *Amador Church* where Linda's father once served as pastor, and meet various people in what was now a thriving congregation. Another joy was witnessing a unique and fruitful soccer ministry led by Mark Wittig, a Medellin missionary Linda often babysat when he was only one to two years old.

When Linda left Medellin for the U.S. in 1956, the population was approximately 400,000, but by the time we made our trip in 2014, the greater metropolitan area of Medellin was rapidly approaching 4 million. The missionary compound Linda remembered as rural was now surrounded by high rise apartments in the center of urban activity. Once we were on the grounds, however, it was familiar to her, including the houses where she had lived, and the places where she and her friends played as children. I loved hearing her memories and was thankful that she could share it with her sister and others from her youth, but especially grateful that I could enjoy it with her.

With dear friends and Colombia missionaries, Howard and Jan Biddulph

Linda's boast of Medellin was of the perfect climate, due to it being on the equator, but with a mile-high elevation. This makes for year round temperatures in the 70's, with beautiful orchids, colorful bougainvillea, and other gorgeous flowers blooming continually While the temperatures were slightly warmer than she recalled, due to Medellin's urbanization, she was correct about the flowers. Medellin also has one of the most efficient transit systems in the world, one we utilized to explore various parts of this uniquely beautiful city. While Medellin was known in previous years as one of the most violent and dangerous metropolitan areas in the world, it now has reduced crime and poverty, and is considered one of the safest cities in the world.

Lauren and Seth's wedding

Another unforgettable event occurred in January of 2015 as our oldest granddaughter, Lauren, was married to Seth Bowser. When they asked me to officiate at the wedding ceremony, I considered it one of the great honors of my life. The site of the wedding was the Porterville Congregational Church which was constructed in 1909, a building listed in the National Register of Historic Places. The dark wood throughout the sanctuary, the beautiful stained glass windows, and a massive pipe organ skillfully played as Lauren walked down the aisle, made for a lovely, extraordinary wedding. Both Lauren and Seth have a heart to experience God's best, and it is a joy to be involved in their lives, and part of the same church family. The Lord has now blessed them with Brielle, who was born on February 13, 2018. Lauren typically brings her to our home one afternoon each week while she goes grocery shopping. One day she said to us, *"When I was little, I was only able to see you a couple of times each year because we lived so far away. Because Seth and I live close by, we want Brielle to be a regular part of your lives!"* No objections on our part; only deep gratitude and delight!

While Linda and I have been blessed with numerous opportunities to serve in missions, our continuing ministry is in the church, seeking to work in a complimentary way alongside Pastor Ken and his wife, Krista. Their story is one I love to tell because it is all about grace. Pastor Ken did not come to know Christ until he was 33 years old. I jokingly remind him that Jesus was finished by that age, while Ken was just getting started! Like his father before him, Ken was in the restaurant business. He owned *The Olive Tree* in Lindsay, about ten miles north of Porterville on Highway 65, considered the gateway to the Sequoias. Many in the area remember him from his non-Christian days. Krista came to faith in Christ approximately two years before Ken when their three daughters were small, and she and the girls began attending Living Word Fellowship. Ken sometimes comments on how he would drive through the parking lot wondering what all those crazy people were doing inside.

His estimate is that well over a dozen people shared the gospel with him before his conversion. He was even the vice president of Fellowship of Christian Athletes at Fresno State - before he was even a Christian. Krista often says that *Ken majored in baseball,* and he was an excellent college player. But he is also a good all-around athlete, and enjoys coaching and encouraging others, whatever the sport. Ken and I play golf together periodically, and he has helped me with my *old man's swing,* determining the type of shaft that works best for me. He can hit a golf ball 300 yards; I tell people that he has all the

Golfing with Ken

shots, and he does; the only problem is he doesn't hit them all the time! After fighting for years against God's call to salvation, his prayer of surrender was simply, *"I give up!"*

Several years ago I heard a missionary say, *"Jesus said, 'Follow Me!' but He did not say where He was going."* When Ken came to faith in Christ, and Krista two years earlier, they had no way of knowing that following Jesus would mean becoming the pastor and pastor's wife at LWF, but this is where the journey has led. Various men and women in the church helped Ken and Krista grow in their faith. Following Jesus in the beginning involved leading worship in the church, working with the youth, and serving others. Two men in particular, Craig Bowser and Dennis Spuhler, sensed that God was likely calling Ken to be a pastor, and mentioned the idea. Ken eventually applied to the Master's Seminary with no assurance that he would be accepted. While he had been a student at Fresno State, he had not graduated. While a college degree was desired, the acceptance policy of the seminary was such that they would admit a small group each year without degrees if they discerned that God had truly called that person to the ministry. After an extensive interview, Ken was accepted and began the journey toward his degree. Because of being asked to step into the role of pastor when the church had an unexpected need, it would be eight years before Ken would complete the seminary requirements for graduation.

When the day arrived, it marked a great achievement for both Ken and Krista; not only had he persevered in his studies, she had typed countless papers and assisted in numerous other ways. Ken's precious mother and others in the family also rejoiced, as did everyone who had prayed for him and witnessed his hard work and perseverance. His graduation was held at Grace Community Church with Dr.

Pastor Ken and Krista

John MacArthur giving the commencement address; many of us from the church were present to celebrate God's grace and faithfulness to Pastor Ken and Krista!

The elders at LWF had been waiting for Ken to receive his degree before he was formally ordained. As the *elder statesman* at the church, it became my honor to preach when he was ordained some weeks later. In addition to addressing his high calling as a pastor, one of the points I enjoyed making came from the words of the Apostle Paul when he made his defense before Festus, the procurator of Judea, with King Agrippa also present. Festus said to Paul, "You are out of your mind! Your much learning is driving you mad!" Paul's response was this: "I am not out of my mind, most excellent Festus, but I utter words of sober truth. For the king knows about these matters, and I speak to him also with confidence, since I am persuaded that none of these things escape his notice, for this has not been done in a corner!" (Acts 26:25-26) Even as the transformation of Saul of Tarsus into Paul, the Apostle, was *not done in a corner*, such was the conversion of Ken Rollans! Many in our part of the county had witnessed the amazing transformation that occurred in Ken, and in Krista; it had not taken place in some obscure corner, but was common knowledge to countless people in our area.

While I love telling Ken's story to people who ask me about our church, one of my favorite parts relates to his wife, Krista, who had no inkling that following Jesus meant that she would one day be a pastor's wife. Even on the day of Ken's ordination, she was still refreshingly honest about her struggles, questioning if she had what it takes to be a pastor's wife. One of the amazing facts about God, however, is that *He does not call those who are already equipped; rather, He equips those He calls!* This is what God has done with Krista; through God's transforming grace, she now joyfully embraces her role as pastor's wife, and does it with excellence!

As I write these words, Pastor Ken is preaching through Paul's epistle to the Romans, the New Testament book that gives the fullest treatment of the Gospel. In his introductory remarks, Paul writes: " I am not ashamed of the Gospel of Christ, for it is the power of God unto salvation to everyone who believes, to the Jew first and also to the Greek" (Romans 1:16). While Pastor Ken was expounding those words, I thanked God that He has blessed us to serve in a church that not only faithfully preaches the Gospel, but one where the pastor and his wife are living testimonies of its transforming power!

Family photo the week of our 50th wedding anniversary

With our two great grandchildren, Ian and Brielle

CHAPTER TWELVE

When the New Chapter Begins that No One on Earth has Read; Going Home

"With a long life I will satisfy him, and let him behold My salvation."
Psalm 91:16

For several years I have jokingly commented that my definition of *old* is always changing; it is just beyond whatever my age happens to be at the time. That lighthearted way of thinking works for a while, but reality eventually sets in, and each one of us has to adjust to what is not going to adjust to us – we are *old!* Linda's father was only 57 when the Lord called him home; my father lived a little longer but only to the age of 62. As I write these words, I have just celebrated my 77th birthday. In comparison to these two significant men in my life, or by any standard of calculation, I now qualify as *old!* For purposes known only to Him, God has kept me here, and I am grateful and immeasurably blessed!

My longevity is certainly not linked to perfect health, or because I have always taken great care of myself; the overarching reason is that God's sovereign purpose for me is not yet complete. There have definitely been health challenges along the way. More than 25 years ago during a physical, my doctor discovered a melanoma on my back, which was soon successfully excised. On two other occasions since our move to California, additional melanomas were discovered, but again they were surgically removed with no further problems. In January of 2017 I was also diagnosed with prostate cancer; my urologist is carefully monitoring it and determining the most appropriate treatment plan for me. In March of 2018 on my way to a knee replacement, a stress test pointed to some irregularities with my heart. The angiogram a few days later revealed 99% blockage in the two main arteries, but amazingly, I had no symptoms. My doctor friend in Indiana, Gary Creed, asked if I were in denial, and may have been, though unknowingly. While my energy level was not the same as it had been ten years earlier, not having been 76 before, I was not sure how much energy an *old man* should expect! Thankfully, my blockage was such that it could be stented, and my cardiologist chose to do that in stages, inserting two stents on March 14, and two additional ones on March 30. On both occasions I spent one night in the hospital, my only overnight stays since hernia surgery in the summer of 1960. While I hope to have my knee replaced at some point, I am still able to hike a mile or more when we go to Sequoia, or on other outings. I also seek to go to the gym four days a week, riding a bicycle five miles in thirty minutes, and working out on other equipment. All things considered, I am doing remarkably well with few limitations.

One of the benefits of aging, and the inevitable health challenges that capture our attention along the way, is an enlarged ability to reflect, especially to look back and appreciate the panorama of God's sovereign design. For a number of years I have loved and identified with God's words in Psalm 91:16: "With a long life I will satisfy him, and let him behold My salvation." To behold involves more than a casual glance; it means to look and reflect deeply on what one is *beholding*. Noah Webster's American Dictionary of the English Language[1] published in 1828, provides this definition: *To fix the eyes upon; to see with attention; to observe with care.* In my later years, I am better able to *behold, to observe with care, and to reflect deeply* on the larger picture of God's salvation in my life, and am greatly encouraged that there is infinitely more still to come.

A comment I have been making for several years is that *the Gospel is far better news than I first thought!* The Gospel itself has not changed, of course, but my appreciation for *God's good news* has certainly increased. This is largely due to having a much greater understanding of Scripture; it also comes from having more years to reflect on God's faithful, ongoing work in my life. I now see that when God called me to Himself by His grace at the age of 16, He was setting in motion countless blessings and benefits I knew nothing about at the time.

One occasion when this came into sharper focus was when Monalta Duffin, one of our loyal friends and a teacher at Strathmore High School, asked me to speak at a baccalaureate service. In addressing this hopeful group of young graduates, including some from our church, I explained that when I was their age, I had already been a Christian for two years. While I was genuinely excited about my faith, there was no way I could have ever imagined as a high school graduate, even in my wildest dreams, the rich future God had for me.

My biblical text for that afternoon gathering was this: "I thank my God always concerning you for the grace of God that was given you in Christ Jesus, that in everything you are enriched in Him..." (I Corinthians 1:4-5) It was only in the years to come that I would see every single area of my life enriched. God would give me a loyal, godly wife, children who are seeking to follow the Lord, each one loving us and showing us honor and respect. We are also blessed with eight grandchildren, and our first two great grandchildren. God would give to Linda and me a ministry that has now spanned six decades, a ministry He would richly bless, giving us friendships with brothers and sisters in Christ in several places around the world where we have been blessed to serve. Through His grace He would also set in motion a spiritual legacy that will impact future generations, as Psalm 78 describes: "that the generation to come might know, even the children yet to be born, that they might arise and tell them to their children, that they should put their confidence in God and not forget the work of His hands" (Psalm 78:8-9). Some of this Linda and I are already blessed to see, but God's Word assures us that the ministry He began in and through us will continue long after He calls us home to be with Him! Ours has been and continues to be, just as the Apostle Paul expressed, *an enriched life because of grace!*

In the fall of 2017, Bible believing Christians around the world celebrated the 500th anniversary of Martin Luther.[2] It was on October 31st in 1517, that Martin Luther courageously nailed his 95 theses to the church doors in Wittenberg, Germany. Luther's bold action that day was to call out destructive errors of the Roman Catholic Church, and stimulate discussion in pursuit of the truth. His intent as a monk was more along the lines of restoration and recovery in the church, and not the sweeping reformation that would result. Through it, however, the entire Western world was taken by storm as the light of authentic Christianity began to again shine brightly, having been taken back to its biblical roots. Church historians consider the Protestant Reformation of the 16th century to be the greatest event in the history of the Christian church since the Day of Pentecost.[3]

In the months leading up to Reformation Sunday, I taught two preliminary Sunday school lessons to our adults, one about Martin Luther, and another on the *five solas of the Reformation*.[4] In the fall, Pastor Ken gave me the opportunity to preach about the significance of that historic event, and I was grateful. My title that day was *Celebrating Five Non-negotiable Truths of the Gospel*. After the message a close friend, David Henderson, came up and said, *"You've been working on that sermon since the beginning of your Christian life, haven't you?"* Though I had not thought of it in those terms, I saw that David was accurate in his assessment. Sheryl Clifton, another friend who was not in church that day but listened to the sermon online the next week, called to make a similar comment, saying that my passion for these five, life-changing truths came through even though she was not present.

Sola is the Latin word which means *only or alone*. The *five solas* are five theological propositions, all interrelated, interconnected truths.[5] They are: *Sola Scriptura, Sola Gratia, Sola Fide, Sola Christus, and Sola Deo Gloria*. One simple sentence expresses their meaning and significance: *it is in Scripture alone where we learn that we are saved by grace alone, through faith alone, in Christ alone, to the glory of God alone*. While these *solas* were correctives to the errors and distortions of the Roman Catholic Church at that time, they continue to stand as nonnegotiable, unified biblical truths which capture the very essence of the Gospel.

In the 62nd of his 95 theses, Martin Luther makes this profound statement, *"The true treasure of the church is the Holy Gospel of the glory and grace of God."*[6] Luther was implying that other things, inferior objects and practices, had replaced the *glory and grace of the Gospel.* Through his diligent study of Scripture, Luther discovered the unchangeable truth of the Gospel of the Grace of God, and it is in the pages of God's Word where we find it as well.

While I had studied Martin Luther in seminary and read other articles and books about him in the years since, as I prepared my sermon for the 500th anniversary of the Reformation in this *reflective autumn season of life,* I came to see that God had been working over the years to deepen my personal convictions in each of the *five solas.*

As to the first *sola*, the one which affirms that Scripture is the final authority in all spiritual matters, this was never a serious issue for me. From the beginning of my Christian life, God gave me a genuine love and respect for His Word. While I know others who have struggled in this area, I never faced any serious questions about the truthfulness of Scripture, and whether or not the Bible was the Word of God.

Because of my love for God's Word, a daily quiet time has been my primary spiritual discipline for the majority of my Christian life. In the early years, I set aside time in the evening, being more of a night person. As the years passed, I moved it to the first thing I do each morning. Here is how I have come to define it: *a quiet time is a time deliberately set aside on a daily basis for the purpose of cultivating my relationship with God. It includes time in His Word for Him to speak to me, and time in prayer for me to speak to Him.* While I have a both a college and seminary degree, and have attended countless Bible conferences and seminars, and read many books, some of them deeply influential, nothing has shaped my life and thinking as much as my daily quiet time. During these private moments of reading and meditating on God's Word, my mind has been renewed and my thinking transformed. The deepest convictions of my life were formed during these daily times along with God in His Word. If you are a Christian and not having a time such as this, beginning one immediately is the greatest encouragement I could give. What I have found most helpful is to simply go through a book at a time, and I would suggest beginning in one of the books of the New Testament, taking one chapter each day, unless it is exceptionally long. My pattern is to set aside approximately thirty minutes daily, though it is sometimes less and at other times more. In addition to the intake of truth, God's Word is also our spiritual food. After fasting for forty days in the wilderness, Jesus was tempted by Satan to turn stones into bread. In response He said: "Man does not live by bread alone, but by every word which proceeds out of the mouth of God" (Matthew 4:4). He was quoting from Deuteronomy 8:3 where God humbled His people during their 40 years of wandering in the desert, feeding them with *manna* (bread from heaven), so they would learn this vital truth Jesus so clearly affirmed.

When I was in college, I majored in Philosophy and Religion, primarily because of the respect I had for Dr. Clarence Hunter, the head of the department. As the years went by, however, Linda periodically heard me comment on how majoring in philosophy had been a poor decision. What benefit was there in knowing what Plato, Socrates, and Aristotle believed? One day she said to me, *"I don't believe it was a waste at all. One of your greatest passions as a pastor has been to make sure that what you say is biblically true, and also to protect the church from false teaching. Just as you evaluated the thinking of the philosophers, as a pastor you carefully evaluate everything you hear and read."* Suddenly I knew she was correct, and I recognized again that God is in the process of redeeming every experience of our lives. The admonition of Scripture is to "examine everything carefully; hold fast to what is good" (I Thessalonians 5:21). The standard by which we examine all things is the Word of God.

Martin Luther and the other reformers resolutely embraced the authority and sufficiency of Scripture. In 1545, the year before Luther died, he wrote, *"Let the man who would hear God speak, read*

Holy Scripture. Here alone, in the pages of the Bible, God speaks with final authority. Here alone, decisive authority rests. From here alone, the gift of God's righteousness comes to hell-bound sinners."[7]

The second of the *five solas* is *grace alone. Sola gratia*, like *sola scriptura,* is nonnegotiable because it is one of the distinguishing truths separating the true biblical Gospel from false gospels that cannot save. From the early months of my Christian life, I learned that *grace is the unmerited favor of God.* Sadly, while I knew the definition in my mind, and was even being transformed by its power, the liberating truth of grace had not yet penetrated my heart. It was not until I was out of seminary that I came to "understand the grace of God in truth" (Colossians 1:6). The breakthrough occurred as I read through Paul's epistle to the Galatians in one sitting during our first year in Texas in 1968. When I finished, I asked myself, *"Is this saying what I think it is saying?"* To make sure it did, I read all six chapters again, and the message was the same! Paul's letter to the Galatians was both corrective and instructive. "I am amazed that you are so quickly deserting Him who called you by the grace of Christ, for a different gospel; which is really not another; only there are some who are disturbing you and want to distort the gospel of Christ" (Galatians 1:6-7). By adding *law* to the Gospel of Christ, which was my fleshly tendency, the false teachers were effectively destroying the liberating message of grace, turning the message of God's undeserved favor toward sinners into a message of earned and merited favor. What I saw that night in Galatians was that the Gospel of Grace is one of freedom; to add anything to grace takes that away. This is why Paul later writes, "It was for freedom that Christ set us free; therefore, keep standing firm and do not be subject again to a yoke of bondage" (Galatians 5:1). Simply put, *sola gratia* is a biblical affirmation that the totality of our salvation, from first to last, is a gift of grace from God!

God has used numerous passages over the years to reinforce and deepen this conviction in my mind and heart, but it is not possible to mention them all. The classic is this: "For by grace you have been saved through faith, and that not of yourselves, it is the gift of God not as a result of works, lest any man should boast" (Ephesians 2:8-9). When you carefully read the entire book of Ephesians, however, it becomes clear that these verses are actually a summary of the doxology of praise with which Paul began his epistle: "Blessed be the God and Father of our Lord Jesus Christ, who has blessed us with every spiritual blessing in the heavenly places in Christ, just as He chose us in Him before the foundation of the world, that we would be holy and blameless before Him. In love He predestined us to adoption as sons through Jesus Christ to Himself, according to the kind intention of His will, to the praise of the glory of His grace" (Ephesians 1:3-6). While it is impossible to fathom and wrap my finite mind around Paul's inspired words, I can nevertheless understand and gratefully accept the good news of God's Word. The incredible actions God has taken toward me and toward all of His children, which began in eternity past, were not based on any good thing in us, or any positive actions He knew we would take to be deserving of salvation. No, as we see so clearly stated, because God is the Sovereign Initiator, and the One who called us, our eternal salvation can only be *to the praise of His glorious grace!*

This is one of the reasons I chose this subtitle for my memoirs: *"The Personal and Pastoral Memoirs of One Called by Sovereign Grace from the Hills of Appalachia."* My works or personal standing had absolutely nothing to do with God's call; as the passage in Ephesians 1 clearly states, everything had its origin in His sovereign grace. This being the case, whatever good that may have occurred in my life, in the marriage and ministry Linda and I have been blessed to share, can only be to the *praise of His glorious grace.*

For additional reinforcement, consider how grace is linked to the second phrase in this classic verse about sin: "For all have sinned and come short of the glory of God, being justified as a gift by His grace through the redemption that is in Christ Jesus" (Romans 3:23-24). As the Apostle Paul nears the conclusion of Romans in what is the most lengthy theological treatise of the Gospel in the New Testament, he writes, "But if it is by grace, it is no longer on the basis of works; otherwise grace is no longer grace" (Romans 11:6). *Sola Gratia!*

The third of the five *solas, sola fide*, which means *faith alone*, is also a prominent theme throughout Scripture. When the Philippian jailer in his desperation cried out to the Apostle Paul, "What must I do to be saved?" Paul's answer was simply, "Believe on the Lord Jesus Christ, and you will be saved" (Acts 16:31). When I first called on the Lord for salvation on May 8, 1958, my faith was that God would hear my cry and not turn me away. While it was a childlike faith, I later learned that this is what pleases the Lord. "Truly I say to you, whoever does not receive the kingdom of God like a child shall not enter it" (Luke 18:17). The Apostle John beautifully links receiving and believing in his words, "But as many as received Him, to them He gave the right to become children of God, even to those who believe on His name" (John 1:12).

The liberating verse God used with Martin Luther, opening his eyes to *faith alone*, was Romans 1:17: "For in it (the Gospel) the righteousness of God is revealed, from faith to faith; as it is written, 'BUT THE RIGHTEOUS MAN SHALL LIVE BY FAITH.'" For Luther, the righteousness of God referred to God's punishment of sinners; this being the case, he was unable to see the good news the verse contained. As a devout, conscientious monk, Luther had a great fear of God and His righteousness, knowing he could never measure up to God's standard of perfection. But in His grace and kindness, the Holy Spirit opened Luther's heart and mind to see and understand the Gospel in verse 17. Here are his words: *"At last, by the mercy of God, meditating day and night, I gave heed to the context of the words namely, 'In it the righteousness of God is revealed; as is written, 'He who through faith is righteous shall live'. Then I began to understand that the righteousness of God is that by which a person lives by a gift of God, namely by faith. And this is the meaning: the righteousness of God is revealed by the gospel, namely the passive righteousness by which a merciful God justifies us by faith! Here I felt that I was altogether born again and had entered paradise itself through open* gates!" [8] Once Luther's eyes were opened, he began to see the simplicity of faith throughout the New Testament. "Therefore, having been justified by faith, we have peace with God through our Lord Jesus Christ, through whom we have obtained our introduction by faith into this grace in which we stand" (Romans 5:1).

This does not mean that works are unimportant; what we must see, however, is that they are the fruit, while grace and faith form the root. After unequivocally declaring, "By grace you have been saved through faith...not of works, lest any man should boast" in Ephesians 2:8-9, Paul goes on to explain, "For we are His workmanship, created in Christ Jesus for good works, which God prepared beforehand so that we would walk in them" (Ephesians 2:10). A faith that gives no evidence of change is a dead faith. While we are saved by grace alone through faith alone, *grace and faith do not remain alone*; they always lead to positive changes in our lives, including good works!

As I have studied God's Word on this issue over many years, I have come to see that in addition to grace being an absolutely free gift, so is faith. Commenting on Ephesians 2:8-9, the MacArthur Study Bible has these explanatory words: *"In the phrase, 'and that not of yourselves,' Paul is referring to the entire previous statement of salvation; not only the grace but the faith as well. Even though we are required to believe for salvation, even that faith is part of the gift of God which saves and cannot be exercised by one's own power."* The writer of Hebrews convincingly makes this point as well when he instructs us to "lay aside every weight and the sin which so easily entangles us, fixing our eyes on Jesus, who is the AUTHOR (SOURCE, ORIGINATOR, INITIATOR, and CAUSE) and PERFECTOR (FINISHER, COMPLETER) of our faith" (Hebrews 12:1-2). What hope and assurance Scripture provides when we accept it for what it is, *"the Word of God, which performs its work in those who believe!"* (I Thessalonians 2:13)

The fourth *sola* is *sola Christus,* or Christ alone. When Luther and the Reformers courageously proclaimed salvation *by grace alone through faith alone,* with equal conviction they also boldly proclaimed that the *object of that faith had to be Christ alone.* In our pluralistic world of relativism, which rejects any notion of absolute truth, people are adamant in resisting the assertion that Christ is the only way. And yet, the claim of our Lord is unmistakably clear and unchangeable: "I am the Way, the Truth, and the Life; no man comes to the Father but by Me" (John 14:6). The first century church embraced and proclaimed this identical truth: "And there is salvation in no one else; for there is no other name given under heaven among men, by which we must be saved" (Acts 4:12).

As I mentioned earlier, one of the first evidences of my new life in Christ was a love for God's Word. While all parts of it were fascinating for me, in the early months of my faith the four Gospels of Matthew, Mark, Luke, and John were especially instructive. In them I saw the Lord Jesus Christ, the One who is the very heart and center of our faith. When I saw how He invited ordinary men and women from all walks of life to follow Him, I was thankful that He had called me as well. Regretfully, I have not always followed as faithfully as I would have liked, and as He deserved, but I have long been convinced that He is worthy of my wholehearted, life-long allegiance.

As I became increasingly familiar with the big picture of the Bible, I learned that everything in the Old Testament was preparatory. From the covenant God made with Abraham, to the sacrificial system, and the writings of the prophets, everything was pointing to Christ. In the four Gospels, I saw a powerful picture of our Lord's eternality, His work in Creation, His life on earth as a man, His teaching, His miracles, and how He trained His disciples. But each of the four Gospels carefully highlighted His final week — the events leading up to and including His death, His resurrection, and His appearances over a period of forty days before His ascension into heaven. I saw how the sermons in the book of Acts and the instruction in the Epistles expanded even more on Christ's identity and what He came to accomplish. Christ alone was at the center of it all, and He must be given preeminence in all things. (Colossians 1:18)

What I discovered was that the more I read and studied God's Word, the more my love and gratitude for Jesus increased. I saw that what He did for me was immensely greater than I had initially understood. While I knew He died for my sins, I did not understand that in doing that, all of God's holy anger and wrath which I deserved because of my sin were poured on Christ. His love for me and for each one of His children was infinitely greater than I could fathom. "He who spared not His own Son, but delivered Him up for us all, how will He not with Him freely give us all things?" (Romans 8:32) Because of His holy, unconditional love for us, God did not spare Christ - *so He could spare us!* In the days leading up to Martin Luther's life-changing discovery, he once declared, *"If I could believe that God was not angry with me, I would stand on my head for joy!"*[9]

At the heart of the controversy in the sixteenth century was the question each one of us must answer: *on what basis can we as sinful men and women ever be declared righteous in God's sight?* If it is based on us, we are in deep trouble, even as the psalmist expressed, "If You, O Lord, should mark iniquities, O Lord, who could stand?" (Psalm 130:3) If I have to stand before God's holy and righteous judgment based solely on my own performance, I could never pass, nor could you. But this is where the good news becomes even greater; not only did Christ pay in full the penalty for our sins, but *by grace alone through faith alone in Christ alone*, God imputes to us the very righteousness of Christ. "He has made Him who knew no sin to be made sin on our behalf that we might become the righteousness of God in Him" (II Corinthians 5:21). In and of ourselves, under God's scrutiny, we all continue to sin in one form or another, whether sins of commission or sins of omission, sins of attitudes or of actions. The question then becomes, will I be judged on my righteousness or the righteousness of Christ? If I have to trust my own virtue and morality to get me to heaven, I am in complete and utter despair, without any possibility of ever being redeemed. But when I embrace the good news of the Gospel, which declares that the righteousness of Christ is mine *by grace alone through faith alone in Christ alone*, like Luther I am ready to stand on my head for joy!

One of the tender, delightful pictures of this truth that encourages me greatly, is found in the prophetic writings of Isaiah, who is sometimes referred to as *the evangelical* prophet, and whose book has been called *the fifth Gospel.* Even though Isaiah wrote approximately 700 years before Christ, he was enabled by the Holy Spirit to see many of the wonderful truths about the Messiah, especially His suffering and death, and the salvation He would bring. Here are Isaiah's words: "I will rejoice greatly in the Lord, my soul will exult in my God; for He has clothed me with garments of salvation, He has wrapped me in a robe of righteousness..." (Isaiah 61:10) What an encouraging picture of the imputed righteousness that is ours *by grace alone, through faith alone, in Christ alone!*

When the Apostle Paul was writing about this glorious news to the church in Rome, he began by reminding them of Abraham's experience: "What shall we say then that Abraham, our forefather according to the flesh, has found? For if Abraham was justified by works, he has something to boast about, but not before God. For what does the Scripture say? 'ABRAHAM BELIEVED GOD, AND IT WAS CREDITED TO HIM AS RIGHTEOUSNESS.' Now to the one who works, his wage is not credited as a favor, but as what is due. But to the one who does not work, but believes in Him who justifies the ungodly, his faith is credited as righteousness." (Romans 4:1-4) In His grace and love, God has done for us in Christ what we could never do for ourselves. This is the truth we see throughout the New Testament, and it is this Gospel that is the great treasure of the church, *"the glory and grace of the Gospel,"* as Luther referred to it.

The seeds for the fifth, *Soli Deo Gloria,* were planted in my heart during the early months of my Christian life. It happened when our small but adventuresome youth group from Baxter made our way into the massive Charlotte Coliseum for the Billy Graham Crusade just as the choir was rehearsing *To God be the Glory!* While I had not heard the song before, as I mentioned in an earlier chapter, the truth of the words were forever implanted in my heart; instinctively I knew this was how it should be; God should always be given the glory!

Later I learned from the Westminster catechism that the chief end of man is *"to glorify God and to enjoy Him forever."*[10] The ones who wrote those oft repeated words arrived at their conclusion because the truth is revealed all through Scripture. Creation itself is designed to declare God's glory: "The heavens are telling the glory of God" (Psalm 19:1). The amazing design in literally everything God created should prompt us to rejoice in what He has made, and give glory to Him. We as His created children are included: "Bring My sons from afar and my daughters from the ends of the earth, everyone who is called by My name, whom I created for My glory, whom I formed and made" (Isaiah 43:6-7). God's purpose in creation extends to everything He does: "God works all things according to the counsel of His will, so that we who were the first to hope in Christ might be to the praise of His glory" (Ephesians 1:11-12). As the Apostle Paul nears the end of his rich theological treatise of the Gospel in his Epistle to the Romans, his grateful response is to the glory of God alone: "From Him and through Him and to Him are all things; to Him be the glory forever" (Romans 11:36). Even the essential routines of daily life are meant to be done for His glory: "Whether you eat or drink or whatever you do, do all to the glory of God" (I Corinthians 10:31).

With profound insight, John Piper has often commented, *"God is most glorified in us when we are most satisfied in Him."*[11] While our flesh is constantly pulling us toward self-gratification, God is ever teaching us to be satisfied, even delighted, in Him and His ways; this brings Him great glory, and it is also where our greatest long-term joy is found.

While these *five solas of the Reformation* may seem to some like deep theology, I make no apology for sharing them, for they are at the very heart of *the Gospel of the Grace of God*. As a pastor, I have known many people over the years that are saved and truly love the Lord, but know relatively little about the life-changing truths of their faith. Nothing would please me more than for you to be encouraged by my comments to make a new commitment to spending consistent time in God's Word. Jesus Himself said to the disciples who believed in Him, "If you continue in My word, you are truly disciples of Mine; and you shall know the truth, and the truth shall set you free" (John 8:31-32).

In seeking to follow God's call over these many years, the truth of His Word has set me free from wrong ideas in countless areas, some I have already shared in my memoirs. One area of liberation, actually the greatest, is how the truth of Scripture set me free from many incorrect ideas I had about God, a process that is continuing. Many years ago I was profoundly challenged by A. W. Tozer's book, *The Knowledge of the Holy.*[13] On the opening page are words I have never forgotten: *"What comes into our minds when we think about God is the most important thing about us."* Dating back to the time before I was saved, as well as in the earlier years of my Christian life, I had many incorrect, humanistic beliefs about God and His attributes. I was like the wicked man in the Psalm to whom God said, "You thought I was just like you" (Psalm 50:21). My tendency was to picture God the way I thought He should be rather than simply accepting the truth the Bible discloses about Him. Tozer went on to explain that *"an attribute of God is what God reveals to be true about Himself."* While we learn many truths about God from His creation, it is in His Holy Word where we see with the greatest clarity who He is and what He is like. There we learn that God is eternal, triune, unchanging, holy, love, light, omnipotent, omniscient, omnipresent, just, wise, merciful, faithful, along with many other attributes.

One of the most significant of these revelations was to see that God reveals Himself as the Absolute Sovereign. Here are two out of numerous examples: "The Lord's throne is in the heavens and His sovereignty rules over all" (Psalm 103:19). "He who is the blessed and only Sovereign, the King of kings and the Lord of lords, who alone possesses immortality and dwells in unapproachable light, whom no man has seen or can see. To Him be glory and eternal dominion Amen!" (I Timothy 6:15-16) My thinking for many years, in my uninformed arrogance, was that the freewill of man is sovereign. While we see the concept of freewill in Scripture, it always ha limitations. I am free, for example, to shake my fist in the face of God, if I should so choose, but because God is sovereign, He determines how many times I will shake it, and whether I will live to shake it tomorrow. In the Epistle of James, he gives this wise instruction to remind his readers to always be aware of God's sovereignty: "Come now, you who say, 'Today or tomorrow we will go into such and such a city, and spend a year there and engage in business and make a profit.' Yet you do not know what your life will be like tomorrow. You are just a vapor that appears for a little while and then vanishes away. Instead you ought to say, 'If the Lord wills, we will live and do this or that.' But as it is, you boast in your arrogance, and all such boasting is evil" (James 4:13-16). This has helped me immeasurably in making my plans, knowing they are always subject to change, based on God's sovereign purposes which I am unable to see. In His sovereignty, He is also able to take the most difficult and disappointing events that come into our lives, and still give this promise: "We know that God causes all things to work together for good to those who love God and are called according to His purpose" (Romans 8:28).

What is also now clear to me is God's sovereignty in salvation, explained in detail in the opening verses of Ephesians. As I mentioned earlier, with my finite mind I cannot grasp how this could be. In my bewilderment, there have been times when I simply ignored the truth, and at other times attempted to explain it away. As the years have passed, however, my response is now one of accepting this astonishing truth with grateful humility.

Another difficult passage on God's sovereignty is the ninth chapter of Romans, where God speaks of His choice of Jacob over Esau, even before the twins were born. Paul continues on in that chapter to apply sovereignty to salvation, while anticipating and then addressing the likely objection of his readers. "There is no injustice with God, is there? May it never be! I will have mercy on whom I will have mercy, and I will have compassion on whom I will have compassion. So then it does not depend on the man who wills or the man who runs, but on God who has mercy" (Romans 9:14--16).

269

For years I was perplexed by this passage, and it became a point of deep struggle for me. In later years I ultimately came to see that what I was actually questioning was *God's right to be God!* He is the Potter and I am the clay, and this is the poignant illustration Paul uses: "Who are you, O man, who answers back to God? The thing molded will not say to the molder, 'Why did you make me this way?' Or does not the potter have a right over the clay to make one lump for honorable use and another for common use?" (Romans 9:20-21) In these autumn years, I am delighted as a finite man to acknowledge God as the Infinite, Absolute Sovereign, with no rivals, especially me!

In His sovereignty, God knows "the days that were ordained for me when as yet there were none of them" (Psalm 139:16). One fact is sure about my time on earth - there is more of my life behind me than there is ahead of me! "As for the days of our life, they contain seventy years, or if due to strength, eighty years, yet their pride is but labor and sorrow; for soon it is gone and we fly away" (Psalm 90:10). Because of the fleeting nature of life, the Psalmist goes on to pray, "So teach us to number our days, that we may present to You a heart of wisdom" (Psalm 90:12). Later he adds this petition, "Let Your work appear to Your servants, and Your majesty to their children. Let the favor (grace) of the Lord our God be upon us; and confirm the work of our hands; yes, confirm the work of our hands." The margin of my Bible explains that the word *confirm* literally means, *Give permanence to the work of our hands.* This insightful, instructive prayer from the heart of the Psalmist was one of the motivating factors which prodded me to finally write my memoirs. If no one ever reads what I have written but my children, grandchildren, a handful of loyal friends, and a few others in future generations, my prayer is that these simple words of gratitude for the grace I have been shown will *give a measure of permanence to the work of my hands.* But as I have said throughout the book, it is all because of grace. That being the case, it is not *the work of my hands*, but the gracious work of God in and through me! To Him alone be the glory and praise!

As surprising as it might appear to some, as the years have passed, one of my favorite parts of being a pastor has been the funerals. Some have been extremely difficult, of course, even heart wrenching. The ones for infants, young children, and teens have been among my greatest challenges. The few I have been asked to do when someone took his or her life have also been extremely sorrowful, as are the funerals when the person has never given any evidence of faith in Christ. Contemplating that someone has passed into eternity without Jesus is one of the most serious and weighty thoughts that could ever enter our minds. Many of the funerals, of course, have been for those who were believers, and a number of these have been family members and close friends. When this is the case, the service can be a time of rejoicing, for we know that the person is with Christ. Any sorrow we experience is more because of our loss, but not for what our loved ones are experiencing.

A favorite passage I use in most funerals is from the Old Testament book of Ecclesiastes from *the Living Bible*: "It is better to spend your time at funerals than at festivals, for you are going to die, and it is good to think about it while there is still time. Sorrow is better than laughter, for sadness has a refining influence on us. Yes, a wise person thinks much about death, while a fool only thinks of having a good time now"[13] (Ecclesiastes 7:2-4 *TLB*). As these verses indicate, anytime we attend a funeral, or in my case, am the one speaking, it forces us to reflect deeply on our own mortality; we are going to die, and *it is good to think about it while there is still time!*

In seeking to bring comfort to family members and friends of the person who died, I always share some of the key truths of the Gospel, pointing to the living hope which belongs to those whose trust is in Jesus Christ as their only hope. He is the One who, as the Apostle Paul succinctly affirms, "abolished death and brought life and immortality to light through the Gospel" (II Timothy 1:10). In our humanity, we naturally fear death. An old Appalachian song expresses it well: *"Everybody wants to go to heaven, but nobody wants to die."*[14] The wonderful reality Jesus brought about through His death and triumphant resurrection was to remove the fear of death, as the writer of Hebrews explains: "Through death He rendered powerless him who had the power of death, that is, the devil, and might free those who through fear of death were subject to slavery all their lives" (Hebrews 2:14-15). Death for believers is simply the doorway by which we enter into the presence of God and into our *Father's house* which Jesus has been preparing for us (John 14:2).

A great encouragement as I think about death is of the grace still to come: "He raised us up with Him, and seated us with Him in the heavenly places in Christ Jesus, so that in the ages to come He might show the surpassing riches of His grace in kindness to us in Christ Jesus" (Ephesians 2:5-7). Because of the incredible future grace awaiting believers, the Apostle Peter gives this admonition: "Fix your hope completely on the grace to be brought to you at the revelation of Jesus Christ" (I Peter 1:13). If we think grace is amazing in this life, and all believers agree that it is, how breathtaking it will be when *the surpassing riches of His grace in kindness to us in Christ Jesus is shown in the ages to come when He is revealed, and we see Him as He is!*

When Joshua, the well-known Old Testament patriarch, was dying, his weighty words were these: "Behold, today I am going the way of all the earth" (Joshua 23:14). Yes, all the earth, each one of us, has an appointment with death which we cannot escape. I sometimes say at funerals, *"Sooner or later, we all have to take our turn."* We don't know when that will be, but we are certain that our time is coming.

One of my favorite stories I love to share at memorial services is from Dr. D. James Kennedy. An old Scottish lady was dying, and as was the custom in those days, the pastor came by to see if the person had true faith. As she lay dying on her bed, he asked, *"Do you still trust Christ?"* *"Ah, yes, I do,"* she said, *"He is my only hope in life and in death."* The pastor then asked, *"Do you believe He will take you to heaven?"* *"Yes, I know He will!"* she replied. The pastor then asked *"But what if He does not take you to heaven?"* The woman though for a brief moment and then replied, *"Ah, God may do what He wills, but if He does not take me to heaven, He will lose more than I. Though I will lose my soul, He will lose His honor, for He has promised that those who trust in His Son will never perish!"* [15] Her testimony gives us an accurate picture of true faith, trusting in Christ alone for our salvation, having come to faith in Christ through the promises in God's Word.

The famous Heidelberg Catechism, that personal creed loved by millions in both Europe and America, begins with the penetrating question to which each one of us must respond: *"What is your only hope in life and in death?"* The essential truth in the answer is, *"That I belong – body and soul, in life and in death – not to myself but to my faithful Savior, Jesus Christ, who at the cost of His own blood has fully paid for all my sins, and has completely freed me from the dominion of the devil...therefore, by His Holy Spirit, He also assures me of eternal life."*[16]

So what will heaven be like? The Bible informs us of a number of marvelous truths including, first and foremost, that we will be with Jesus, our precious Savior who purchased us at the cost of His own blood. The Lord Jesus Christ will be eternally preeminent, for He alone is worthy to receive the glory and praise; He is the One who redeemed us, including brothers and sisters from "every tongue and tribe and people and nation" (Revelation 4:9). We will also be eternally reunited with family and friends who were believers, and how marvelous this will be! The book of Revelation also gives this incredible description: "Behold, the tabernacle of God is among men, and He will dwell among them, and they shall be His people, and God Himself will be among them, and He will wipe away every tear from their eyes; and there will no longer be any death; there will no longer be any mourning, or crying, or pain; the first things have passed away. And He who sits on the throne says, 'Behold, I make all things new!'" (Revelation 21:3-5)

Our family first caught a glimpse of the magnificence of heaven many years ago around a camp fire in Colorado, when our children were still young. It came as we were finishing the classic children's series, *Chronicles of Narnia,* each book packed with profound spiritual truth by C. S. Lewis. The series revolves around the adventures of children in the world of Narnia, guided by Aslan, a wise and powerful lion (who represents Christ) who can speak, and who is the true king of Narnia.

In the final book of the series, *The Last Battle,* C. S. Lewis chronicles the end of the world of Narnia, which opens the door for Aslan to lead the children into the *true* Narnia (Heaven). Aslan is explaining that while their parents indeed died in a train wreck, an event which ended their life in *Shadowlands* (Earth), their death was actually only the beginning.

These are the climactic words from Lewis which I read to our family in a tender and teachable moment around that Colorado campfire: *"And as Aslan spoke, He no longer looked to them like a lion; but the things that began to happen after that were so great and beautiful that I cannot write them. And for us, this is the end of all stories, and we can most truly say that they lived happily ever after. But for them it was only the beginning of the real story. All their life in this world, and all their adventures of Narnia had only been the cover and title page; now at last they were beginning Chapter One of the Great Story which no one on earth has read; which goes on forever; in which every chapter is better than the one before!"* [17]

My prayer is that I will see you in the eternal heaven where we will experience those breathtaking, enthralling new chapters together. The only way to assure your presence there is to respond to God's gracious call, and place your trust in Jesus Christ alone for your eternal salvation. His promise is this: "All that the Father gives Me will come to Me, and the one who comes to Me, I will certainly not cast out!" (John 6:37) And it is all because of grace!

NOTES

Chapter One

1. Marcos Sampaolo, "Tennessee Encyclopedia of history and culture," *Encyclopedia Britannica,* 2018.

Chapter Two

1. Francis Thompson (1859-1907), "The Hound of Heaven," *The Oxford Book of Mystical Verses,* ed Nicholson (1917).
2. Fred R. Shapiro, Editor, *Yale Book of Quotations* (New Haven, CT: Yale University Press, 2006).
3. John Bradford, English evangelical preacher and martyr, (circa 1510-1555).
4. Darrell Scott, *"*You'll Never Leave Harlan Alive*," Aloha from Nashville,* (1997).
5. Bruce Carroll, "The Great Exchange," *The Great Exchange,* *(*Word, 1990) 6.
6. The Living Bible, (Wheaton: Tyndale House Publishers, 1971), 60187.
7. Francis Thompson, "The Hound of Heaven".

Chapter Three

1. "History of Camp Meetings," newworldencyclopedia.org 2008.
2. Mrs. Charles E. Cowman, *Mountain Trailways for Youth* (Los Angeles: Cowman Publications, 1956), 151.
3. Norman Clayton, "Now I Belong to Jesus" (Norman Clayton Publishing Co., 1943).
4. Fanny Crosby, "To God be the Glory," *Brightest and Best* (Lowry and Doane, 1875).

Chapter Four (None)

Chapter Five

1. William A. Gillam, "True Love," 1963.
2. Darrell Scott, "You'll Never Leave Harlan Alive.*"*

3. Helen Keller, Most commonly attributed to her, but sometimes referred to as an Arabic Proverb.
4. Robert A. Traina, *Methodical Bible Study* (Grand Rapids: Zondervan, 1952),

Chapter Six (None)

Chapter Seven

1. Andrae Crouch, "My Tribute," *Keep on Singing* (Santa Monica: Universal Publishing Group, 1972).
2. Karen Burton Mains, *Open Heart, Open Home* (Elgin, IL: David C. Cook Publishing Company, 1976), 25.

Chapter Eight

1. Don Francisco, "I'll Never Let Go of Your Hand, *"He's Alive"* (New Pax Music, 1980), 7.

Chapter Nine

1. Jay Adams, *Christian Living in the Home* (New Jersey: Presbyterian and Reformed Publishing Co., 1972), 10-13.
2. R.C. Sproul, *The Invisible Hand* (Sanford, FL: P & R Publishing Company,2003)
3. Bill Hybels, *Leadership Journal* – Spring 1991

Chapter Ten (None)

Chapter Eleven

1. Wikipedia, Central Valley (California)https:/en.wikipedia.org/wiki/Category: Central Valley (California)
2. Discover Central California Website
3. Mark Bittman, *"Everyone Eats There"*, *The New York Times Magazine*, October 10, 2012.
4. U.S. Census 2010 Porterville, CA – *The Porterville Recorder*, May 10, 2011.

Chapter Twelve

1. Noah Webster, *American Dictionary of the English Language,* Republished in Facsimile Edition by Foundation for American Christian Education, Post Office Box 9588, Chesapeake, Virginia 23321-9588
2. Steven J. Lawson, *The Heroic Boldness of Martin Luther* (Sanford, FL: Reformation Trust Publishing, 2013).
3. Phillip Shaff, *History of the Christian Church, Volume 7: The German Reformation* (Grand Rapids: Eardmans, 1910), 1.
4. John Piper, *What are the Five Solas?* desiringgod.org, October 3, 2017.
5. John Piper, *Why the Reformation Remains Relevant after 500 Years,* (From an interview – *Ask Pastor John,* October 16, 2017)
6. Steven Lawson, *The Heroic Boldness of Martin Luther,* 11.
7. John Piper, *The Legacy of Sovereign Joy – God's Triumphant Grace in the lives of Augustine, Luther ,and Calvin,* (Wheaton: Crossway Books, 2000).
8. John Piper, *How Does the Gospel Save Believers?* desiringgod.org, August 9, 1998.
9. Sinclair Ferguson "Grace Alone: Luther and the Christian Life," *The Legacy of Luther* (Sanford, FL: Reformation Trust Publishing, 2016)
10. Westminster Catechism (The Westminster Presbyterian, 1649).
11. John Piper, *Desiring God* (Portland: Multnomah Publishers, 1986), 9.
12. A.W. Tozer, *The Knowledge of the Holy* (New York: Harper Collins, 1961), 1, 12.
13. The Living Bible.
14. Jim Collins and Marty Dodson, "Everybody Wants to go to Heaven, but Nobody Wants to Die" *I Know Who Holds Tomorrow* (Alison Krauss and the Cox Family, 1994), 7.
15. D. James Kennedy, *This is the Life* (Glendale, CA: Gospel Light Publications, 1973), 13—14.
16. Ibid., 10-11.

17. C. S. Lewis, *The Last Battle* (New York: Harper Trophy, 1994), 228.

WORKS CITED

Adams, Jay. (1972). *Christian living in the home*. Phillipsburg, NJ: Presbyterian and Reformed Publishing Company.

Bradford, John. English evangelical preacher and martyr (circa 1510-1555)

Bittman, Mark. (2010,October 12). Everyone Eats There. *The New York Times Magazine.*

Carroll, Bruce. (1990) The great exchange. *The Great Exchange*. Waco, TX: Word.

Clayton, Norman, (1943) Now I belong to Jesus. Norman Clayton Publishing Company.

Collins, Jim. Dodson, Marty. (1994) Everybody wants to go to heaven, but nobody wants to die. [Recorded by Alison Krauss]. *I Know Who Holds Tomorrow.* Rounder Records. 7

Cowman, Mrs. Charles E. (1956). *Mountain trailways for youth.* Los Angeles: Cowman Publications.

Crosby, Fanny. (1875) To God be the glory. *Brightest and Best.* Song collection by Lowry and Doane.

Crouch, Andrae. (1972). My Tribute. *Keep on Singing.* Universal Publishing Group.

Discovercentralcalifornia.org

Ferguson, Sinclair. (2016). *The legacy of Luther.* Sanford, FL: Reformation Trust.

Francisco, Don. (1980). I'll never let go of Your hand. *He's Alive.* London: New Pax Music. 7
Gillam, William A. (1963). *True Love,* lyrics and music.
Hybels, Bill. (Spring 1991). *Leadership Journal.*

Keller, Helen. Most commonly attributed to her, but sometimes referred to as an Arabic Proverb.

Kennedy, D. James. (1973). *This is the Life.* Glendale, CA: Gospel Light Publications.

Lawson, Steven J. (2013). *The Heroic Boldness of Martin Luther.* Sanford, FL: Reformation Trust Publishing.

Lewis, C. S. (1994) *The Last Battle.* New York: Harper Trophy.

Mains, Karen Burton. (1976). *Open Heart, Open Home.* Elgin, IL: David C. Cook Publishing Company.

(2008). A History of Camp Meetings. Newworldencyclopedia.org.

Piper, John. (1986). *Desiring God.* Sisters, OR: Multnomah Publishers, Inc.

Piper, John. (2017, October 3). What are the five solas? desiringgod.org

Piper, John. *Why the Reformation Remains Relevant after 500 Years,* (From an interview – *Ask Pastor John,* October 16, 2017)

Piper, John. *The Legacy of Sovereign Joy – God's Triumphant Grace in the lives of Augustine, Luther, and Calvin.* Wheaton, IL: Crossway Books.

Piper, John. (1998, August 9). How does the Gospel save believers? desiringgod.org.

Sampaolo, Marco. (2018). Tennessee encyclopedia of history and culture. *Encyclopedia Brittanica.*

Scott, Darrell. (1997) You'll never leave Harlan alive. *Aloha from Nashville.*

Schaff, Phillip. (1910). *History of the Christian Church, Volume 7: The German Reformation.* Grand Rapids: Eerdmans.

Shapiro, Fred R. Editor. (2006) *Yale Book of Quotations.* New Haven, CT: Yale University Press.

Sproul, R.C. (2003). *The Invisible Hand.* Sanford, FL: P & R Publishing Company.

The Living Bible. (1971). Wheaton, IL: Tyndale House Publishers.

Thompson, Francis (1917). The Hound of Heaven. *The Oxford Book of Mystical Verses.* Nicholson & Lee.

Tozer, A. W. (1961). *The Knowledge of the Holy.* New York: Harper Collins Publishers.

Traina, Robert A. (1952,1980). *Methodical Bible Study.* Grand Rapids, MI: Zondervan.

(2011, May 10). U.S. Census 2010, Porterville, CA – *The Porterville Recorder.*

Webster, Noah, *American Dictionary of the English Language,* Republished in Facsimile Edition by Foundation for American Christian Education, Post Office Box 9588, Chesapeake, Virginia 23321-9588

Westminster Catechism, 1647, *The Westminster Presbyterian*

Wikipedia, Central Valley (California)

Made in the USA
Columbia, SC
08 June 2019